# In the
# Hands of Fate

# In the
# Hands of Fate

## The Story of Patrol Wing Ten

8 DECEMBER 1941 – 11 MAY 1942

By Dwight R. Messimer

NAVAL INSTITUTE PRESS
Annapolis, Maryland

Second printing, 1986

Library of Congress Cataloging in Publication Data
Messimer, Dwight R., 1937–
  In the hands of fate.
  Bibliography: p.
  Includes index.
    1. World War, 1939–1945—Naval operations, American.
  2. World War, 1939–1945—Aerial operations, American.
  3. United States. Navy. Patrol Wing 10—History.
  4. World War, 1939–1945—Campaigns—Pacific Ocean.
  I. Title.
  D773.M43   1985        940.54'4973        85-3069
  ISBN 0-87021-293-1

Printed in the United States of America

To my parents

# Contents

# Foreword

Dwight Messimer's *In the Hands of Fate*, which recounts the story of Patrol Wing Ten during the early months of World War II, is a remarkable book and should become a principal source for researchers who want to know more about the navy's air operations in the Philippines, the Netherlands East Indies, and Australia at the time U.S. forces were being overwhelmed by the Japanese.

The wing operated from Olongapo and Sangley Point (in Manila Bay) for perhaps a week and then commenced a long retreat through the Indies and eventually to Perth, Australia. There was a pause in the Indies when operations were conducted from Surabaja, the major Dutch naval base, from Ambon, a secondary base, and from a number of other places where seaplane tenders supported the flights. One squadron of reinforcements from Pearl Harbor joined the wing in early 1944.

Because the PatWing-10 aircraft and crews were so scattered, the individual crews knew nothing about the adventures of others. Never after the early departure from the Manila area was the wing assembled at a central point where everyone could be privy to all that went on. When some of us finally arrived in Perth, many of the earlier arrivals had already left for the United States to take up other assignments, and I, for one, never saw many of my close Olongapo squadron mates until months and even years later.

Messimer has succeeded in identifying and getting pertinent information from virtually every survivor of Patrol Wing Ten. From their testimony and from the formal navy reports, he has pieced together the whole story, and I will wager that prior to his fine work nobody knew it all and very few knew very much about it.

There is an impressive amount of detail about the air operations. At the same time, he shows an understanding of the overall picture in the Far East during those eventful months just before and after the start of hostilities. Patrol Wing Ten had existed for almost exactly one year. My squadron (VP-26) was ordered from Pearl Harbor to the Philippines in December 1940 to become the second of two squadrons, VP-101 at Sangley Point, and VP-102 at Olongapo. Our dependents were not permitted to go with us, and the navy dependents then in the Philippines were being ordered to return to the United States. The army and army air corps were not so conservative, and the fact that their families were still there was an irritant to most of us during that year before the war. For a few months prior to December 1941, there were repeated alerts—everyone ordered to remain at base—and weekend jaunts to Manila and Baguio had to be postponed. These repeated cries of "wolf" resulted in many of us becoming cynical about the likelihood of war. How would a small nation like Japan ever dare to attack the United States? Why was General MacArthur living in that penthouse in the Manila Hotel if war was imminent? These and other questions were answered when we were awakened at midnight to be told that Pearl Harbor had been attacked.

One of the things that impressed me in retrospect after it was all over was the fact that in the Asiatic Fleet there was hardly a single person, officer or man, who had ever experienced a shooting war. None of us really knew what was expected of us. I can recall a message we were shown on the first day from old Admiral Tommy Hart, the fleet commander, saying, "We are at war. Conduct yourselves accordingly." Each of us looked at the squadron mates on each side of him wondering privately just what that meant. We had no yardstick and no combat experience. We really did not know for sure what could or should be done by a PBY crew. All things considered, the way the wing did perform was highly creditable.

The book is full of exciting stories about individual exploits. As I said earlier, I had never known about many of them because of the very wide dispersal of our forces. I'm proud to say that I was a member of Patrol Wing Ten. I think that we did all that we could, and several turned out to be heroes. I think we did "conduct ourselves accordingly" as we were admonished to do by Admiral Hart's message, and that our performance stood up well when examined later on.

This is not to say there weren't failures in leadership and individual performances. The author has soft-pedalled these in his story, and I believe it is best that way. Messimer told me that he had no desire to be a "head hunter." After any very complex operation in war, it is always easy to find disgruntled people who want to "expose the truth" and tell the "real" story. These stories come almost always from the poor performers. We did wonder about some of our orders and were puzzled about the performance of a few leaders. Now that I am older, I realize much more fully that troops really never fully understand "the reasons why." It wasn't until about May of 1944 in Perth that I learned the full story of our losses at Pearl Harbor. During our action in Southeast Asia, we actually did continue to hope for and even to expect reinforcements, but none came except for the single PBY squadron from Hawaii. So when it became clear that we were going to have to make do with what we had, I suppose it's fair to say that our morale wasn't always the highest. A patrolling crew couldn't help but wonder why it mattered if they did sight advancing Japanese forces, for they knew that almost nothing could be done about it. However, the flights went on as regularly as possible with the diminishing numbers of planes, and individual heroics were not uncommon.

One of the good things that has transpired is that there is a bond among most of the survivors. I have a feeling that I was among a really fine group. The chiefs, especially, were absolutely outstanding.

A gratifying number of the officers went on to become flag officers. One of our most outstanding performers, who had perhaps the most harrowing experience of any of us, was Admiral Thomas H. Moorer. He eventually became chief of naval operations and later chairman of the joint chiefs of staff.

Later on in the war, patrol plane operators surpassed whatever we managed to do, but for the most part, they had better aircraft and were part of the great steamroller of military power we had built and trained after those early setbacks. The knowledge that something has been done only leads to someone deciding that he can do it better, and usually he does. However, that is getting beyond the purpose of this foreword.

I have read most of the published material about the war in the Pacific. A good deal of it describes the actions in superlative terms, and based on my own experience, I've wondered how accurate those accounts really were. This excellent book happens to be about operations in which I participated and knew quite a bit about. It is very accurate when it describes the things I know about, and based on that, I believe that the events and adventures I didn't know about are also described accurately. There is no attempt made to glamorize anything beyond what it deserves, yet the book was to me exciting reading. It captures very well the general tone of our attitudes as they were just previous to hostilities and as they changed along the way.

If anyone is curious about what went on in those early months of the war, he might try talking to people who were there, but by far the best he can do is read this book, which tells the whole story in an exciting, entertaining, and yet very accurate way.

John J. Hyland
Admiral, USN (Retired)

# Preface

During my research for *Pawns of War*, I came across repeated references to Patrol Wing Ten. That was because the USS *Langley* was the wing's flagship. The bits and pieces of information I heard convinced me that there was a story worth telling. In fact, once I started the research I found that there are literally dozens of stories worth telling about PatWing-10 and its many members.

What has been written here is a "big-picture" overview of the wing's dramatic operations against Japan during the war's first twenty-two weeks. To get the information I interviewed over fifty survivors, read a dozen personal diaries and flight logs, and drew from over one hundred official reports, log books, narratives, and war diaries.

The knowledgeable reader may complain that some episodes have been left out. That is true. Many of the smaller episodes were left out to keep the main story moving along at a quick pace. Similarly, some readers will look askance at some of the facts. But everything said in this book is true, even though there are some points that disagree with popularly accepted ideas.

For example, PBY-4s did not have waist blisters. One plane may have been modified at Cavite before the war, but the other twenty-seven in PatWing-10 had sliding hatches.

Another technical point that will raise some eyebrows is the assertion that the PBY-4's bow gunner stood up in an open turret ring. He did. Interviews with several officers and NAPs who manned the bow gun confirmed that point. In fact, Jack Martin, a pilot in VP-22, recalled that he stood in the open bow for twelve hours during the evacuation flight from Dobo to Darwin.

Every effort has been made to correctly identify the airplanes by their assigned numbers. The problem is that the numbers were changed from time to time, so that some planes had as many as three different assigned numbers. When the squadron went to the Philippines, the planes bore squadron numbers. VP-21's planes were 21-P-1 to 21-P-14, and VP-26's planes were 26-P-1 to 26-P-14. When Patrol Wing Ten was formed, and the squadrons were redesignated VP-101 and VP-102, they continued the practice of using squadron numbers. For example, 21-P-1 became 101-P-1, and so on. At some point before the war the numbering system was changed from a squadron to a wing system. Thus, in the wing's records the planes were numbered 101-P-1 to 101-P-14 and 102-P-16 to 102-P-29. There was no plane numbered 15. But the Patrol Wing Ten War Diary uses the wing numbering system, as do most of the patrol reports. Some pilots, however, continued to use the old numbers when identifying their planes. The problem became more complicated as the planes were destroyed. In many cases the surviving planes were given the number of the lost planes, such as 101-P-13 becoming 101-P-7 and 102-P-22 becoming 101-P-2. The planes in VP-22 underwent similar number changes as they were integrated with Patrol Wing Ten's remaining planes. To make matters even more confusing, the five Dutch PBYs turned over to the wing are referred to in the War Diary by both their Dutch numbers and the wing's number.

The aircraft numbers used in this book are according to the wing numbering system, except in a few instances in which the plane was still identified by its original squadron number. Those instances occurred shortly after VP-22 arrived in Australia, and during Operation Flight Gridiron.

I am grateful to everyone who contributed material for this book. All their names appear in the bibliography. Special thanks go to

Kirk Autsen for his excellent drawings, and to Joanne MacDougal for helping with the typing. I am particularly grateful to my wife for the hundreds of hours she contributed toward getting this book ready.

# In the
# Hands of Fate

# I

# Patrol Wing Ten

---

The sky was splotched with flak bursts, the air filled with the drone of aircraft engines coming from the Vees of Japanese bombers high overhead. Heavy explosions shook Surabaja, thick black smoke rolled skyward from raging fires on the navy base, and civilians scurried for the beehive-shaped air-raid shelters. Between the sky and the earth, Japanese fighters rolled and looped, pursuing the few Allied fighters that rose to oppose them.

Two men, dressed in khaki shorts and shortsleeved shirts, leaned against a building, looking up at the battle being fought above them. They were unshaven, their uniforms tattered. Each had a pair of gold wings over his left shirt pocket.

An old woman hurrying toward an air-raid shelter paused as she passed the two thin men slouched against the wall in their threadbare uniforms. Shaking her finger at them she snapped, "Young men, you're supposed to be out there fighting." Before the surprised officers could react, the old woman darted away.

The two men looked at each other and burst out laughing. Behind them the wall shuddered and heaved as a bomb exploded down the street. The men were PBY pilots in Patrol Wing Ten. The wing had been fighting the Japanese continuously for eight weeks.

Though it had retreated nearly 1,500 miles and had lost 66 percent of its aircraft, the wing's aircrews were still flying back-to-back patrols in planes that were barely fit to fly. Dead tired, dressed in rags, and poorly equipped, the men in PatWing-10 faced the Japanese during the darkest weeks of the war.

This is their story.

The view through the cockpit windshield was obscured by thick grey clouds and heavy rain. Alone in the PBY's cockpit, Ensign Gordon Ebbe sat in the right-hand seat, a partially folded chart on his lap, his side window open. Rain blew through the open window, soaking the flyer and causing rivulets of water to run down his face. Peering downward through the gloom, Ebbe could barely make out the island's coastline two hundred feet below. As the plane sped past the island, the ensign compared the twists and turns of the shoreline to the wet chart on his lap. Despite the poor visibility, Ebbe was satisfied that he was still on course and there was no need to awaken his PPC (Patrol Plane Commander), Lieutenant Harvey Burden, who was asleep on the berth aft.

Another PBY flew beside Ebbe's plane, keeping station on his left wing. In that plane's cockpit Ensign Duncan ("Duke") Campbell and Ensign Edgar Hazelton were concentrating on staying with

PBY-4s were used by VP-101 and VP-102. The airplane shown here bears designation 12-P-4 showing that the plane was based in Hawaii before it was sent to the Philippines. (National Archives)

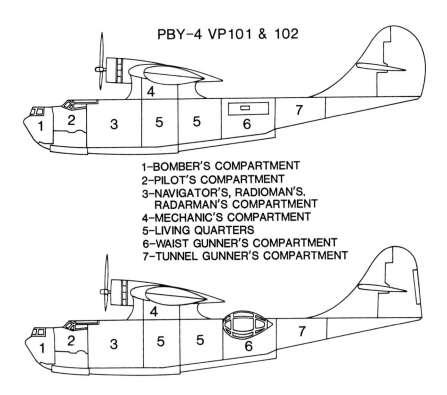

PBY-4 VP101 & 102

1–BOMBER'S COMPARTMENT
2–PILOT'S COMPARTMENT
3–NAVIGATOR'S, RADIOMAN'S.
   RADARMAN'S COMPARTMENT
4–MECHANIC'S COMPARTMENT
5–LIVING QUARTERS
6–WAIST GUNNER'S COMPARTMENT
7–TUNNEL GUNNER'S COMPARTMENT

PBY-5 VP22 & DUTCH PLANES

Ebbe. Their concentration was motivated by more than just a desire to keep formation—Campbell and Hazelton had no idea where
they were going. Understandably, Campbell was uneasy and slightly
irritated. He recalls:

> Harvey Burden and his crew had whatever secret information there
> was to be delivered, and all we were along for was to pick-up Bur-
> den if he broke down. During our refueling stop in Palawan, I
> asked Harvey where we were going, but the mission was so hush-
> hush that he wouldn't tell me. All he told me was to fly wing on
> him. It was a night flight from Palawan, and after takeoff we
> learned we were headed south into the China Sea. I got really con-
> cerned then because I didn't have any charts for that area. All I had
> was a five-inch by seven-inch map I had found in a book. It covered
> everything from the Dutch East Indies, clear through the Philip-
> pines. If I didn't stay with Burden, we'd never get back.[1]

Campbell's worst fears almost came true when the two planes became separated in the dark. Hurrying ahead to catch up, Campbell
and Hazelton searched the black sky for some sign of Burden's plane.
For a moment they thought they might have passed Burden, until
Hazelton spotted a faint glow ahead to the right. It was the glow of
the other plane's exhaust. The sighting had been fortunate. Just as
Campbell closed up on Burden's left wing, it started to rain.

As the two PBYs neared their secret destination, the Kapuas
River on Borneo's west coast, the four pilots faced several unknowns.
Campbell and Hazelton still did not know their destination, and
none of the pilots knew that the war they all expected was just a
month away. But those things were really unimportant compared to
the third unknown. They did not know that the map on Ebbe's lap
was wrong and they were about to hit a mountain.

The first warning came when Ebbe lost sight of the shoreline. It
just disappeared, swallowed up in the dark. He stuck his head out
of the window for a better view, but the rain beat his face with such
violence that he jerked back inside. But Ebbe had seen why the
shoreline had disappeared. Ebbe saw trees.

The chart was all wrong. It showed the coastline continuing
straight ahead and then curving off to the right. In fact, the shore-

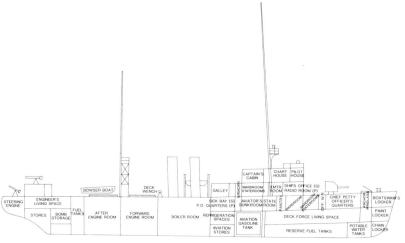

USS CHILDS AND USS PRESTON

PBY-4 belonging to VP-21, the squadron that became VP-101 after it arrived in the Philippines. (Courtesy Gordon Ebbe)

line made a ninety-degree left turn. A chunk of tree-covered land, three or four hundred feet high, was directly in front of the PBYs.

Ebbe kicked the rudder hard left and buried the column in his lap. Banking sharply, the PBY struggled upward as Ebbe rammed both throttles forward. Campbell and Hazelton saw the trees and Ebbe's violent maneuver at almost the same time. Desperately, Duke Campbell hauled his flying boat around, trying to stay with Ebbe. It was a losing proposition. Campbell's plane was on the inside of the turn, and to stay there it had to fly more slowly than Ebbe. But Ebbe was just barely hanging on as he struggled to clear the trees. Campbell and Hazelton were starting to stall.

Unable to stay with Ebbe, Campbell fell off and the two planes crossed, Ebbe above and Campbell below. Trailing from Ebbe's plane like a giant fishing line was a steel, aerial antenna. As Campbell passed beneath Ebbe's plane, the cable slid along the trailing edge of Campbell's right wing and jammed in the aileron. There was a hard wrench and a loud snap as the antenna parted, leaving six feet of steel cable wedged between the aileron and the wing.

Campbell was in trouble. With his right aileron jammed, he had to use maximum left aileron to keep his plane under control. The PBY lacked any mechanically assisted controls, and under the best conditions was a heavy plane to fly. With a jammed aileron Campbell's plane was nearly unmanageable. Only with the greatest effort were Campbell and Hazelton able to keep their plane in the air and stay with Ebbe.

The plan called for Burden to land and deliver the documents, while Campbell circled overhead. It was a plan that had to be changed, and Campbell lost no time getting on the radio to Burden.

> While we struggled with the damn thing Burden landed on the river. The reason I wasn't supposed to land was because the river was full of rocks, and they didn't trust a young aviation cadet with a river landing. But I told him I couldn't make it back to Manila with the aileron jammed the way it was. Hell, it was a real struggle just holding the plane level.

It was obvious to Burden that Campbell had to land. The river conditions were bad, and landing even a healthy plane took skill and careful attention. Sweeping around to the left, Campbell lined up on the river and started down. Sweat poured off the pilots as the plane settled toward the water, nose up. They were concentrating so hard on controlling the plane that they were nearly on the water when Campbell realized that his floats were still up. His hand shot toward the switch on the instrument panel, and the floats dropped down. It had been a close thing.

While Burden delivered the secret messages, Campbell's badly shaken crew cleared the fouled aileron. The whole operation was quickly finished. In less than thirty minutes both planes were off the water and climbing back into the rain and clouds. Campbell never did find out what Harvey Burden had delivered.

The aircrews of Patrol Wing Ten (PatWing-10) had not always been involved in such cloak-and-dagger missions as this one. In fact, PatWing-10 did not even exist until December 1940. Nevertheless, as early as 1939 navy planners, having long recognized the possibility of a war with Japan, decided something had to be done to prepare for that possibility. In order to provide the aging Asiatic Fleet with an efficient long-range reconnaissance capability, a squadron of fourteen PBYs was sent to the Philippines.

The big, twin-engine flying boats' mission was to find the enemy at sea, an indispensable part of the Philippine's defense plan. The navy's role was to intercept the oncoming enemy offshore, and either drive him back or maul him so badly that his weakened forces could be chewed up on the beaches by General Douglas MacArthur's American and Filipino troops. It was the PBYs' job to scout ahead of the fleet, report the enemy's strength, course, and speed, and if necessary, attack with bombs and torpedoes. The PBY was an excellent patrol plane, but wholly unsuited for its role as a daylight, horizontal bomber.

The army was steadily reinforcing the Philippines with B-17s. Since the bomber flew faster, farther, higher, and was more heavily armed than the PBY, one might ask why were not B-17s used instead of PBYs. There were several reasons why.

In the first place, the fleet depended upon observations and reports made by its naval aviators. The soundness of that fundamental requirement had been demonstrated time and again since 1917. Secondly, the B-17s could only operate from land bases in the Philippines. That meant when fuel ran low, the army bombers would have to return to their base to refuel or rearm. The PBY, on the other hand, could land and refuel anywhere a tender had set up shop. In fact, with prior planning, the PBYs could refuel themselves from fuel caches stashed on dozens of small islands. It was the PBY's ability to go anywhere in the Pacific, without relying on prepared airfields, that made its presence in the Philippines necessary.

In its day, the PBY was a big airplane, capable of lifting tremendous loads off the water and carrying them long distances. It was also a rugged airplane, able to withstand rivet-popping landings on rough water, a feature that was particularly appreciated by downed airmen being rescued. But the PBY-4s and -5s suffered two deficiencies that made them very vulnerable in combat. They lacked self-sealing fuel tanks and sufficient armament.

There were four machine guns in a PBY, two .30-caliber guns and two .50-caliber guns. The .30-caliber gun in the bow looked like an arrangement out of World War I, in that it was fired by a man who stood in an open hatch, half his body outside the airplane. On the PBY-4, the two .50-caliber waist guns were fired through rectangular openings in the fuselage. The fourth gunner lay on his stomach peering through a slot in the bottom of the fuselage, between the step and the tail. His field of fire was very limited, so much so that the position was sometimes left unmanned, reducing the crew to seven instead of the full complement of eight.

In the PBY-4, the exposed positions of the bow and waist gunners seriously interfered with their shooting accuracy. The problem was the 110-knot wind, caused by the plane's movement through the air, that buffeted guns and gunners.

There were three pilots in the crew, usually two officers and an enlisted man called a Naval Aviation Pilot (NAP). The senior officer was usually the PPC, but not always. Prewar requirements were that a pilot needed up to 1,000 hours of flight time before he could take the qualifying, practical examination for PPC. That meant that a newly assigned lieutenant, lacking the minimum flight time, could be assigned as the second pilot in a plane commanded by an ensign, or a lieutenant (j.g.). One of the long-standing gripes voiced by re-serve officers during the prewar period was the practice of allowing regular navy officers to become PPCs with only a few hundred hours of flight time, compared to the 1,000 hours minimum set for reserve officers. The 1,000-hour requirement was dropped when the war started.[2]

An NAP was nearly always the third pilot. They were excellent pilots, often with much more experience than the officers. As a re-sult, a good NAP was worth his weight in gold, and some PPCs insisted on having two NAPs aboard instead of another officer. The enlisted pilots were usually radiomen or machinist's mates, which is one reason they were so valuable.

On long patrols, often up to seventeen hours, the three pilots took turns flying. Similarly, the rest of the crew was made up of two radiomen and three machinist's mates who took turns manning the radio or sitting in the tower. When not at one of those positions, they rested, made coffee, or manned a gun position. In combat, one of the pilots went into the bow to act as bombardier and man the bow gun. Usually the senior radioman was on the radio, and the senior machinist's mate, the plane captain, was in the tower. The other crewmen manned the waist and tunnel guns.

The tower position requires an explanation, since it is frequently mentioned in the events covered in this book. The plane captain, usually a chief machinist's mate or a machinist's mate first class, was the flight engineer. He sat in the pylon that supported the wing above the fuselage, monitoring fuel consumption, engine tempera-ture, and a host of other gauges.

The PBY crew was an integrated team of specialists, most of

whom were cross-trained. The prewar practice of keeping the crews together, assigned to specific planes, resulted in closely knit companies of eight men each. That situation already existed in VP-21 when it made the move west from Pearl Harbor to the Philippines.

In September 1939, VP-21 flew to the Philippines via Midway, Wake Island, and Guam. The flight was uneventful except for a typhoon between Guam and the Philippines. Had the typhoon extended all the way to Manila, the situation might have gotten serious, because the charts being used to navigate did not show the heights of the mountains on the approach to Manila Bay. Therefore, the pilots were depending on clear weather for the flight across Luzon and into Manila Bay. Before there were any problems, they luckily broke out of the storm, and their arrival at Sangley Point was without incident.

Because the seaplane base at Sangley Point was unfinished, the planes moored to buoys that had been set by the tender USS *Langley* (AV 3). The *Langley* was an ex-aircraft carrier; in fact, she was America's first flattop, commissioned in 1922 after being converted from a coal collier. After having been converted a second time, this time from carrier to tender, she was sent out to join the other elderly ships that made up the U.S. Asiatic Fleet.

Though old and slow, the *Langley* was probably the finest seaplane tender in the world. But her spacious work areas, well-equipped machine shops, and ample stores were not really appreciated by the aircrews of VP-21, who had to live aboard her until the seaplane base an Sangley Point was finished.

Living aboard the *Langley* was not a popular arrangement with the aircrews. There was a certain amount of friction between the ship's crew and the "airdales," whose presence tended to disrupt the ship's routine. On the other side of the coin, the aircrews complained that their quarters were cramped, hot, and noisy. But strained relations were not limited to airmen and sailors.

By mid-1940 relations with Japan were becoming increasingly bad, and what a few described as a "do-nothing routine" had become one of regular training flights and practice bombing missions. The practice bombing missions were primarily against ships, and the emphasis, until the war started, was on horizontal bombing from 10,000 to 12,000 feet. Torpedo practice was done only "to a very small degree," and gunnery practice was done "very infrequently."[3] The prewar training exercises revealed faults in the PBY that were either overlooked, or ignored.

From mid-1940 on, there were occasional exercises with PBYs against fighters. The fighters were to attack the PBYs, using gun cameras to record "hits." The PBYs' guns were similarly equipped. Film analysis showed that the fighters were scoring 1,300 "hits" for each six scored by the PBYs.[4] Part of the problem stemmed from the open-to-the-elements arrangement of the PBY-4's guns. Gunners had a hard time concentrating on the target while being battered by a 110-knot wind. But regardless of the reason, the fact was clear that the PBYs were very vulnerable to fighter attack. Curiously, the one-sided score did not alarm anyone.

Maybe the results were overlooked because the exercises were "only practice." More likely, they were overlooked because there was nothing that could be done about it. The PBY was the only plane available, and besides, the army was supposed to provide fighter escort. That would certainly even the score. In the meantime, the most important task was to complete the seaplane base at Sangley Point and move ashore. That day finally arrived; VP-21 moved ashore, and a second squadron was selected for assignment to the Asiatic Fleet. The squadron selected was VP-26, which, like VP-21, was equipped with the PBY-4.

USS *Childs* AVP 14). The *Childs* was a converted destroyer that acted as a tender to PatWing-10.

USS *William B. Preston* (AVP 20). Another converted four-piper that tended the PBYs in PatWing-10.

The PBY-4 had been in service since 1938, and VP-21's planes were due for a major overhaul. Since the overhauls had already been completed on VP-26's planes in Hawaii, the squadrons exchanged aircraft. The trade was made in June 1940 when VP-26 flew its reconditioned planes to Sangley Point, and returned to Hawaii with VP-21's planes. In December 1940 VP-26 made the trip back to the Philippines with the newly overhauled planes, and joined VP-21. The two squadrons were redesignated VP-101 and VP-102, and PatWing-10 was established.

Eight days after VP-102 had arrived in the Philippines, the USS *Childs* (AVD 1) joined PatWing-10 as the wing's second seaplane tender. A few months later the USS *William B. Preston* (AVD 7) had also come west. The *Childs* and the *Preston* were converted "four-pipers," ex-destroyers with the forward fireroom removed and the space converted to aircrew quarters and aviation fuel storage. Much of the superstructure abaft the bridge had been cleared away creating a fairly open work area. The most attractive feature, however, was their speed. Even with two boilers gone, the ex-destroyers could still make twenty-five knots.[5]

The fourth tender in the PatWing-10 organization was a bird-class seaplane tender, the USS *Heron*. The *Heron* was responsible for the utility squadron's four Grumman J2F "Ducks," five Vought

OS2U "Kingfishers," and one Curtiss SOC "Seagull." The *Heron* had been in the Asiatic Fleet "since 1926 or earlier."[6]

PatWing-10's main base was at Sangley Point, on a small peninsula that juts north into Manila Bay. Just south of this base was the Cavite Navy Yard, and Manila lay eight miles to the northeast. Across the entrance to Manila Bay was Corregidor, and behind that, the Bataan Peninsula. A second base was established at Olongapo on Subic Bay.

Generally, VP-102 was at Olongapo and VP-101 at Sangley Point. But because Olongapo lacked maintenance and recreation facilities on a par with Sangley Point, the two squadrons traded places according to a prearranged schedule. The schedule called for a trade every six months, but it did not always work out that way. To relieve some of the tedium sometimes associated with Olongapo, liberty flights were flown to Manila on the weekends, a thirty-minute hop one way.

USS *Heron* (AVP 2) was a Bird-class tender that had once been a minesweeper. The *Heron* had been in the Asiatic Fleet since the 1920s. (Courtesy Gordon Ebbe)

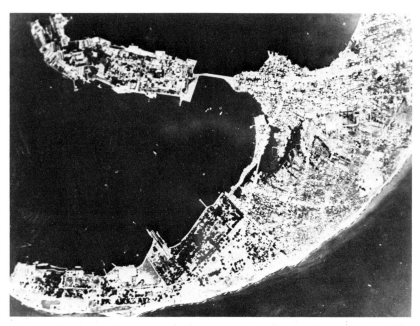

Sangley Point and Canacao Bay, 25 August 1941. The seaplane base was still not completed when this picture was taken. (Courtesy Tom Pollock)

The whole organization was commanded by Captain Frank D. Wagner, a capable administrator who set high standards for himself and expected the same of his pilots. Under Wagner's command, the wing began flying patrols as soon as Sangley Point became operational. Initially, the patrols were limited to the Philippines, with a few to Borneo and the Celebes. As American-Japanese relations deteriorated, the patrols were extended farther west and north. The flights were a mix of training and operational missions, with the operational aspects becoming more pronounced in the spring of 1941.

Patrol missions to Cam-ranh Bay, French Indochina (now Vietnam), had been started on 20 April 1941. The purpose was to check on Japanese fleet movements, the information being shared with the British and the Dutch. As Ensign Robert ("Hawk") Barrett observed, the flights were "a new and dangerous trend." They also were a good indicator that war with Japan was becoming more likely every day.[7]

The early patrols were made with two planes covering adjacent patrol sectors. The flights were generally uneventful, the monotony

Sangley Point, 25 August 1941. The seaplane base, though uncompleted, is already in use. VP-101's planes and the utility squadron's planes are clearly visible. (Courtesy Tom Pollock)

Olongapo, 27 October 1941. The white arrow on the right of the picture is a Philippine fish trap. Composed of bamboo poles driven into the mud and lashed together, the fish traps were navigational hazards to the PBYs. The ship in the lower right corner is the USS *Rochester*, a relic of Admiral Dewey's fleet. Olongapo was also used as a base by PatWing-10. (Courtesy Tom Pollock)

broken by the occasional sighting of a Japanese ship. In those days ships flying the red-ball flag were mostly freighters and fishing boats. But small passenger ships were being seen in greater numbers throughout the islands, and the pilots wondered how many of the civilian-clad passengers were actually officers in the Imperial Japanese Navy.[8]

But training patrols were not always dull affairs. Sometimes the pace picked up when an engine quit, or a pilot got his plane into some sort of problem. Though these occurrences eased the boredom, the crews were not exactly pleased. The most memorable example of this happened on 5 August 1941.

What had started out as a rather dull, routine training patrol had suddenly become a pressure-cooker experience for Ensign Lowell Williamson. Two PBYs had taken off from an advance base at Balabac on a photo mission to the Sarangani Islands, east across the stormy Sulu Sea. On the return trip they ran into "dense squalls with high cumulus build-ups" and spent most of their time flying on instruments. Lieutenant John Hyland and Hawk Barrett were in the lead plane. Williamson was flying on Hyland's wing, with AMMc (NAP) Donald Dixon in the right-hand seat. Williamson's PPC was asleep in a berth aft.[9]

Spotting a hole overhead, Hyland and Barrett climbed toward it. At 10,000 feet they broke out of the pea soup and found themselves among towering cloud columns and deep holes that formed a series of canyons and hollows. Barrett was flying and "dodging one build-up after another." Flying "up, around, and then down into the deep holes," he banked sharply around the fleecy columns, standing the PBY on its wing tip in what were called "flipper turns." While Williamson was still struggling to stay with him in the turn, Barrett would abruptly roll over on the other wing and drop down into a deep hole. At the bottom of the hole he pulled up so sharply that his plane nearly stalled. Williamson swore as he fought to stay with Barrett.

> I had to keep giving full throttle and then no throttle, trying to keep up with his gyrations. He'd drop into a hole and then do a two- or three-G pull out at the bottom, and a negative-G pushover at the top. We were flying around like a roller coaster.

Williamson heaved, kicked, and hauled his plane around trying to stay with Barrett.

The ramp by Olongapo, and VP-102's planes. The *Rochester*'s masts and funnels can be seen above the roof line. (Courtesy Gordon Ebbe)

The strenuous follow-the-leader game lasted an hour until both planes found themselves in clear air. At that point Lieutenant Hyland relieved Barrett in the left-hand seat and started looking for an opening through which to let down. As he did this, the roller-coaster ride started again.

Williamson stayed with Hyland as long as he could, but the ensign was growing tired. At 5,000 feet he called it quits and leveled off. At that point Williamson was relieved by his PPC just as the lead plane disappeared around a tall cloud column.

Williamson had just started aft when he felt the plane roll over into a flipper turn. The PPC had gone to full power and was trying to turn inside Hyland in order to catch up quickly. As he turned, the plane flew into the cloud, and visibility dropped to zero. At that moment something went wrong. As Williamson entered the crew compartment, the plane rolled over on its back.

> Everything in the airplane, people, mattresses, bedding equipment, ammo boxes—everything hit the roof of the airplane. Holes were punched in the top. We wobbled around for a while and then started down. You could hear the airspeed building up. I thought for sure we were going to crash.

The plane had entered the cloud at about 5,000 feet, and Williamson is not sure how far the plane fell out of control. As quickly as the plane had rolled over, it came back on an even keel and flattened out. Everything that had hit the ceiling crashed to the floor. Williamson was hit on the wrist by something that bent his identification bracelet.

Though again upright, the plane was still buried in the thick cloud and not fully under control. Williamson grabbed a parachute and had clipped only one snap to his chest when the plane rolled over again. This time Williamson thought the plane was in a tail-down attitude because everything that had hit the ceiling on the first roll was now tumbling aft. Again Williamson hit the ceiling and then slammed down on the deck. At that point he made a serious effort to get out.

> The second time we got back to the floor I decided that if I could get out, I would. I could see the plane captain trying to put a chute on. We were diving at about a twenty-three degree angle, when I started to get up. But then the plane made a three- or four-G pull-up that pinned us down on the floor. I couldn't move. I couldn't even get the second snap clipped on my chute.

By now the entire crew was battered nearly senseless, and events are recalled only hazily. What is clearly recalled, however, is that after making the crushing pull-up, the plane rolled over a third time. Completely out of control, the PBY tumbled down through the clouds toward the sea. Suddenly, the plane straightened out, and seemed to be under control. Williamson and the plane captain, however, still believed they were going to crash. Their fears were reinforced when the plane suddenly nosed over into a deep dive.

The sudden nose-over created "negative Gs that sent everything half way to the ceiling." As abruptly as the dive had started, the plane leveled out again. Williamson and the plane captain scrambled to the waist escape hatch and slid it open. Both men were ready to jump, but hesitated long enough to sense that "maybe" the plane was under control. While they stood by the open hatch the PBY burst through the bottom of the clouds and leveled off. Looking down, Williamson estimated their altitude at about a thousand feet.

With a sigh of relief, Williamson and the plane captain moved foward, helping the bruised crewmen back into their places and checking for damage. Overhead there were several six- to eight-inch holes in the fuselage, and the interior of the plane was a shambles of jumbled, broken equipment. But other than that, everything seemed to be holding together.

The training continued, but by October 1941 the patrols had been stepped up and were now full-blown war patrols. Instead of flying in twos, the planes flew alone along the coast of China, checking remote islands for signs of Japanese military activity. Sighting reports became frequent, and the PBYs were often shadowed by Japanese patrol planes and fighters.

Many of the patrols were flown from advance bases scattered throughout the Philippines. Typically, these bases were nothing more than fuel and ammunition caches on remote islands to which three planes were sent for about a week. Sometimes a tender was there to service them, and sometimes not. Usually, one plane was kept on patrol during the day while the other two were serviced by their crews. Those prewar advance base exercises provided experience that was very useful after the war started.

In October 1941, Ensign H. ("Bob") Swenson and Ensign John Sloatman were at an advance base in the southern Philippines. The senior pilot, Lieutenant John Hyland, was out on patrol, and the *Langley* was anchored near the mouth of the small harbor. While taxiing his plane toward the beach, Sloatman hit a coral head hard enough to punch a hole in the hull. Luckily the plane grounded on the coral and did not slide off into deep water and sink.[10]

Swenson and his crew were sprawled on the beach taking a break when the bow of Sloatman's plane suddenly reared up out of the water. They knew at once what had happened. Wasting no time, Swenson's crew clambered into a motor whaleboat and headed toward the stricken plane.

On the *Langley*'s bridge no notice was taken of the plane's abrupt halt. Even the motor whaleboat hurrying away from the beach did not attract anyone's attention. From the *Langley*'s bridge everything looked normal, and that is exactly what Sloatman and Swenson wanted.

Airmen are generally an independent bunch, and the airmen in PatWing-10 were no exception. In fact, the nature of their assignment probably made them more independent than many of their fellow flyers. PBY crews were expected to look after their planes themselves when operating from primitive, advance bases. And those expectations were not limited to refueling and general maintenance. There are many examples of crews repairing or replacing engines, patching hulls, and replacing wing fabric without the aid of an established seaplane base or tender.

The pilots surveyed the damage and agreed that the situation was not as serious as had been expected. The hole was well forward, and could probably be raised out of the water if enough weight could be shifted to the after part of the plane. The main problem would be pulling her off the reef without doing more damage. Once off the reef, they would use the motor whaleboat to tow her to the beach, while maintaining a tail-down attitude that would keep the hole above the water.

Everything that could be moved was shifted as far aft as possible, and four men sat on the tail. The hole rose above the water. A line was passed to the motor whaleboat, while the rest of the men stood in the water along both sides of the hull. Slowly the slack was taken up. The motor whaleboat pulled, the men heaved and shoved, and a light blinked from the *Langley*'s bridge. WHAT IS THE MATTER OVER THERE.[11]

"Mr. Swenson, the *Langley*'s signaling."

"What do they want?"

"They want to know what's happening."

"Oh Christ! The last thing I want is help from the *Langley*. Come on, you guys, let's get this thing done before they find out and come over here!"

With renewed vigor the men struggled to unstick the big flying boat. Slowly the plane moved a few inches toward deep water and stopped. Hurriedly a man was sent out on one wing to roll the hull on its side a bit. That maneuver bought a few more inches—nearly a foot.

"Mr. Swenson, *Langley* wants to know why we haven't answered the last message."

"Tell them we didn't see it. Come on you guys, heave! Or we'll have Felix Stump himself over here."

Commander Felix Stump, the *Langley*'s skipper, had a reputation for roasting young ensigns. Swenson's last threat must have done the trick. With one tremendous effort the men pushed the plane off the reef and into deep water. While two more men climbed up on the tail to ensure that the hole stayed well above the water, the others were loaded into the motor whaleboat. With the damaged

PBY in tow, fourteen exhausted airmen headed toward the beach.

"Mr. Swenson, *Langley* wants to know what we're doing."

"Tell them we're towing a PBY."

Having arrived at the beach, there remained only the job of attaching beaching gear to the plane's hull, and hauling her up on the sand. It was a ten-minute job that took an hour. The problem started when the starboard beaching gear got away from the crewmen and plunged to the bottom. The men were standing in water up to their chests when the heavy leg and wheel assembly slipped out of their hands. At first it did not appear that the fumble would cause any real problem, since the water was relatively shallow and crystal clear. Unfortunately, directly beneath the plane was a hole about fifteen feet deep, and that is exactly where the beaching gear went.

At first the men were stumped when they looked down, expecting to see the gear lying on the sandy bottom, and saw nothing. A hurried dive, and a quick search revealed the gear's hiding place. Had it gone down in just five feet of water, the men would have simply picked it up and hooked it to the plane. But it was too heavy for two men to bring to the surface from fifteen feet down. Clearly, the solution to the problem was to pass a line around the gear, and haul it up on the beach.

While everyone else waited on the beach, Swenson waded out to the plane, dragging a line with him. Hauling out enough slack to be sure he had enough to pass around and make fast to the gear, he dove. At the other end, the men on the beach were lined up like a tug-of-war team. At the head of the line, nearest the water, was Ensign Sloatman.

Swenson was a pretty good swimmer, but he had underestimated the time it would take to bend a line on the beaching gear. In fact, he had just enough time to run the line under the leg before he had to surface for air. Not wanting to lose the line, Swenson was still gripping the end when he popped to the surface.

As he broke the surface and opened his mouth to take a deep breath, Sloatman shouted, "Are you ready?" Swenson was still blowing and gasping as he tried to get enough air in his lungs to go back and finish the job. Mistaking Swenson's walrus-like noises for an affirmative answer, Sloatman bellowed, "Haul away."

Thirteen sturdy airmen gave Sloatman's order everything they had. Swenson, still gripping the line with his right hand was jerked beneath the surface, and almost reached the bottom before he let go. Abruptly relieved of what little weight there was at the other end, the men on the beach collapsed like a row of dominoes. The line whipped away from the beaching gear, and settled to the bottom.

After a brief conference to establish signals and procedures, the salvage operation was successfully completed. The damaged PBY was hauled up on the beach, the hole was quickly patched, and the following morning she was ready to go on patrol.

It was probably a good thing that the two crews had repaired Sloatman's plane themselves, since the experience would be put to good use in the near future. Signs that war was fast approaching were clearly evident. All navy dependents had been sent home in November 1940, Manila Bay and Subic Bay had been mined in July 1941, and in September 1941 PatWing-10 was ordered to shoot *first* at any German raiders sighted. The fact that there were not any German raiders to shoot at "lessened the impact of the order," but things were clearly "near gun point with Japan." [12]

By November 1941, the wing was already on a "seventy-five percent war footing," the missions they flew becoming more and more dangerous and more likely to cause an incident that would open hostilities between the United States and Japan. One month before the war Lieutenant John Hyland flew a group of Chinese generals from Manila to Hong Kong. Another pilot flew a load of tires to Chennault's Flying Tigers. Two weeks before the war Hyland flew a photoreconnaissance mission over a Japanese-held island. There was always the chance that a PBY would be fired on by a Japanese plane during one of those flights. And as the war came nearer, and tension mounted, instances in which Japanese planes made menacing advances toward the PBYs became more frequent. [13]

These developments caused many of the airmen to consider what might happen if they were shot down in the Philippines. Contrary to wartime propaganda describing the Filipinos as flag-waving, staunch friends of Americans, many of the men of PatWing-10 considered them as "unscrupulous, treacherous, and not to be trusted." [14]

There was particular concern about the Moros. Nearly everyone had been told, and believed, that a Moro's sure ticket to heaven was to kill a Christian. It was, therefore, assumed that the Moros were safe to be around only so long as they were outnumbered and outgunned.

Headhunters were another concern. Frequent references were made to them, and in 1940 Gordon Ebbe had written an aunt, "Headhunters still flourish sixty miles north of Manila. Every now and then they go on a rampage and lop off a dozen heads. Pleasant country, this."

Though overstated, the men's fears occasionally proved to be legitimate. During the war there were cases in which Filipinos, Moros, and headhunters attacked Americans, or turned them over to the Japanese. And for several months before the war started, an active fifth-column movement steadily supplied information to the Japanese. There is no doubt that the disastrous losses on the first day of the war were, in part, the result of fifth-column activity.

The relatively poor quality of their equipment bothered them too, particularly as it became increasingly evident that they were going to have to fight a war with it. Lieutenant Commander J. V. Peterson described the material condition of the wing just prior to the war.

> The aircraft tenders, that is the *Langley, Childs, Preston,* and *Heron,* were old converted ships which had been docked during the preceding six months. That is, they had been in dry dock, bottoms had been scraped, some repairs and alterations had been made and generally they were in fairly good seaworthy condition. All tenders were short on personnel, both enlisted and officers, as were the squadrons. . . . The ships were fairly well stocked as to provisions and fuel, both gasoline and bunker, and ammunition. Generally, they were in good condition considering their age and shortage of personnel. The patrol planes were PBY-4's which had no armor or self-sealing gas tanks. However, these planes were in fairly good condition. The fabric had been changed on most of the aircraft during the preceding summer and we had saved as much engine time as possible in order to be prepared for an emergency. The Utility Wing, that is, the OS2U's and the J2F's were in fair condition. However, they were very short-legged and it was difficult for them to make the long flights between bases.
> We were critically short of spare engines, in fact I think we had only four. One for each tender. There were some structural parts,

that is nuts, bolts, cotterkeys, and so forth. The whole Wing and the ships were all short of engine accessories, batteries, floats, fuel-pumps, and such gear.[15]

At the time Peterson made that evaluation, the United States was delivering new PBY-5s to the Dutch in the Netherlands East Indies. The new planes were flown into Manila by Consolidated Aircraft crews, where they were picked up by the Dutch crews and flown to Surabaja. Understandably, the men in PatWing-10 were irritated that the Dutch were getting the latest model PBY, while American crews had to make do with rebuilt, outdated planes.

Captain Wagner had described his pilots as "the best aviators in the world." And in many cases he was right. The Dutch were, by comparison, often poorly trained, a situation that later put a heavy burden on the American flyers. An early clue was picked up by Duke Campbell and his copilot, Ensign Al Armbruster, in November 1941.

Campbell and Armbruster, in the air over Manila Bay, watched one of the new Dutch PBYs take off. As the Dutch plane climbed, Campbell slid in beside it to look the plane over. There was no one in the cockpit.

> We did a double take, and sure as hell, the cabin was empty. We figured we weren't seeing right so I crossed under the Dutchman and came up on the other side. We were at a thousand feet, headed south, and there was still no sign of life in that plane.[16]

Puzzled, Campbell pulled away. Later he ran into a Dutch pilot at Sangley Point and told him about the incident. The Dutch pilot's explanation floored him. The Dutch pilot told him that as soon as he got off the water, he put the plane on auto-pilot and adjourned to the navigator's table to play cards with his only other crewman, a mechanic. He concluded that the other pilots probably did the same thing.

One reason for the high quality of the PatWing-10 aircrews was the high quality of the two prewar squadron commanders. Lieutenant Commander J. V. Peterson had assumed command of VP-101 in June 1941. Peterson was a charismatic leader who made a lasting impression on every man in the squadron. His leadership qualities

Interior of Officer's Quarters "N" at Olongapo. The man in the chair on right is John Sloatman. (Courtesy Lowell Williamson)

were put to the hardest test just six months after he took command, and he more than passed the test.

Lieutenant Commander A. N. Perkins had been in command of VP-102 since June 1940. Like Peterson, Perkins was enormously popular with his squadron. He has been described as a "thoroughly southern gentleman" who was easygoing and very considerate of his subordinates. In fact, in the eyes of the senior brass he may have been too easygoing and too considerate. One thing is certain, as long as Perkins was VP-102's skipper, the officers' huts at Olongapo were the scene of high-spirited activities.[17]

But throughout November, and into the first week of December 1941, there were several personnel changes in both squadrons. Enlisted men and officers who had completed their tours went home, while others were transferred to the ships of the Asiatic Fleet. There were also several promotions. The result was that the squadrons were filled with a lot of "fresh-caught ensigns," the over-whelming majority being reservists.

Among the officers replaced was Lieutenant Commander Perkins, his replacement being Lieutenant Commander Edgar T. Neale. The new squadron commander was an energetic, hard-driving man much like Captain Wagner. But he found it difficult to get along with people, largely because of his terrible temper. As a result, few of his subordinates were able to see past his unpleasant personality and recognize his several good points.

Neale knew there was very little time left in which to adjust to his new command. It is a measure of the man's drive and energy that when the war came he and VP-102 were ready. And Neale had no doubt that war was about to start. Two weeks before the attack on Pearl Harbor he called his pilots together and told them, "It's coming in two weeks. Here are your wartime codes; start your patrols." [18]

Lieutenant Commander Neale's warning was well founded. His counterpart in VP-101 recalled that:

> Just prior to the war . . . we received orders to carry out a series of special patrols . . . [a]cross the South China Sea, and along the coast of Indo-China. Reports had come thru that the Japs were moving south along the coast of Indo-China. . . . A good many ships were observed making progress down the coast [of Indo-China]. Because the pilots in PW-10 had seen the movements of the transports, we were, as a group relatively certain that war was at hand. . . . On all these flights the planes were armed defensively, but had instructions not to fire unless fired upon. Many pilots reported that the Jap planes . . . made practice runs on our planes. [19]

Liberty was now restricted to short periods away from the bases at Olongapo and Sangley Point. But during those brief outings the men saw ample signs that something was up. Japanese-owned businesses advertised rock-bottom clearance sales, and Filipinos, in rare acts of generosity, bought drinks for the airmen. When asked why, they answered that they did not want to leave anything for Tojo. [20]

In Manila Bay, the crew of the *Childs* rigged a canvas tarp between the bridgehouse and the forward funnel to alter the ship's appearance. It was a futile effort, and the rig was taken down. At Olongapo CM1c George Gaboury was building two plywood PBY

VP-102 officers at Olongapo. Left to right, J. C. Watson, Andrew Reid, Schmuck, and Lowell Williamson.

decoys. When finished, the pilots told Gaboury that from 5,000 feet the decoys looked real.[21] The Japanese, however, did not attack from 5,000 feet, and when the day of reckoning came, the decoys were ignored.

With Japanese intentions becoming clearer every day, Patrol Wing Ten and its ships moved out to their advance bases.

The *Preston* with three patrol planes was in the Gulf of Davao, and her planes patrolled the eastern approaches to the Celebes Sea. The *Heron*, with four light planes, was at the southeastern tip of Palawan Island. These planes covered the western approaches to the Celebes Sea. The Dutch were patrolling along the northern edge of the Netherlands East Indies, covering the territory contiguous to that covered by us, while the rest of our planes from Manila searched the area to the west as far as the coast of Indo-China, to the northwest to Hainan, and to the north to Formosa;

thus, to all intents and purposes, we started fighting the war a week before the Pearl Harbor incident.

Up to the second of December, our planes had sighted nothing alarming. On the second of December, twenty Jap merchant ships, including transports, were found in Cam Ranh Bay.[22]

Lieutenant (j.g.) William Robinson and Ensign Andrew Burgess were the pilots who made the sighting. Burgess recalled:

> It was a ten-hour flight, five of which were made on instruments in pea-soup weather. We had just broken out of the soup when we saw thirty or forty ships, mostly freighters and transports. Several single-engine floatplanes were flying cover, but they didn't spot us. We hung around for ten or fifteen minutes and then headed home. We had orders not to transmit until we were at least two hours out of Cam Ranh Bay.[23]

The next day another plane reported fifty ships, including destroyers and cruisers. Clearly, the Japanese were making their move. But on the third day, the Japanese fleet disappeared, and the Americans were unable to relocate them.

On 4, 5, and 6 December Japanese patrol bombers were encountered off the coast of Luzon. No shots were fired, but on 7 December a twin-engine "Nell" tried repeatedly to work in behind a PBY flown by Ensign Leslie Pew. It was a maneuvering game, for which both planes were unsuited. After several fruitless tries, the Nell turned away toward Formosa.

The narrowly avoided confrontation convinced many men that it was time to settle their personal affairs. Tom McCabe had been sending regular allotments to his wife, but decided early in December to send her a particularly large check. It might be the last he could send. The problem was how to get it to her. The last China Clipper flight from Manila to San Francisco had left, but Ensign Bob Etnire's wife, Ema, was still in Manila. Certain that she would be taken out before the war started, McCabe gave Ema Etnire the check. He felt a lot better knowing that his wife would have it in a short time. In fact, she never saw the check.[24]

Ema Etnire was not evacuated. She was, instead, captured by the Japanese, and spent the entire war imprisoned in Santo Tomas.

Throughout her ordeal she hung on to the check, trying on several occasions to have it smuggled out and sent to Tom's wife. When Manila was liberated in 1945, she returned the check to Tom McCabe.

By Saturday 6 December, the lid was firmly clamped on all non-war activities. There was no liberty, and everyone, including officers, was restricted to the bases. But that did not stop Bill Robinson and Andy Burgess from slipping away to enjoy a meal in Manila. Their expectations of a pleasant time were dashed when they had dinner at one of Manila's largest Japanese restaurants. Not only were they the only people in the restaurant, but the Japanese waitresses cried openly while serving their meal. They ate quickly, and hurried back to Sangley Point.[25]

While the two officers were hurrying through their meal, Vice Admiral Sir Tom Phillips, RN, arrived in Manila. He had come to ask Admiral Thomas Hart and General Douglas MacArthur for aircraft and ships to support HMS *Repulse* and HMS *Prince of Wales*. While the men met in Hart's headquarters the next morning, word arrived that a powerful Japanese force had been spotted off the coast of Malaya, headed for Thailand. The RAAF Hudson that had reported the sighting had been shot down.

Admiral Phillips immediately left the meeting to return to Singapore. But the crew of his Sunderland flying boat could not be found, and the word went out to find them. While the admiral fumed, a growing manhunt was carried out through Manila's bars, brothels, and back alleys. The British aircrew was nowhere to be found.

Unable to wait any longer, Admiral Phillips asked Admiral Hart for a lift back to Singapore. Hart gladly provided a PBY from VP-101, flown by Duke Campbell and Al Armbruster. Several hours after Campbell and Armbruster had taken off, the search for Admiral Phillips's crew was still in progress. It seemed that all the obvious places had been searched at least twice, and the men had even been asked to reveal other "secret getaway spots." Surprisingly, the men willingly named places that were wholly unknown to the authorities, but even in those hidden places there were no signs of the missing British crewmen.

The problem was that the searchers had based their search on the false assumption that the British airmen would be chasing the jaded pleasures of Manila's bars and brothels. Actually, they were in a movie house watching Rita Hayworth and Tyrone Power in *Blood and Sand* and the fifth episode of *The Green Archer*. In fact, they sat through the whole show three times.[26]

Before the search was over, Campbell and Armbruster had already delivered Admiral Phillips to Singapore where they stayed just long enough to eat and refuel before heading back. Landing at 1500 on 7 December, they taxied up to the ramp, expecting to have the plane hauled out for its scheduled maintenance. Instead, the plane was refueled and Campbell was told to move out into the bay. When Campbell protested, he was told, "Don't argue. Just do as you're told." War was exactly twelve hours away.[27]

# 2

# The Philippines
# 8–13 December 1941

---

*8 December*

"JAPAN STARTED HOSTILITIES GOVERN YOURSELVES
ACCORDINGLY."[1]

In Cavite, the duty officer, Ensign Arthur Jacobson, received the
decoded message and immediately notified Peterson and Wagner.
The time was 0315. His next step was to spread the alarm to VP-101.

Lights snapped on, whistles blew, sleepy men rose from the
depths of sleep and stared dumbly at the man shouting through
the open door. Many voices shouted the same message.

"Hit the deck. We're at war with the Japs."

"The war's started."

"Off yer ass and on yer feet, there's a war on."

Out of the confusion and noise an annoyed airman's voice angrily
demanded, "Can't the duty section handle it?"[2] PatWing-10 went
to war.

In the officer's quarters Duke Campbell and his copilot Al
Armbruster quickly dressed and headed for their plane. The third
roommate, Lieutenant Joseph Antonides, awakened by the noise,
peered bleary-eyed at his watch. Because Antonides was the engi-
neering officer in charge of aircraft overhaul, he was not actually a

Prewar life in the Philippines afforded ample opportunity for recreation. Until just before the war, the duty day ended at 1300 hours unless the aircrews were out on patrol. This photo was taken 8 August 1941 on Tawitawi. (Courtesy Lowell Williamson)

Hunting was another popular pastime among the PatWing-10 aircrews. Shown here is Robert "Hawk" Barrett and his three gun bearers. (Courtesy R. Barrett)

member of PatWing-10, but belonged to the navy yard. Reasoning that, war or no war, his civilian employees would not come to work until 0800, Antonides dressed and reported to ComPatWing.

A similar scene unfolded in Olongapo. Ensign Frank Ralston, the duty officer, received the war message and went directly to his skipper, Lieutenant Commander Edgar Neale. The squadron commander looked quickly at the message and told Ralston to have the pilots assemble in the hangar. At 0400 the first sleepy airmen were abruptly awakened by the bright room lights and a bellowed, "Hit the deck."³

Tom McCabe was already up and shaving. He was scheduled to

fly an early patrol that morning and was surprised when his friend, John Hyland, came in.

"What are you doing up so early, John?"

"They woke us all and said we're to report to the hangar."

"I guess that means us too."

"Yea, they said everybody."

Though both officers suspected what the early morning assembly meant, neither one knew for sure. Ensign Lowell Williamson was not sure what the early call meant either, and assumed it was "just another early morning drill." He had been suffering from dysentery for three days and decided to ignore the drill.

Pig roasts were another activity they enjoyed. This four-pig feast is being supervised by John Hyland and an officer from the *Childs*. The man on the right is Captain Gallard, Philippine scouts. Photo taken October 1941. (Courtesy T. E. L. McCabe)

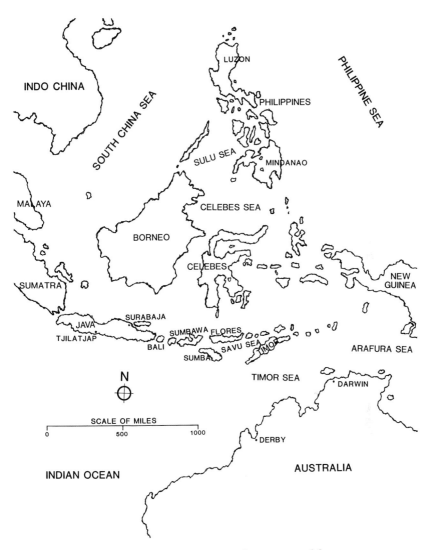

PatWing-10's area of operations, 8 December 1941–9 May 1942.

At both Olongapo and Sangley Point, ground crews shackled four 500-pound bombs to each plane. Plane captains supervised last-minute checks, while other crewmen loaded boxes of .50- and .30-caliber ammunition into the planes. None of the ammunition belts had any armor-piercing rounds. The ammunition being loaded

into the PBYs on the first day of the war was all training ammunition. The situation did not result from oversight born of
haste. There simply was not any other ammunition available to
PatWing-10.[4]

On the water, VP-101 planes went to the *Langley* to draw bombs
and ammunition. They had the more difficult job of bombing-up
their planes from an open boat beneath the wings. But by 0600 the
first patrols were taking off.

In Olongapo the VP-102 pilots gathered in the hangar to hear
Lieutenant Commander Neale read Admiral Hart's war message.
When Neale had finished, John Hyland turned to the man next to
him and asked, "What the hell does that mean, conduct yourselves
accordingly?" The other pilot just shrugged.

Lieutenant Al Gray, a former Annapolis football star, told Tom
McCabe that the Pacific Fleet would soon be arriving and make
short work of the Japanese. The forecast made sense to McCabe,
and underscored the fact that no one in VP-102 knew that Pearl
Harbor had been bombed. A few in VP-101 might have heard
something about the attack at that early hour, but none of them even
suspected how badly the fleet had been hurt. In fact, the collective

Still another hunting expedition, this time for crocodiles, in August 1941.
(Courtesy Lowell Williamson)

It was not all play for PatWing-10, particularly as the war drew nearer. The presence of Japanese freighters, such as this one photographed from a low-flying PBY, became a common affair. Many of the ships' crewmen and officers were actually Japanese naval officers sent to obtain information. (Courtesy Gordon Ebbe)

state of mind in both squadrons was confidence and optimism. Ensign Jack Grayson summed it up when he said, "We were too naive to be scared."

Prewar training was paying off. Despite some confusion, the two squadrons were quickly armed and deployed. Seven PBYs, designated as a scouting group, were held at Olongapo. Seven more were sent to the *Childs* in Manila Bay to act as an attack group. Five formed another scouting group at Cavite, and four were sent to Laguna de Bay, eighty miles south of Manila, to form a second attack group. Three planes were already in Malalag Bay, at the south end of Mindanao, with the *Preston*. The only two planes not operational on 8 December were undergoing overhaul in hangar X-34.

The planes were deployed to give them the best coverage of the Manila area and to reduce losses. But there was one feature of the war plan that seemed odd, even at the time. Both squadron commanders had fully equipped headquarters at their home bases. But when the war started, both were uprooted and sent off to tem-

porary bases. Neale went from Olongapo to Cavite, and Peterson
went from Cavite to Los Baños. The planners could have cut the
movement in half by simply sending Neale to Los Baños, and leaving Peterson in Cavite. Better yet, they could have left them both
where they were.

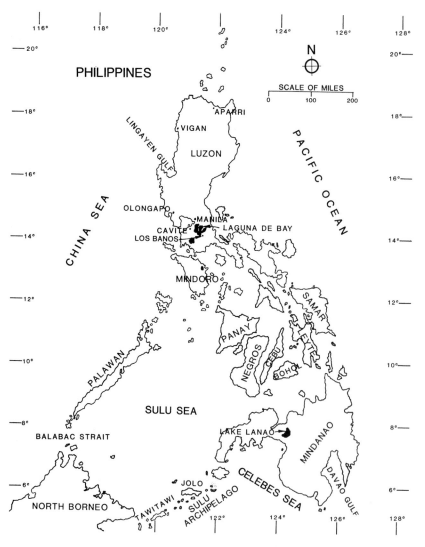

PatWing-10's area of operations until 14 December 1942.

By late 1941 PatWing-10 had camouflaged its airplanes a mottled jungle green and brown. The camouflage scheme was abandoned by the time the war started. (Courtesy Gordon Ebbe)

As the deployment took shape, Tom McCabe was preparing to take off on a patrol to Cam Ranh Bay. As his PBY went down the ramp, he was told that the Japanese had bombed Pearl Harbor. "Nonsense," he responded, and started his takeoff run.

In Manila Bay, Ensign Donald Chay was taking off in an OS2U "Kingfisher" to fly an antisubmarine patrol at the entrance to the bay. As the plane rose up on the step, one of his bombs broke loose and plunged into the water. The safety system worked, and the bomb did not explode.

At about that same time Bob Swenson was also experiencing a slight hitch in plans. His copilot, Ensign William Gough, had not made it to the plane, and Swenson was having to leave without him. Like several others, Gough had not really believed that the alert was genuine, and he chose this day to protest what he felt was a serious grievance.

Because the junior officers were berthed on Sangley Point, some distance from the ramp, a station wagon was supposed to pick them up. Sometimes the car got there, but most of the time it did not. When it did not, the junior officers had a long hike to the ramp. On 8 December the station wagon did not get there, and Gough vowed not to budge until it did. By the time he realized that the alert was real, Swenson's plane was already in the water. While Gough trudged up the road toward the ramp, Swenson was starting his takeoff run.[5]

In Olongapo Lowell Williamson was unaware of the frantic activity around him. The sick pilot was still asleep when, at 0610, Ensign Andrew ("Andy") Reid shook him awake.

"Come on. Get up," Reid urged, "There's a war on." Engine noise and shouts underscored Reid's message, and Williamson thought, "I'd better get up if I don't want to be left behind." Feeling terrible, he dressed and went out to his plane. It was 0640.[6]

In Malalag Bay, on the south end of Mindanao, the *Preston* had just shifted her anchorage. The war message reached the ship at 0340, and the first patrol plane had taken off at 0515. The other two PBYs were still moored to buoys near the beach. Lieutenant Commander Etheridge Grant had his ship at condition two, half the guns manned.[7]

Cullen Bray, an NAP, stood by the boarding ladder watching the motor whaleboat that had just pulled away from plane number four (P-4). The boat was bringing Gordon Ebbe, who had just been relieved as the onboard plane watch, back to the ship for breakfast. Bray was to be taken out to plane number seven (P-7) to relieve Ensign Robert Tills.[8]

At 0710 the boat came alongside the tender, Ebbe started up the ladder, and the general quarters alarm blared. Just as Ebbe stepped on deck, six fighters swept in under the low overcast, machine guns firing. Together Bray and Ebbe dove for cover as the *Preston's* anti-aircraft guns opened up.[9]

Ignoring the ship, the fighters pounced on the two PBYs. Unable to fight back, the flying boats were easy meat for the cannon-armed Zeros. As the fighters roared over, both PBYs exploded and burned in expanding pools of flaming gasoline.

In P-7 Ensign Tills died instantly, a bullet in the head. RM3c Albert E. Layton leaped from the inferno, his body wrapped in flames. The men from P-4, who had gone over the side as the

Part of PatWing-10's prewar training included operations from advance bases. This is John Sloatman's plane pulled up on the beach after it hit a coral head. Sloatman's crew, assisted by Bob Swenson's crew, is repairing the hole in the hull just forward of the wing. (Courtesy of Lowell Williamson)

fighters started their run, swam back and pulled the badly burned Layton to the beach.

The *Preston* was already underway, racing for the harbor entrance. As she dashed toward open water, seven Japanese carrier-based bombers attacked her. All around the ship the sea exploded and foamed, concussion rings racing out as water rose in columns a hundred feet high. Maneuvering to avoid the bombs, the tender twisted and turned, slalom-like between the columns.

For nearly half an hour the Japanese attacked the ship, coming close but never hitting her. Their bombs expended, the Japanese headed back toward their carrier, and the *Preston* came about to look for survivors. As they were picking up the survivors, P-6, the lone patrol plane, flashed a warning. Three unidentified destroyers were fifteen miles south of Davao Gulf, headed toward the *Preston*. They had to be Japanese. If the *Preston* did not leave now, she would be trapped inside the harbor. Commander Grant lost no time getting underway, glad that the *Preston* was a 25-knot ex-destroyer instead of the plodding 13-knot *Langley*.

One thousand feet above the tender, Ensign Ira Brown and his copilot, Ensign Doug Norris, knew nothing about the attack. They assumed that the missing PBYs were out on patrol and the *Preston* was moving to a new position. What bothered them was the garbled signal that repeatedly blinked up at them from the tender.[10]

A few minutes later P-6 received a coded radio message from Commander Patrol Wing (ComPatWing), directing them to search east and then fly to Polloc Harbor, on the west side of Mindanao. The message also ordered them to avoid the Gulf of Davao.

"Hell. We were right in Davao Gulf and it was impossible to go east without going right over it," Brown recalled, "so I turned north a little before heading east."

Fifteen minutes later ComPatWing sent, "REPORT WHEN TENDER LAST SIGHTED AND HER CONDITION." Apparently the *Preston* had maintained radio silence after the initial report that she was under attack.

P-6 replied, "TENDER LAST SIGHTED 1020 GETTING UNDERWAY. CONDITION NORMAL."[11]

The report reassured ComPatWing, but the whole exchange bothered Brown and Norris. What was going on? Swinging south they again spotted the three destroyers, noting that they were headed straight for the Davao Gulf. In answer to their contact report, ComPatWing sent "PROCEED POLLOC AND REPORT ARRIVAL."[12]

As P-6 turned toward Polloc Harbor, the *Preston* was hurrying to clear Davao Gulf before the Japanese closed the door. Aboard were the survivors of P-4 and P-7, including the badly burned radioman.

Meanwhile, at Cavite Captain Wagner could only wait. PatWing-10 had patrols out that covered areas northeast and northwest of Manila. So far they had reported nothing. But the attack on the *Preston* reinforced the widely held belief that the Japanese would attack from carriers. In fact, only the light carrier *Ryujo* was operating in the Philippines.[13]

Lieutenant Antonides never got to his office in the Cavite Navy Yard. After he reported to Captain Wagner, Antonides was put to work as a messenger, with the understanding that he would be relieved when his civilians came to work at 0800. It was now long past 0800, and Antonides was still delivering messages. Understandably anxious to get over to his own battle station, he told Wagner that he had "things to do besides carry messages." It was just after noon when he spoke to the captain. Wagner's reply caught him by surprise.[14]

"You've been transferred to PatWing-10 because you've got no damn business being in the navy yard wearing a pair of wings." Wagner pointed to the gold aviator's wings on Antonides' breast. He told the startled lieutenant that "arrangements have already been made with the Chief of Staff." Actually, nothing changed in regard to his duties, but the transfer probably saved Antonides' life.

While Antonides was adjusting to his new billet, MacArthur's bomber commanders were tearing their hair over MacArthur's apparent indecision. They were urging him to order a bomber strike at the Japanese airfields on Formosa, but getting nowhere. Among the several reasons given for the turn down was the report that MacArthur was waiting for the Japanese "to commit a hostile act in the Philippines." Apparently the general did not know about, or chose to ignore, the attack on the *Preston*. Whatever the reason, the order to bomb Formosa was not given, and when the Japanese attacked later that morning the B-17s were on the ground.[15]

Another change in plans was taking place out on the water where Duke Campbell and Al Armbruster were fueling P-3 from the USS *Langley*. They had returned from an early patrol and expected to be fueled and bombed up. Instead, they were told to unhook the one bomb that had already been shackled on and return to the ramp.

At the ramp they were told to fly Rear Admiral William Glassford to his flagship, the *Houston*, in Iloilo Bay. The admiral and his staff had not yet arrived at the ramp, so Campbell took the opportunity to change a defective starter cable. They were about half way through the job when Admiral Glassford showed up with ten or twelve people and a truckload of baggage. The passengers and baggage had been taken aboard, and the new starter cable was being hooked up, when the air raid alarm started to wail. Looking up, Campbell saw a large formation of bombers and fighters coming in from the north. They were the planes that should have been destroyed on the ground in Formosa, had General MacArthur acted in time.

"Never mind hooking that cable up," he shouted to his plane captain AMM1c William Gannott. "Pull it out and we'll crank it by hand."[16]

Hurriedly a crewman buttoned up the cowling, Gannott grabbed the engine crank, inserted it in the engine and gave it a "hell of a turn." Gannott was a big man, 6 feet, 4 inches tall and well over 240 pounds. He was already as strong as an ox, but the threat that was now clearly visible in the cloudless sky must have given him even greater strength. The "hell of a turn" snapped the crank off inside the engine.

Campbell's situation had gone from not good to desperate. And what started out to be a fifteen-minute job looked like one that might never be finished. The cowling was jerked open and Gannott shoved the starter cable inside. Joined by a third crewman, the men held the six cable connections in place while Campbell and Armbruster started the engines.

As the three crewmen dove back inside, Campbell turned into the wind. The overloaded PBY plowed across the bay on what seemed to Campbell to be an endless run. Behind them smoke marked the destruction of Clark and Nichols fields, blackening the

Before the war, the American star insignia had a red ball in the center as shown here on the bow of 21-P-10. When the war started, many anti-aircraft gunners mistook the red ball for a Japanese "meatball" and fired on the planes. The red ball was removed shortly after the war started. (Courtesy Gordon Ebbe)

sky. Slowly the PBY rose off the water as more Japanese bombers moved across the sky in a precise V of Vs. Staying low, the PBY shot across the water toward the open sea and safety.

Long before Campbell delivered his passengers to Iloilo Bay, the Japanese had effectively smashed United States air power in the Philippines. Nearly all the army's B-17s and most of its fighters were caught on the ground that day. It was as disastrous a blow to PatWing-10 as if they had been the target. Without the army's fighter protection the PBYs were virtually defenseless against the Japanese Zeros. And the loss of the B-17s meant that the PatWing-10 PBYs—poorly armed, slow, lacking in armor and self-sealing fuel tanks—would be expected to shoulder even greater responsibilities. Captain Wagner summed it up when he wrote, "This attack put out of action, on the first day of the war, about two-thirds of our Army pursuit strength. It was a very disappointing blow."[17]

At the end of the day, the patrol planes returned empty-handed, to find dramatic evidence that the Japanese had gotten through. The problem was that the PBYs had been looking for a fleet, or more specifically, a carrier force. In fact, on 8 December 1941, there was nothing out there for them to find. The Japanese bombers and fighters were coming from Formosa, but the invasion fleet would soon be on the scene. In the meantime there were dozens of rumors about fifth-column activity and the presence of German pilots and planes among the Japanese formations.

The fifth-column rumors stemmed from reports by army pilots that just prior to, and during, the attack on Iba, Clark, and Nichols fields, their radios had been jammed. Additional evidence was found in a report made by Lieutenant W. E. Strathern, operations officer at Clark Field, that Japanese transmitters were found near Clark and Nichols fields.[18]

There may have been some truth to the rumors. There was a group of Philippine nationalists who wanted the Americans out of the Philippines, and many of those people looked to the Japanese for the means of accomplishing that goal. There were also hundreds of Japanese nationals living in the Philippines, and some were probably spies.

There was, however, no truth to rumors about German pilots and planes being among the Japanese formations. Nevertheless, stories about Messerschmitts at Clark Field and sightings of downed enemy pilots with blond hair and blue eyes were accepted without question.[19]

The facts, and the rumors, made the men in PatWing-10 uneasy, but did not shake their confidence or diminish their optimism. Tomorrow would be a better day—they would find those Japanese carriers.

*9 December*

The presence of fighters with the bombers convinced the Pat-Wing-10 flyers that Japanese carriers must be operating in Philippine waters. And it was frustrating for them to have ended the first day without a single sighting. The attack on the *Preston*, Tills's death, and the drubbing the army air force had taken made the frustration worse.

Before dawn, patrols were again sent out to locate the enemy. About eighty miles out, P-19, flown by Al Gray and Frank Ralston, spotted a small freighter. They were northwest of Olongapo when they saw the ship, apparently steaming toward Manila. She flew no flags so they were unable to determine the freighter's nationality by looking at her, and when they challenged her by lamp, she did not answer.[20]

Al Gray, a careful man who rarely jumped to conclusions, wanted a better look at the ship before he did anything. Circling and dropping to wave-level, he came up on the ship from astern. They were amidships, one hundred feet out, when machine-gun fire burst from the bridge. A closely spaced stream of bullets chopped up the rudder, cutting a control cable. Ralston poured on the coal, Gray hauled back the column, and the starboard waist gunner poured a stream of .50-caliber slugs into the ship.

"HAVE BEEN OPPOSED BY ENEMY VESSEL RIGHT RUDDER CONTROL BROKEN TAIL DAMAGED REPAIRABLE. I AM RETURNING TO BASE . . ."[21]

The message gave the ship's position, but no other information. Still, it was an enemy contact, and appeared to be the break that PatWing-10 was hoping for. Three PBYs flown by Lieutenant Bill Deam, Lieutenant (j.g.) Leroy Deede, and Ensign Bob Swenson, took off from Laguna de Bay to attack the enemy.[22]

Meanwhile, on the bridge of the Norwegian freighter SS *Ulysses*, the captain and his men were congratulating themselves on having driven off a Japanese bomber. There was no doubt that it was a Japanese plane. They had clearly seen the large red "meatball" on the fuselage, and the plane had fired at them. The fact that the large red "meatball" was in the center of a large white star on a blue field, apparently went unnoticed.

Bill Deam's three-plane section arrived over the target at 10,000 feet. What the pilots saw did not look much like an invasion fleet, but then the message had only mentioned one vessel. Deam's bombardier peered through the Norden bomb sight at the now zigzagging target. Satisfied that the problem was set up correctly, he released his bombs.

Twelve 500-pound bombs plunged toward the *Ulysses*, now scrambling frantically to get out of the way. The outcome of the attack was recorded in the PatWing-10 *Diary*. "They found an allied freighter in the vicinity and attacked, but missed—fortunately."

The next morning the *Manila Bulletin* ran two, side-by-side, headlines, "PBYS BOMB JAP SHIP" and "FREIGHTER REPELS JAP BOMBERS." A few days later the *Ulysses'* captain told Bob Swenson, "Before we were bombed, I had a hell of a time getting my men to go to their battle stations. I don't have that problem now."[23]

The *Ulysses* incident at least gave some of the people in PatWing-10 something to chuckle about, but there was no humor in another case of mistaken identity on 9 December.

P-21, flown by Ensign Earl McConnell and Ensign J. C. Watson, was returning to Olongapo from patrol. Approaching Subic Bay from landward, the PBY descended to 300 feet, setting up for the approach to Subic. Suddenly a Filipino antiaircraft battery opened up. Tracer streams poured up from the jungle, converging on the low-flying PBY. Rounds slammed into the plane smashing instruments, radios, and puncturing the fuel tank. Watson was hit in the right elbow. AMM2c Thomas Marbry was hit hard in the knee, the slug nearly severing his leg. Another crewman, RM2c James Gray, doubled over with a round through his groin.[24]

His plane shot up, leaking fuel, and two crewmen badly injured, McConnell quickly set down on the water. George Gaboury watched the PBY come in low over the shore and hit the water right at the ramp. "There was a hell of a splash when he hit hard, sort of a three-point landing."[25] The hull was full of bullet holes.

The uninjured crew members shouted for stretchers and a truck to transport the wounded. Inside the PBY, fuel, water, and blood sloshed in the bilges. McConnell tried to staunch the flow of blood from Marbry's shattered leg. Gray was in terrible pain, and of the two appeared to be in the worst shape. In fact, Marbry died of shock and loss of blood five hours later. Gray survived and returned to duty.

When the second day of the war ended, PatWing-10 was still largely unscathed. Morale was good, the men eager to strike a blow at the enemy. Though the patrols had again returned empty-handed, they were certain that the elusive Japanese were out there somewhere. They were right. The Japanese were about to knock on the door, and when they did the roof would fall in.

*10 December*

At dawn 4,000 Japanese troops started coming ashore at Vigan and Aparri. Their objectives were airfields close to their landing areas. While the invasion fleets moved in, and Japanese soldiers prepared to go over the side, bombers and fighter crews on Formosa were being briefed for a massive raid on the Cavite Navy Base.

Patrol Wing Ten was unaware of these developments when they sent out their first patrols on 10 December. At 0500 three PBYs took off from Manila Bay, fanning out over patrol sectors that swept from east to west across the seas north of Luzon. Al Gray covered the left-hand sector, Lieutenant Clarence ("Nick") Keller had the center, and Lieutenant Leslie Pew had the right-hand sector. At 0645 Nick Keller and his copilot Andy Reid found the Japanese.

They knew they were getting close at 0630, when they saw a float-equipped biplane below them on the opposite course. They did not recognize the plane as Japanese, but they stayed clear of it anyway. Fifteen minutes later they saw what they thought were two battleships, a heavy cruiser, and four destroyers.

Reaching for his notepad, Reid said, "I'll make out a contact report."[26] Keller shook his head. "No, those are the British—*Repulse* and *Prince of Wales*." Reid stopped writing, and Keller continued northward on patrol. They did, however, notify ComPatWing-10 about the sighting. Whether or not they suggested the ships might be British is unknown, but they obviously were not too concerned that they might be Japanese.

There was at least some basis for Lieutenant Keller's line of reasoning—but not much. Probably Keller was more concerned about locating the Japanese aircraft carriers that were believed to be operating off Luzon. And that preoccupation, coupled with a vague idea that the powerful British warships would have sailed north to meet the Japanese, made him overlook the more obvious conclusion. Whatever Keller's line of reasoning was, it was not shared by Captain Wagner. Thirty minutes after sending the sighting report they were ordered to relocate the ships, and "make MOs," two dashes followed by three dashes, sent continuously for other planes to home in on.

Thirty minutes later the PBY approached the fleet from dead astern and a bit off to starboard. Banking the PBY, Keller cut across the stern of the last ship in line.

I passed astern of the force, distance about 7,000 yards, altitude 50 feet. The cruiser, which was in the rear of the column, and two destroyers, turned and opened fire with antiaircraft and secondary battery. The bursts of antiaircraft were about 200 yards astern. The detonations could be felt in the plane.[27]

As the PBY raced across the water, flak dotted her path. More deadly were the thick columns of water thrown up by the secondary and main batteries. The gunners were firing ahead of the low-flying plane, hoping that it would run into one of the columns. Radioman Edward Bedford, peering through a small port, thought that the gunfire "looked exactly like long, black snakewhips reaching out ahead and behind us." To Andy Reid "the volume of fire was so great that it looked like the ships were on fire."

The PBY was under fire for three minutes before Keller climbed to 2,500 feet and ducked into some scattered cumulus clouds. Using the clouds for cover, he worked around until he had the sun at his back. Then he sent his contact report.

"1 KUMA CLASS CL 4DDS 2 KONGO CLASS BBS POSITION 6-40x8-10 COURSE 180 SPEED 10." The message was received by ComPatWing-10 at 0800, and Wagner ordered Peterson's Los Baños attack group to attack the target. The five PBYs were already bombed up and ready to go when a decision was made to rearm the planes with torpedoes.[28]

In the meantime Keller and Reid were tracking the Japanese and sending a constant stream of MOs. The signal, sent in Morse Code, was broadcast on 440 kc, a frequency that required a lot of power. Ed Bedford lowered the trailing antenna and pounded out the repetitious signal.

Forty-five minutes later Peterson's five PBYs had been rearmed with torpedoes and were nearly ready for takeoff. But again the takeoff was delayed by a new decision—change back to bombs. Finally, at 0910, the five bomb-laden PBYs lifted off Laguna de Bay, swung out over Mariveles, and settled on course 310 degrees true. At 1050 they picked up Keller's MOs. At 1105 they changed course to 328 degrees, homing on the signal.[29]

Keller had been tracking the Japanese for over three hours, and everyone in the plane was wondering "where in hell is the attack group?" Peterson's group should have shown up a long time ago. But a new development pushed thoughts about Peterson's group aside. Eight floatplane fighters were rapidly climbing toward the PBY.

"Here they come! Looks like two seaplane fighters." The shouted warning was from AMM1c Joseph Durham in the starboard waist gun.[30]

Keller dove into a cloud, performing a maneuver that would shortly become a standard defensive tactic for PatWing-10 pilots. Keeping an eye on the fleet, watching for fighters, and ducking into the nearest cloud, Keller and Reid joined in a deadly game of "hide-and-seek." Abruptly, the game was made more complicated by a new problem.

Beneath the violently maneuvering plane the trailing antenna swung and snapped like a huge steel whip. Unable to withstand the forces exerted on it, the antenna shorted out, starting a fire in the hull near the tunnel gun. Smoke and flames filled the after part of the plane, choking and blinding the crewmen stationed aft. Quickly the antenna burned through, sending 175 feet of steel cable tumbling toward the sea. Ed Bedford jumped up from his radio set, grabbed a $CO_2$ bottle, and emptied the contents on the fire. Its source gone and smothered in $CO_2$, the fire went out. Switching over to the emergency antenna, Bedford again started pounding out MOs.

At that moment, Peterson's group spotted the enemy ships about ten miles away. They also spotted enemy fighters 9,000 feet below. The area was dotted with low, fleecy clouds that partially obscured the ships, but afforded the PBYs some cover. Peterson led his group up to 15,000 feet and started the bomb run.

The ships were making twenty-three knots, and zig-zagging, with the PBYs approaching from their starboard beam. Not satisfied with the setup, Peterson led his group around in a "turn through 360 degrees, and headed for the largest enemy battleship in the center of the disposition."[31] The attack was made out of the sun.

As the PBYs approached, the enemy opened up with heavy anti-aircraft fire. Edgar Palm, an NAP in one of the planes, recalled that "there was AA all over the place; above us, below us, all around."[32] To Jack Dawley and Arthur Jacobson the "AA fire was close."[33] At 1205 the PBYs unloaded twenty 500-pound bombs in salvo.

"Let's get the hell out of here."

No one hesitated. Edgar Palm said that it was the first time he had ever seen five PBYs do a clover leaf "like the Blue Angels do." As the five PBYs broke formation and dove for the clouds, Japanese fighters were already among them, the sky black with flak. But instead of heading for home, Peterson circled back to watch the bombs hit.

> I noted that the pattern was good, but the mean point of impact was about twenty-five yards astern. Three bombs hit very close on the port quarter, about ten to twenty feet away, and one burst fifteen feet astern. The target turned through 360 degrees to port, slowed, and took up an erratic course about 20 degrees true. No smoke or flame was seen.[34]

Later there would be a claim that one bomb had hit on the fantail, and that the damaged ship was a *Kongo*-class battleship. Actually, they had damaged a cruiser, though no direct hits had been scored. The ship was clearly hurt, probably rudder damage and a sprung shaft. She was soon left behind by her consorts, who were last seen zig-zagging away at high speed.

Peterson did not hang around any longer than he had to. Having seen what he needed to see, he headed for cloud cover and called the rest of his group to join up. Five miles astern of the enemy formation they formed up and headed home. At 1230 Peterson sent, "ATTACK COMPLETED."[35]

Peterson's message was unclear. Was the attack completed because the target had been destroyed, or were the planes just out of bombs? Ordering two of Peterson's planes to relieve Keller keeping watch over the enemy, Wagner called in the other planes from patrol. He intended to mount a second five-plane attack.

But Wagner's follow-up raid ran into trouble from the start. P-12, flown by Ensigns Robert Snyder and William Jones, had just come across an unescorted freighter. Whether it was another *Ulysses*-type incident or a lone Japanese ship is unclear. Whichever it was, P-12 bombed and hit the ship, leaving it dead in the water and listing. They were recalled shortly after the attack, but P-12 never got back.

Snyder was coming in to land on Laguna de Bay. Knowing they were so close to home and elated about their successful bombing attack, his crew may have dropped their guard. On the other hand, the Japanese pilot may have been so good that he was able to approach the PBY undetected. The Japanese pilot, attacking from low and behind, waited until he was at point-blank range before opening up with machine guns and cannon. Holes were blown in the hull, wings, and engines. P-12 shuddered, black smoke belched from both engines, and she exploded. One minute she was an airplane, and the next she was a rolling ball of fire, smoke, and debris tumbling toward the lake. None of the crew survived.[36]

The other four planes, already rearmed with one torpedo and two 500-pound bombs, were starting their takeoff runs. As the heavily laden planes rose up on their steps, the Japanese attacked Cavite. Swarms of bombers, flying in precise formations, bombed from altitudes well out of reach of the few American antiaircraft guns. While the bombers were blasting the Navy Yard into a flaming ruin, the fighters came down on the deck to chew up anything that moved. Out on the water floatplanes and flying boats were racing every which way, trying to get airborne.

Ensign McConnell, in P-28, had just taken off when his plane was pounced on by a swarm of Zeros. In an instant P-28 was reduced to a barely flyable sieve, one engine dead, gasoline spewing from the wings. How anyone survived, and what kept the plane from burning, is a mystery. Hugging the tree tops, McConnell staggered to Laguna de Bay where he put the crippled plane down as fast as he could.[37]

Lieutenant Harmon Utter's P-5 was barely airborne when someone shouted, "We're being attacked by three Zeros."[38] The warning was accompanied by the rattle of hits along the fuselage. Cannon rounds exploded in the hull, control cables were shot away, and Plexiglas panels glazed. NAP Payne stood in the bow firing at the fighters with the .30-caliber machine gun. Ensign Richard S. Roberts, in the right-hand seat, watched him fire a long steady burst at a fighter coming in on their beam. Roberts started to bank right.

"Stay flat and straight so the gunner can line up and shoot," shouted Utter.[39]

Roberts watched the fighter bore in, red flashes sparking along its wing. "I just wrapped the damn airplane around until the wing was damn near in the water." The PBY turned into the fighter, Payne firing the bow gun in an uninterrupted burst. For a moment everything slowed down to a crawl. Roberts watched the line of tracers from Payne's gun climb over the fighter's nose, pounding into the cockpit. Abruptly the fighter nosed down and exploded on the water.

Another Zero came in bow on, high, chewing up the starboard engine, knocking it out, and puncturing the fuel tanks. Fuel ran from the wings, and oil poured from the starboard engine. Utter and Roberts went down onto the water so fast that the Japanese pilots figured they had a kill. P-5 was still plowing across the water when the fighters wheeled away in search of new targets.

At the same time that McConnell and Utter were taking off, the Utility Squadron's single-engine floatplanes were also scrambling to get away. Three Grumman J2F "Ducks" and a Vought OS2U "Kingfisher" took off, heading across the tree tops for Laguna de Bay. The fourth J2F, flown by Ensign Don Chay, was almost caught on the water when its engine refused to start. Chay kept trying while his gunner beat off two twin-engine fighters that swooped down on what was literally a sitting duck. At the eleventh hour, the

engine kicked over and Chay went for broke without waiting to
warm up. After he landed safely on Laguna de Bay he recorded in
his diary, "I was really clipping the tree tops and zig-zagging."

Chay was not the only one caught on the water with a stubborn engine. Lieutenant (j.g.) Robinson and Ensign Burgess were
headed toward their torpedo-armed PBY when the fighters came
in. Things already looked bad as they dropped into their seats, but
things looked a lot worse when the starboard engine would not turn
over. While the Japanese attacked targets around them, two crewmen climbed out on the wing to hand-crank the engine. Looking at
the situation later, Burgess decided that the faulty engine may actually have saved them, since the Japanese were only going after
planes that were obviously trying to take off.

Finally the balky engine kicked over and caught. Robinson and
Burgess took off, heading for the last reported position of the dam-
aged Japanese cruiser. Their PBY, and another flown by Lieutenant
Commander Clayton Marcy and ACMM George Webber, an NAP,
were all that remained of Captain Wagner's second strike attempt.
And they failed to find the target.[40]

The sky over Cavite was clear except for scattered black puffs of
flak that burst well below the large Japanese bomber formation.
The bombers, in a tight V of Vs, made several passes over the Navy
Yard before they dropped their bombs. Without opposition, they
were taking their time to do the job right. Captain Wagner and his
executive officer, Commander Frank J. Bridget, stood on the bal-
cony of their office watching the bombers approach.

As the first salvo hurtled down, Captain Wagner suddenly re-
membered that Peterson's returning attack group had to be warned
about the raid. A messenger was sent to locate Lieutenant Tom
Pollock, VP-102's communications officer, to tell him to put out a
warning to Peterson. At that moment the first salvo hit the water
between Canacao and the Navy Yard, sending up a "solid curtain of
water, over one hundred feet high and a half-mile long."[41]

The bombers passed over, turned, and lined up for a second
run. Pollock and RM1c Kenneth Cox were already in the radio-
room, Pollock encoding and Cox sending, when the second salvo
struck. Just before the explosion, Pollock heard a sound "like a train
crossing a trestle." For a moment he had a vision of himself being
picked out of the wreckage, but the somber image did not last long.

A tremendous explosion slammed into the concrete building, blowing the blackout covers off the windows, shattering glass, and violently shaking the building. The same stick of bombs smashed the power station, destroyed the telephone exchange, and knocked out most of the water system.

Without power the transmitters were dead, and there was no way of warning Peterson. Pollock and Cox had gotten some of the message out, but there was no way of knowing if any of it had been picked up by the homeward bound PBYs.

Lacking water to fight them, fires started to burn unchecked through the Navy Yard. Dead and injured were scattered everywhere. Panic-stricken civilians rushed from shelter to shelter, many being caught in the open and cut down. Sailors fired at the planes with any weapon they could find; pistols, Springfields, and automatic rifles popped and chattered adding to the growing battle noise.

The third salvo fell with deadly accuracy. Buildings collapsed, docks burned, and the Asiatic Fleet's entire supply of torpedoes exploded with an earth-shaking blast. When bombs fell into the crowded wooden buildings that made up the yard's industrial area, the fires really "started rolling."

Through skill and "superhuman effort," an electrician restored power, which put the transmitters back on the air. But the success was short-lived. The next salvo took out the power station for good, bringing down one of the tall antenna masts.

Unable to transmit, Pollock and Cox took cover in an open trench. As more bombs fell, the ground convulsed and black, acrid smoke fouled the air. The dead lay where they fell, many remaining unburied for days after the attack. Through the noise of exploding bombs and falling buildings, the living could hear the screams of people trapped in the flaming debris.

The sky belonged to the Japanese, who just two days earlier had virtually destroyed the army's fighters on the ground. Seeing the bombers making slow, unopposed runs made the sailors feel helpless and angry. Pollock heard a man voice the feelings they all shared.

Where the hell is our fighter protection? If the damn AA guns can't reach them, why can't we get a little help from the army guys?

They been roasting us about our waddling ducks, and where are they now? Yeah, Where?[42]

After what seemed an eternity, the bombers and their fighter escort disappeared, leaving Cavite smashed and untenable. The loss of life was enormous. But PatWing-10 had come out of the disaster in surprisingly good shape. One plane, with its entire crew, had been lost, and two had been shot up. One of those was written off as a "washout," but the judgment proved to be premature.

McConnell and his crew had landed P-28 in one piece on Laguna de Bay. But looking at the shot-up engine, the leaking fuel tanks, and watching water rising in the bilge, they concluded the plane was a total loss. Stripping the plane of guns and other useful equipment, they destroyed the bomb-sight and slashed the electrical cables in the two junction boxes behind the pilots' seat. They then abandoned P-28 to her fate. Unknown to the crew, P-28 would get out of the Philippines before most of them did.[43]

Utter and Roberts made the opposite decision. Like P-28, P-5 was a mess. One engine was out, some of the control cables had been shot away, the hull was full of holes, and fuel was dripping from both wings. Nevertheless, they managed to taxi from Fortune Island, about twenty miles southwest of Corregidor, to a cove on southern Luzon. Working all night, they patched up their wreck and flew it back to Cavite the next day. But because Cavite was untenable, they were sent down to Laguna de Bay.

Sangley Point was, by and large, spared. A few scattered bombs had hit the seaplane base, but no serious damage had been done "except to put the fear of God into any reasonably loyal civilian workmen."[44] The overhaul hangar, X-34, was superficially damaged, but the two planes inside appeared to be in pretty good shape. In fact, one, P-13, would be ready to fly the next day.

But the wing's luck would not hold forever, and Captain Wagner observed that, "since the Navy Yard was out of commission we expected to be the next target, by being the largest naval aviation base."[45] To prevent what was obviously the inevitable, Wagner dispersed the PBYs at Los Baños on Laguna de Bay, and at Olongapo on Subic Bay. PBYs still operated out of Manila Bay, but only on an as-needed basis. Having disposed of his planes, the wing commander moved his headquarters aboard the *Childs*.

At 1500 Peterson's attack group landed on Laguna de Bay. They had missed the raid by about two hours, but clear evidence of the Japanese success had been visible from fifty miles away. The two-plane, follow-up force searched until approaching night forced them to return empty-handed. When he landed, Robinson was steaming mad about having been given the wrong position in which to search. That may or may not have been the case. More likely, the cruiser had simply gotten underway and had cleared the area.

Morale was high in both squadrons as the war's second day closed. But the cockiness that had characterized most Americans' prewar attitude toward Japanese fighting qualities was gone. Everyone knew that the Japanese were ashore in two places, but there was little concern about what those landings meant. The main concern was about fifth-columnists who were reportedly active during the Cavite raid. Some were described as Japanese "colonists," while others were said to be pro-Japanese Filipinos. Some of the stories were pure fabrication, but several were based on fact.

Everyone now expected a hard, uphill battle, but no one expected to be run out of the Philippines. There was also common agreement that the Pacific Fleet would show up any day, after which things would straighten themselves out. Clearly they misread the situation and were unaware just how weak their position was.

The Japanese had nearly destroyed the army air force in the Philippines. There were only seven B-17s and twenty-two P-40s still in commission.[46] The Japanese were virtually uncontested in the air, and the troops that had come ashore at Vigan and Aparri had already seized fighter bases near the beaches. The surface fighting units of the Asiatic Fleet had gone south, and there would be no reinforcements coming from Pearl Harbor, or anywhere else.

What was also not yet fully clear to the men in PatWing-10 was the extreme vulnerability of the PBY, and its unsuitability for the role of a high-altitude horizontal bomber. It would take another month for those lessons to be painfully learned. In the meantime, another sort of lesson was being learned at Polloc Harbor on the west side of Mindanao.

After delivering Admiral Glassford to the *Houston*, P-3 was ordered to join the *Preston* at Polloc Harbor. On 10 December while out on patrol, Campbell and Armbruster spotted a Japanese four-engine flying boat. They reported the contact and returned to Polloc

Harbor. When they landed they found everyone packing up to go as a result of their contact report. The *Preston* was understandably anxious to clear the area and avoid another Malalag Bay incident.

The other planes had already left by the time P-3 had been refueled, and the *Preston* got underway. Campbell was taxiing out to start his takeoff when P-3 started having carburetor problems that quickly progressed to the point where the engine quit. Not wanting to be left behind, Campbell tried a one-engine takeoff, but gave it up when he saw he was not going to make it. Taxiing back to a sheltered area, he threw out an anchor, and radioed ComPatWing that he needed a new carburetor. Then he sat down to wait.

## 11 December

The next day, 11 December, Campbell figured that they had better get themselves as ready as possible, in case the Japanese showed up. His main concern was to have all the guns in good shape, and he told the crew to tear them down and clean them. Since Armbruster normally manned the bow gun, he elected to clean it.

Because it was hot inside the hull, Armbruster wanted to take his gun up on the wing where it was cooler. Campbell did not want him to work up there because he was afraid that Armbruster would lose part of the gun over the side.

"I told him that if he lost a piece of that gun we'd be in a hell of a fix if we needed it. But he kept insisting so I finally let him go up there."[47]

Of course it had to happen. Armbruster had the gun torn down and the parts spread out on the wing. He was reassembling the trigger group when a small spring-loaded part popped out, arched over the edge of the wing, and splashed into the water. There was a moment of dead silence before Campbell exploded. The entire crew peered down into the crystal clear water, searching for some sign of the wayward part on the bottom twenty feet below. It was, of course, too small to be seen.

"Go down and get it," Campbell growled.

Armbruster knew when not to argue, and quickly stripped down. He had been an All-American swimmer at the University of Iowa, so the dive was not a problem. Inasmuch as the water was very clear and the bottom hard, he figured he had a pretty good chance of finding the small part. As he dove in, Campbell shouted, "Don't come back aboard till you find the damn thing."

Fifteen minutes later he was back aboard with the part in his hand, and Campbell was feeling a lot better. While P-3 swung to her anchor in Polloc Harbor, P-2 was becoming the wing's latest casualty. John Ogle and Bob Swenson had made a single-engine emergency landing on Laguna de Bay and were taxiing toward Los Baños. As they taxied across the huge lake, a lone Japanese twin-engine plane strafed them and unloaded a bomb that hit well ahead of the PBY. All the bomb did was make a lot of noise, but the machine-gun bullets reduced what had been a salvageable engine to trash. That left the wing with only twenty-one planes in commission. After three days at war nearly 29 percent of their planes were out of action—damaged, destroyed, or broken down. It would get worse tomorrow.

## 12 December

On 12 December the airmen at Olongapo received word from Filipino coast watchers that five Japanese battleships, escorted by five destroyers, were off the Luzon coast, headed toward Manila Bay. Soon after the first report, a new one came that said the Japanese group included an aircraft carrier. Given the fleet's last reported position, its estimated course and speed, the Olongapo command calculated that the Japanese would be off Subic Bay by dawn.

Acting on the information, Lieutenant Commander Marcy, the senior officer at Olongapo, ordered every plane bombed-up and he then led the flight in search of the Japanese. He had seven planes in his group, including two that had been involved in the "Kongo Raid" on 10 December. For four hours after their 0500 takeoff, they searched the coast from Mindoro to Lingayen Gulf without finding any sign of a Japanese force, large or small. In fact, the report was entirely false.

Some people later came to the opinion that the report had been a set-up. But Captain Wagner recalled that it "was typical of the reports received from earnest, patriotic, enthusiastic natives whose imagination at times got out of hand."[48] Admiral Hart was less generous, describing it as "unjustifiable, bad information."[49] Wagner was probably right. But nevertheless, the false report did set the stage for the heaviest losses suffered by PatWing-10 on any one day.

By 0900 the first PBYs were landing at Olongapo, taxiing to buoys, or throwing out anchors. At least one, Andy Reid's P-29, anchored in a spot intended to provide some shelter and concealment. For the next hour the planes were refueled, while the crews settled down in their planes to wait.

The seven PBYs were strung out across the water in a rough line near the seaplane ramp. The fourth plane in line belonged to Pew and Williamson, who were sunning themselves on the wing. At about 1010 they saw several fighters fly over at 6,000 feet, headed north. Frank Ralston, on P-19, also "saw planes in the distance" as did Art Jacobson. Everyone who saw the planes knew they were Japanese, and tension was high until they had passed. As soon as the planes were out of sight everyone relaxed.[50]

Reid's plane was in a cove on the south side of Subic Bay, near the old cruiser USS *Rochester*, which was tied up at the navy base. The cruiser, a relic from Admiral Dewey's fleet, had an old-fashioned cylindrical crow's nest that Reid could see sticking up above a low strip of land that separated his plane from the ship.

Suddenly gunfire erupted from Fort Drum at the entrance to Subic Bay. Turning to see what was happening, Reid saw five Zeros pop up over a low hill near the entrance to the bay and swoop low across the water toward the row of helpless PBYs. Machine gun and cannon fire advanced across the water, lashing Reid's plane. Caught flat-footed, the crew went over the side as the plane burst into flames.

The other PBYs were already starting to fire back as the fighters roared over. Pew and Williamson were standing on the turtleback between the engines, watching the show. Williamson noticed that their guns only made a "pop-pop noise" and frequently jammed. He did not realize it at the time, but PatWing-10 had been issued prewar practice ammunition. There was an abundance of tracer, but little punch, on those belts of partially corroded ammunition.

Farther up the line, Tom McCabe had ordered his crew over the side when the first run started. He knew that, bombed-up and loaded with fuel, the flying boats were floating bombs. But for some reason, McCabe elected to stay, and he ran forward to the bow gun.

Art Jacobson and two crewmen were standing on the wing when

they saw the fighters heading straight for them. While the men inside opened up with the waist guns, Jacobson and his partners dove into the water.

As the Japanese swept down for their second run, Andy Reid was still too close to his burning plane. He tried to dive under the water to escape the strafers, but his uninflated Mae West prevented him. Looking back he could see a marine in the *Rochester*'s crow's nest blazing away at the fighters with a BAR. Then, to his horror, he saw that the paint on the 500-pound bombs was starting to blister. His first instinct was to thrash more energetically toward the shore. After a few moments he reconsidered.

"Why hurry?" he thought to himself. "If they blow up before they sink into the water and cool off, I won't make it anyway." It was a question of which inner voice to heed, the pragmatist or the one that urged survival. Survival won and Reid struck out for shore.

By now three of the PBYs were burning, but some of the PBYs were still returning a pretty good fire. Williamson and Pew were inside when the second run on them was made. Bullets punched through the thin skin, and a 20-millimeter cannon round exploded in the flare locker. Instantly the plane was on fire.

"Abandon ship. Everyone over the side." The shouts and the fast-spreading fire sent men leaping through every available opening.

Tom McCabe was still hammering away with the .30-caliber bow gun. His plane had been hit several times and was taking water. Five of the planes were burning, and he could see several swimmers heading toward shore and others already taking cover behind rocks and bushes. The small bow gun was obviously ineffective, and his number was clearly just about up. At that point he said, "I'd better leave."

The Japanese were starting their final run when McCabe started to leave. But his departure was delayed when the trousers he was trying to shed got hung up in the straps of his Mae West. Rounds were smashing into the plane and exploding along the wings by the time he got the tangle straightened out and hit the water.

After the first strafing pass, Jacobson had climbed back aboard his plane. While the gunners kept up a steady stream of fire, he and the others tried to staunch the flow of water through the numerous holes in the hull. It was a losing battle, a fact that became dramatically evident when the port wing tip float sank, and the plane settled on its side. As they abandoned the plane the Japanese made another pass, setting it afire.

Ensign Jack Grayson was also one of the last to leave. Like McCabe he had stayed to fight the plane, along with the rest of his crew. The last run turned their plane into a bonfire that sent everyone over the side through the nearest exit.

Andy Reid had reached the beach, but looking back he saw one of his crewmen, RM1c Linsey Wells, struggling in the water several yards out. Reid quickly dove back in and pulled the radioman to shore. Once ashore Reid soon learned that his copilot, Ensign J. C. Watson, had been killed as had another crewman, ACMM George Seeke.

Lowell Williamson also went back for a foundering crewman. After pulling the man ashore, he stood on the beach and watched his plane sink. It gave him a sense of deep, personal loss. In her blackened hull was his best pair of Florsheim shoes, and his personal, pearl-handled Smith and Wesson revolver.

After the attack, forty-seven survivors gathered in the hangar to exchange experiences and rumors. There were claims that one, two, or three Zeros had been shot down. The successes were attributed vaguely to "the .50-calibers" or shore-based antiaircraft guns. When Don Chay heard the claims the next day, he commented that it was "about time the AA shot down something. All they've done is shoot at us, so far."[51] In fact, it does not appear that any Japanese planes were shot down that day over Olongapo.

Other rumors described the attackers as "cannon-firing Messerschmitts," a claim supported by the "fact" that two had been shot down and identified. Similarly, there was a rumor that one of the Zeros was found in the jungle behind Olongapo, with a German pilot in the cockpit. Keller, who was not too sure about the report's accuracy, suggested that "it was some tale that the marines were putting out."[52]

Captain Wagner arrived at 1300 to assess the situation, and what he saw was not pleasant. The lesson taught at Cavite on 10 December had been underscored at Olongapo on the 12th. For patrol operations the island of Luzon was untenable. Ten of his twenty-eight PBYs had been destroyed since the war started just five days earlier. Four were damaged and not flyable. His force had been cut in half without having done any appreciable damage to the enemy. The bright side was, however, that casualties among the aircrews had been astoundingly low—eleven dead and four injured.

After completing his inspection, Wagner told Marcy to move his people to Los Baños, the only place left where they were reasonably safe from air attack. They would be driven there that night in an eight-truck convoy, after they had been fed and issued small arms. Williamson drew a Springfield rifle and a bandolier of ammunition. He did not know it at the time, but he would have plenty of opportunity to use that rifle in the weeks to come.

Out on the water the fires had burned out, but black smoke hung over the bay. Debris littered the surface, and an occasional piece of wreckage jutted out of the water. All seven PBYs were gone, but George Gaboury's two wooden decoys remained afloat and untouched.

Captain Wagner returned to Manila and discussed with the army a proposal for a joint raid against Palau.[53] The idea was dropped, and the next day what was left of PatWing-10 remained in hiding, except for the scouts operating from the *Childs* in Manila Bay.

Not everyone went directly to Los Baños. Among those given special assignments was Andy Reid, who was sent to Sangley Point to pick up another plane. The plane he signed for was P-13, just out of overhaul. Reid was glad to have another plane, especially one that had just been overhauled, and the discovery that some instruments were missing did not dampen his enthusiasm a bit.

Nick Keller also went to Sangley Point to draw a replacement PBY, but his was one already being tended by the *Childs*. While Andy Reid was sent to Laguna de Bay to await further orders, Keller was told that he and John Hyland would be hunting for the Japanese Fleet.

As their planes were being armed with a torpedo under one wing and two 500-pound bombs under the other, Hyland asked Keller, "What should we do, torpedo first or bomb first?"[54]

"I don't know," answered Keller, "take your choice."

In the meantime Captain Wagner and Admiral Hart were discussing the situation. In Hart's opinion the situation was grim.

By 13 December our Army planes were no longer keeping the air, except for one or two fighters at a time flying for reconnaissance purposes. We had a little less than one squadron of patrol planes, and with little prospect of gaining further results commensurate with losses.[55]

Admiral Hart's assessment of the situation was similar to that of the men who flew the planes. On 13 December, Hawk Barrett wrote in his diary:

To date four officers have been killed plus unknown numbers of enlisted men and nine planes totally destroyed. Two others are out of commission. We have never had a single fighter as escort. We never had more than a few ante-dated AA guns for protection. It seemed miraculous that more have not been killed. At present we are waiting in hiding, so at last they have learned that these planes cannot fly and return without protection. We are living in a cave on the wooded shores of Laguna de Bay, and the plane is covered with jungle growth.

Today the Japs got Manila again. It will only be a matter of days or hours before they find us here, and then who knows? We hear nothing but gossip and rumors. But it is certain that unless we receive aid in short order the U.S. will lose the Philippines. As I write this note here on the water's edge, Manila is smoking, tanks are pushing ahead from Legaspi, and troops are engaged in Lingayen Sector. There is possibility of our being surrounded. In that event we may have to fight our way south. When we will move again is uncertain, perhaps tomorrow. When we do it will be at extreme peril, and there is no joking about it. We are the mice and we are as vulnerable as they to the lurking tomcat!

Admiral Hart, making the only logical decision, ordered Wagner to move PatWing-10 to Java. Keller and Hyland were still discussing the best opening shot, torpedoes or bombs, when the order to move reached them.

"Dump your load and prepare to evacuate."

# 3

# The Retreat
# 13–24 December 1941

On the night of 13–14 December nearly all the wing's PBYs were hidden along the shore on Laguna de Bay, the crews sleeping aboard their planes. Two hours before dawn, messengers went from plane to plane alerting the crews to prepare for takeoff. In the dark the messengers missed at least three planes, hidden in the foliage along the shore, and the crews were not alerted.[1] At 0430 the crews of planes 1, 8, 9, 11, 23, and 25 stripped off the camouflage branches, started the engines, and moved out to the offshore buoys. Thirty minutes later they started taking off. Along the shore of Laguna de Bay slept three crews, ignorant of the fact that the move south had started.

The first five planes got away without a hitch, but John Hyland's P-23 was acting up. Like the other planes, P-23 carried 1,200 gallons of fuel, four 500-pound bombs, and nine men. The extra man was a passenger. It was a heavy load, but one that was usually not a problem to get off the water.

Hyland and Barrett knew they were in trouble the moment they started their takeoff run. As P-23 thundered across the bay, the cylinder-head temperature on the port engine was already too high and climbing. And no matter how hard they pushed, the plane would not reach takeoff speed. Two miles down the run, Hyland, thinking she might be close enough to yank off, hauled back on the column. P-23 leaped off the water, crashed back down with a bone-jarring smack, bounced back into the air, and splashed down again.

Hyland cut the power, a broken engine cowl flapping wildly. While the plane captain removed the damaged cowl flap, and pitched it into the water, the two pilots decided to lighten the load by dumping one of the 500-pound bombs. According to the manual the bomb should not explode. Despite those assurances, no one ever dropped a live bomb into the water alongside his plane without harboring some doubts and grim expectations. But there was no time to do it any other way. So, putting their faith in the experts, they dumped the bomb. P-23 was nearly on the step when the bomb fell away, splashed into the water, and plunged harmlessly to the bottom. Five hundred pounds lighter, the PBY rose on her step and lifted off.

Duke Campbell, Ed Bergstrom, Edgar Neale, and Dick Roberts. Neale was VP-102's squadron commander,. having assumed command just before the war started. This picture was taken after the war. (Courtesy T. E. L. McCabe)

With the departure of P-23, there were nine PBYs still in the Manila area. Three were unflyable. One of the damaged PBYs was McConnell's P-28, which he and his crew had abandoned on Laguna de Bay on 10 December. Two or three days later Lieutenant Joseph Antonides, hearing about a stray PBY drifting on the lake, drove up to have a look at it.

Actually, the plane was not drifting. P-28 was anchored near Los Baños, completely covered with foliage lashed in place with copper wire. While Antonides examined the plane, an elderly Filipino came aboard. He told the navy officer that he had found the plane adrift several days ago and "figured it belonged to someone." To conceal it from the Japanese, he had covered the plane with branches, using wire he had found on board to secure the camouflage in place. Thanking the man, Antonides dug out ten Philippine pesos, the only cash he had, and gave it to the old man for his help.[2]

Completing his survey, Antonides found that, though badly damaged, the plane could be made flyable fairly quickly. The most severe damage had been done by the crew during their attempt to render the plane unusable to the approaching Japanese. They had successfully deactivated the entire electrical system.

Battle damage consisted of shot-up fuel and oil tanks, a smashed magneto in the starboard engine, and a bullet hole in an intake manifold on the same engine. Fixing the battle damage enough to fly the plane back to Manila did not pose a problem. In fact, the biggest chore in getting the plane airborne was cutting all the carefully twisted wires that held the camouflage in place.

The second unflyable PBY was Bob Swenson's P-2. His plane also had a shot-up engine, but it was beyond repair. A replacement was needed. But spare engines were in short supply, and by the time his request reached Sangley Point on the evening of the 13th, the last of the spares was being hoisted aboard the *Childs*. The tender, loaded to capacity with all the spare parts she could hold, was preparing to head south to Java. In addition to spare parts, she was to take Captain Wagner, his staff, and as many pilots as could be packed aboard.

The last spare engine was left ashore, and a call went out for volunteers to deliver it to Los Baños. Among those who answered the call was Sk2c Arthur Burkholder, Jr. Even though the pullout was clearly about to start, Burkholder figured he would be back before the *Childs* left. After all, Los Baños was only about sixty or seventy miles south of Manila. His mistake became apparent several days later, a realization that made him feel he had done "something stupid by volunteering."[3]

That night a three-vehicle convoy left Sangley Point for Los Baños. The lead car was filled with armed sailors, followed by Burkholder driving the engine-laden truck, followed by another car filled with armed sailors. Burkholder recalled:

> We drove all night without any lights and if the lead car had gone into a ditch or over a cliff, I'd have gone right after him. We couldn't see a thing in the dark, and it was taking us a lot longer to get there than we had thought. To make things worse, we were stopped at every bridge, crossroad, and culvert by jumpy Filipino soldiers. We arrived the next morning after a long, slow trip, and unloaded the engine.[4]

1. J. C. Watson, 2. Les Pew, 3. Dennis Szabo, 4. Earl McConnell, 5. Hawk Barrett, and 6. J. Thanos. Watson was killed at Olongapo on 12 December 1941. Earl McConnell's uncle was the skipper of the *Langley* when the tender was sunk on 27 February 1942. Earl McConnell was killed after the war in a flying accident. (Courtesy R. Barrett)

The convoy arrived shortly after the first six PBYs had taken off. While the engine was being hoisted off the truck, Lieutenant Commander J. C. Renard and Ensign A. L. Seaman took off in two utility squadron J2F Ducks. Loaded with as many 5-gallon cans of gasoline as they could carry, the single-engine Ducks were heading south on a "me-too" basis.

Some distance ahead of the J2Fs, the six PBYs had formed up at 12,000 feet, heading south. Hyland's port engine had started to cool down, allowing P-23 to hold its own for most of the flight. But as the formation neared Mindanao, the engine started to cut out and the cylinder-head temperature on number two cylinder shot up to 330 degrees (F). Unable to keep up, P-23 fell behind, losing altitude. To add to his troubles, a breather now started throwing a cloud of oil, and the engine hacked and sputtered. "With parachutes in place and enough altitude to glide seven miles, we started across the mountains."[5]

At about the time John Hyland and Hawk Barrett were struggling to clear the mountains, a little known event was taking place in Manila. On 14 December two Vichy French ships were taken into "protective custody" on orders from Admiral Hart. One, an old freighter loaded with flour and other provisions, was sent to Mariveles where her cargo was to be put ashore at the navy construction base. The other was the modern motor vessel MS *Maréchal Joffre*. Hart rated the passenger ship as "valuable" and because "she could not be protected in Manila it was decided to get her away."[6]

The seizures were made by force, though with help from some members of the French crew who supported De Gaulle. In the pre-dawn grey, Lieutenant E. R. Little led an armed group aboard the *Maréchal Joffre* to meet with the crew's Free French representative. The meeting quickly concluded, the crew was hurriedly assembled on deck and was given five minutes to choose between "Vichy or De Gaulle." Those who chose Vichy, or were undecided, were sent ashore to an internment camp. In all, sixty-three Frenchmen voted to stay aboard, knowing their ship would be pressed into American service.[7]

Inspecting the ship, the Americans found examples of how deeply divided the crew was. One member of the crew was a

French spy working for the Americans. On trips to Saigon he had carefully noted Japanese activity, passing the information on to U.S. Naval Intelligence in Manila. On the other hand, a ship's officer had the main injection needles ready to throw overboard. Apparently he had expected the American takeover, but had been caught off guard before he could act.

But the most disturbing discovery was evidence that a Vichy supporter had tried to sabotage the ship by destroying the auxiliary switchboard. It was, therefore, with considerable concern that Lieutenant Little and five sailors stood watch over the *Maréchal Joffre*. Admiral Hart, also concerned, ordered the ship to head south as soon as possible.

While Little was securing the ship for the night, the *Childs* was already set to head south. Aboard were Captain Wagner, his staff, and several PatWing-10 pilots. The tender was scheduled to stop for fuel at Cebu before proceeding to Menado where she would refuel and tend the PBYs en route to Surabaja from Lake Lanao. That evening, "running at 25 knots through unlighted channels and straits," the *Childs* departed the Philippines.[8] As the darkened ship steamed through the night, Don Chay recorded in his diary:

> Told to get all the spare parts I could, and get on the tender *Childs*. Renard, Seaman and the PBYs headed south. I wonder where in hell we'll base. The Pacific Fleet better get here pretty soon. Left Manila with what clothes I could get.[9]

Chay's short diary entry spoke for all the pilots on board that night. Back in Manila, however, George Burkholder had more on his mind than wondering about where PatWing-10 was going to base.

Burkholder and the engine-delivery crew had returned to Cavite to find the base nearly deserted. His boss, Paymaster Snow, and the entire headquarters staff gone, it quickly dawned on Burkholder that his volunteer duty had cost him his ticket out of the Philippines. Disgusted, and feeling "stupid for having volunteered," he set out to locate whatever constituted the remaining PatWing-10 authority. He soon found the man in charge, Lieutenant Commander Frank Bridget, and reported to him.

Burkholder, like nearly everyone who had been left behind on 14 December, was still optimistic. The Japanese main landings had not been made, and there were plenty of rumors about the Japanese being clobbered by the Philippine scouts. Burkholder, and most of the others, expected the Pacific Fleet to show up any day. In fact, it was widely believed that the PatWing-10 people had been left behind to service the carrier planes that would arrive with the Fleet. The real reason they were left behind was considerably different.

Admiral Hart did not share MacArthur's optimism in regard to defending the Philippines. He was, however, obligated to support the army to the best of his ability. But by 14 December the only naval combat units that could operate out of Manila were the submarines, and they were courting disaster. Hart knew their days in Manila were numbered and had already "decided to stay in Manila for as long as the submarines could."[10]

Despite his realization that there would be no reinforcements sent to the Philippines, he was duty-bound to continue providing MacArthur with naval support. Therefore, when he started to send navy units south to the Netherlands East Indies, he had to be careful not to pull out so many that it would appear that the navy had abandoned MacArthur. In fact, he left too many behind, four to five hundred officers and men by his own estimate.[11] Among those left behind were about half of PatWing-10's complement.[12]

Several hours before the *Childs* headed south, Peterson's six PBYs had already landed on Lake Lanao. The three planes from the *Preston*, already there, had scattered buoys near a long, wooden pier. Gordon Ebbe had been in one of the planes that had flown up from the *Preston*, and had helped set the buoys. The method used was haphazard and established the aircrews' amateur standing in matters regarding establishing a buoy system.

> We put the buoys and anchors in a Moro banca, and they damn near sank the boat. At first we had the Filipinos dive down and estimate the depth, but that took too long. So we used the pragmatic method of throwing the buoy and anchor over the side. If the buoy stayed on the surface, it was OK.[13]

Having set the buoys, Ebbe, Ira Brown, and the others looked forward to a well-earned rest. But though the early bird may get the worm, early arrivals get the jobs, and the two aircrews were put to work refueling the seven PBYs as they arrived from Manila.

Refueling was a time-consuming, back-breaking job. A long wooden pier that extended into the lake would accommodate only one plane at a time. Fifty-five gallon gasoline drums stored on the beach were rolled to the end of the pier, and stood upright. A PBY taxied up to the pier, was made fast, and the fuel was pumped into its tanks by hand. The plane then cast off, restarted its engines and taxied out to a buoy, while another PBY took its place. The work went on all afternoon until, "every damned one of them" had been gassed.[14]

At one point Ebbe and his sweating crew watched a pilot shut down his engines as he taxied to the pier. But the PBY was too far from the pier when the power was cut, and it started to drift toward a bridge and a waterfall just two hundred yards away. As the plane headed down river, the pilot frantically tried to restart the engines. But the propellers just turned over slowly, lazy puffs of smoke popping from the exhaust stacks. The anchor was thrown out, but just bounced along the bottom refusing to bite. Propellers continued turning slowly, the anchor line angled away from the bow, and the powerless PBY headed for the falls. The plane was literally on the brink of disaster when the engines fired, the propellers becoming a circular blur. Under control again, the PBY moved quickly toward the pier while the anchor was hastily brought in.

Shortly after the last plane was fueled, the wind started to pick up. Soon the lake was covered with whitecaps, and the planes were straining at anchor rodes and buoy lines. The plan had been to send the crews ashore to Dansalan (now Marawi) for the night, leaving only an anchor watch aboard each plane. But as the wind increased, it became apparent that a storm was building. The crews were ordered to stay with their planes.

Pressed by the strong wind, the planes started dragging their anchors as night fell. In the dark the cough and roar of engines starting were evidence that many anchor and buoy lines were parting. Throughout the night the PBYs taxied into the wind, trying to avoid being blown ashore onto the rocks, over the waterfalls, or into each other. By dawn, when the storm finally passed, the crews were exhausted, and the fuel tanks had to be topped off again.

During the storm, the J2Fs had not been manned, and in the morning Ensign Seaman's plane was missing. There was no sign of

Lowell Williamson with VP-102's osprey mascot. (Courtesy Lowell Williamson)

wreckage in the immediate area, so Lieutenant Renard and Seaman took off in Renard's J2F to search the lake. They expected to find the plane wrecked along the beach. Instead, they found the J2F drifting, undamaged, about fifteen miles away. Renard landed, and Seaman went over the side. The ensign quickly swam to, and boarded, the drifting plane, and found it to be in perfect shape. In less than an hour, both J2Fs had returned to the anchorage.[15]

While Renard and Seaman were hunting for the missing plane, Hyland's plane, already lame, was suffering more problems. After pouring fresh oil into the ailing port engine, AMM1c John Wilson threw the empty oil cans over the side. He was standing on the wing when he pitched the cans, and his aim was off. Instead of flying clear, they hit the aileron and the antenna, tearing the fabric and breaking the antenna. The damage was annoying but not critical, and was much less severe than what happened next. Hawk Barrett recorded the event in his diary. "With all of this, the motor launch approached and got under our tail, smashing the rudder guard, and rumpling the rudder."[16] Hyland and his crew were beginning to wonder if the fates had it in for them.

On 15 December those PatWing-10 units that had gotten out of Manila were either resting on Lake Lanao or headed for Balikpapan on Borneo's west coast. The Dutch oil port was to be the next stopping place in the wing's route south. The *Heron*, *Preston*, and *Langley* were all moving toward Balikpapan where they would refuel. While the *Heron* and *Preston* waited there for the arrival of the PBYs from Lake Lanao, the *Langley* was to continue south and set up a fueling stop for the PBYs in Makassar. In the meantime, the *Childs* put into Cebu to refuel, arriving just after the Japanese had bombed and strafed the port.[17] Quickly refueled, the tender headed south to Menado where she would act as a filling station for the PBYs en route to Surabaja.

On the morning of 16 December there were eleven PBYs on Lake Lanao and seven in the Manila area. Of the seven still in Manila, three were still unflyable, but being repaired. The other four had been held back to fly out senior army and navy officers, including Admiral Hart. The departure dates had not been set, but it was already apparent that the various headquarters would be leaving soon. Most were simply waiting for the situation to reach the point at which the need to move south became unquestionable. For Admiral Hart that would be when the harbor became untenable for the submarines.

But on the morning of the 16th, he decided to send his chief of staff, Rear Admiral William P. Purnell, to Surabaja. Hart reasoned that "so much of the entire fleet had gone to Task Force-5 [Glassford] that the Chief of Staff and six key officers should be transferred to ComTaskForce-5."[18] One of the three PBYs was brought up from Laguna de Bay to Manila to pick up Admiral Purnell.

In the predawn darkness, John Sloatman and his crew pulled the camouflage foliage off P-29, cast off the tail line, and hauled in the anchor. With the engines throttled down, he and Jack Grayson eased the plane through the fish traps and into clear water—so they thought. The mountains were silhouetted against the early dawn, the lake surface was black as the PBY started its takeoff run.

The plane was charging across the surface, gaining speed, when the pilots felt and heard a heavy thump. The plane continued to race forward, but she was sluggish and would not get up on the step. Sloatman knew something was wrong.

"Jack, go aft and see what's going on."[19]

Climbing quickly out of the right-hand seat, Grayson stepped down into the navigator's compartment. He found himself "waist deep in water." Climbing back into the pilot's compartment, he told Sloatman they were sinking. Sloatman cut the power and swung toward the shore to beach the plane in shallow water. They did not make it.

P-29 sank lower in the water as she churned toward land, and finally Sloatman ordered everyone over the side. As the crew paddled ashore in their rubber boats, the PBY went under until only her propeller blades showed above the lake's surface.

While Sloatman and his soggy crew trudged back to Los Baños, Ensign Dennis Szabo was having a similar experience on Lake Lanao. Szabo was taxiing P-24 along the beach close to shore when he hit a submerged rock. The moment he hit, Szabo firewalled the throttles in an effort to reach the beach. But as in Sloatman's case, it was too late. P-24 quickly sank and was a total loss. The rest of the day was spent salvaging everything useful off the wreck.[20]

That afternoon, Clayton Marcy flew P-22 up to Manila to pick up Admiral Purnell. Because of Japanese fighter activity, departure from Manila was delayed until dark, giving P-22 the cover of darkness for the flight to Java. Everything went as planned, and the flight was uneventful—quite an accomplishment, considering how things had gone up to then.

There were now five PBYs in the Manila area, one flyable and four under repair. On Lake Lanao there were ten flyable PBYs, but Hyland's P-23 was a lame duck. That meant that after just eight days at war, PatWing had lost nearly half its planes, either damaged or destroyed. There was hope, however, that the four damaged planes in the Manila area could be repaired and sent south. In fact, only one would ever leave Manila.

After the hard work of refueling, battling the storm, and salvaging what they could from Szabo's plane, the aircrews at Lake Lanao were sent to the hotel in Dansalan for a much-needed rest. Hawk

Barrett recorded in his diary that they enjoyed "heavenly sleep on soft mattresses, in furnished rooms." Before turning in, Barrett spent some time looking at 1937 issues of *Life* magazine, the only reading matter in the Dansalan Inn. In the 7 June issue he was surprised to find a picture of himself.[21]

On the morning of 17 December, Commander Peterson received orders to proceed with all his planes to Lake Tondano near Menado. The Dutch maintained a small seaplane base on the lake, and it was

Gordon Ebbe and Marvin Berg. (Courtesy Gordon Ebbe)

T. E. L. McCabe is on the left and Dennis Szabo is on the right. Szabo was a very popular officer in PatWing-10. (Courtesy T. E. L. McCabe)

planned to refuel and service the American flying boats there. Actually that was a bad plan because the facilities at Tondano were wholly inadequate, but no one knew that at the time.

But Peterson had a more immediate problem to resolve. There was doubt that Hyland's plane (P-23) could make the trip, and the question was whether or not to scuttle her. Finally he gave in to Hyland's protest, and at 0900 led ten planes toward the Celebes.

In Menado, the *Childs* was "maneuvering on various courses and speeds upon approaching an anchorage . . . ," as three Dutch tri-motor seaplanes flew over.[22] Standing on the *Child's* bridge, Lieutenant Commander J. L. ("Doc") Pratt watched the three planes "fly over us, quite low, as a salute."[23] He continued to watch the three planes as they began to circle some distance away as though to come back. But Pratt's attention was needed for the job at hand, and he momentarily forgot the three Dutchmen.

RM1c Elmer Kuhn was standing on the forecastle when he heard someone topside, aft of him say "let's shoot this guy." And another cautioned, "No. No. He's friendly." Kuhn looked to the right and saw a four-engine flying boat coming in about five hundred feet off the water.[24]

Andrew Burgess was standing with several other PatWing-10 people on the deckhouse just abaft the bridge, manning the ship's water-cooled .50-caliber machine guns. Burgess looked over and saw the plane coming, but "thought nothing of it, because everyone thought it was a Dutch plane."[25]

SM1c Rodney Nordfelt thought the plane was a China Clipper, and he and several others started waving. On the bridge, Captain Wagner heard someone shout, "Here comes that four-engined Dutchman again."[26]

"Four-engined!" Wagner yelled. "That's a Jap! Open fire, commence firing!"

"Look, she's dropping leaflets."

"Leaflets hell, those are bombs!"[27]

Machine guns hammered away at the onrushing enemy bomber, and men dove for cover. A string of bombs tumbled from the plane's wings, exploding fifty to one hundred yards to port. Machine-gun fire raked the plane's belly as it passed over the *Childs*, reaching out for the plane as it sped away. Converging lines of tracers touched the tail, tearing off pieces, silencing the Japanese gunner. The bomber kept going until it was out of sight.[28]

One hundred and sixty miles out to sea, P-23 was doing "pretty well," but she was having a hard time keeping up. P-26 was flying wing on the cripple, prepared to land and pick up the crew if 23

Dennis Szabo and Bob Etnire. Etnire's wife, Ema, had come to the Philippines after the dependents had been sent home. She was captured by the Japanese and spent the war in Santo Tomás Prison. (Courtesy Tom Pollock)

folded up and went down. But the insurance afforded by the escort was canceled by the report of the attack on the *Childs*.

Fearing additional attacks, Wagner ordered the flight to change course for Balikpapan. For P-23 the order was impossible to follow. Hyland had no choice but to try for Menado and the uncertainty of what might be waiting there. At 1115, Peterson led the nine healthy PBYs on a new heading toward Balikpapan, while P-23 continued toward Menado alone.

An hour and forty minutes later lookouts on the *Childs* spotted more incoming aircraft. But it was no Japanese attack. The planes were P-23 and the two J2F Ducks. The Ducks could not have reached Balikpapan even with the extra fuel carried in their five-gallon cans. In fact, the Ducks had been forced to land at sea and refuel from their canned reserve in order to reach Menado.

At 1315 the planes landed and taxied to the *Childs*. For the next two hours, while the planes were refueled, the pilots discussed their next move. In view of the recent bombing, no one wanted to hang around Menado, and Hyland especially was "in a hell of a hurry to refuel and get out of there."

> We gassed in a hurry, and took eighty gallons of oil aboard. Our port engine was burning oil at the rate of five gallons an hour, and we found the oil strainer full of metal particles. But by then it was too late to continue the flight, so the *Childs* left us buoyed in the bay.[29]

It was also too late for the Ducks to continue. After refueling they flew to the Dutch base on Lake Tondano to spend the night.

At 1515, after the *Childs* "stood out of harbor" on course for Balikpapan, Hyland and his crew were again on their own. Their frustrating isolation was recorded in Hawk Barrett's diary:

> We spent most of the remainder of the day waving to the Dutch girls on the beach. But no one sent a boat for us, so we stayed in the plane.[30]

Meanwhile Peterson's main group had reached Balikpapan without incident. But Patrol Wing Ten was now strung out along a line 1,200 miles long, with less than a third of its planes and three tenders in Borneo, one tender at sea, and half its personnel still in the Philippines. Some of the men who had been left behind were already being alerted to move out the following day. Their dash south would be made aboard the MS *Maréchal Joffre*.

During the predawn hours of 18 December, fourteen officers and sixty-two enlisted men from PatWing-10 were selected to go aboard the French ship. On what basis the men were chosen is not known, but the selection process was at the least haphazard. Frank Ralston recalls someone came into his area and shouted, "Who wants to get out of the Philippines?" Ralston quickly volunteered.[31]

Jack Grayson and John Sloatman had a similar experience. According to Grayson someone came along and said that a Vichy French ship had been seized, and Admiral Hart wanted volunteers to take it to Surabaja. Both men eagerly volunteered.

"I would have volunteered to take a rowboat. I wanted out," Grayson said.[32]

There was, however, one officer to whom the offer was unattractive. Joseph Antonides held the opinion that the *Maréchal Joffre* did not have a chance. On that point he was in general agreement with Admiral Hart and the ship's new captain, Lieutenant Thomas G. Warfield. But as Warfield said, "What chance did we have in Manila?"[33]

Not all the PatWing-10 officers had a chance to volunteer. Those officers and NAPs who were assigned to the remaining PBYs had to stay, and there were a few who did not get the word. In fact, it appears that only four veteran pilots went aboard the ship. The other ten officers were freshly assigned ensigns and one lieutenant commander who was not regularly assigned to PatWing-10.[34]

While the PatWing-10 evacuees were being trucked up to Manila, John Hyland and the two utility squadron Ducks were headed for Balikpapan. Other than the need to make an open-sea landing to refuel from their on-board, five-gallon cans, the fight was uneventful for the two small planes. The trip was considerably hairier for P-23.

From Menado, Hyland flew west along the Celebes coast to Stroomen Kaap, and then across the Makassar Strait to the Borneo coast. As they neared Borneo at Talok, the port engine started to heat up. Soon thick, black smoke was pouring from the exhaust stacks as the engine got hotter and hotter. The oil pressure dropped as the engine lost power, sputtering and popping. Two hundred miles out of Balikpapan Hyland shut down the sick engine.[35]

Slowly the PBY started losing altitude. Hawk Barrett watched the manifold pressure on the starboard engine climb to 34 inches as more power was given the remaining engine. At 34 inches the manifold pressure was well above the maximum allowed for a prolonged period. In fact, it was about what would be used during a maximum rate of climb from 6,000 to 9,000 feet. The pilot's manual warned that while a manifold pressure of 39 inches could be used in an "extreme emergency," there was the danger that "cylinder head temperatures might reach 260 degrees centigrade." At that temperature the engine could not operate "more than five minutes."[36] P-23 had a problem.

For three hours Hyland and Barrett nursed the crippled plane down the Borneo coast toward Balikpapan. Fuel was dumped and equipment was thrown out to lighten the plane. Still the plane sank toward the water losing 11,000 feet before Hyland and Barrett spotted the silver oil tanks on the hill above Balikpapan.

At about the time that Hyland was landing in Balikpapan, the *Maréchal Joffre* was getting underway in Manila. After coming aboard that morning, the PatWing-10 people had been assigned to duties throughout the ship. Most were stationed as lookouts, but some of the officers were assigned to stand watches in the engine room. Their job was to guard against acts of sabotage by the French, Chinese, and Indonesian crewmen.

Lieutenant Warfield, not fully convinced they were loyal, remarked several days later:

> Of course it was against the law to shoot any of them if they did something that we considered might be sabotage. But at the same time who was going to worry much about the law in these days?[37]

Shortly before getting underway, Lieutenant Al Gray requested to be put ashore. Warfield tried to convince Gray to stay with the ship. But the pilot steadfastly insisted he wanted to return to the hospital. There is no doubt that Gray was ill. But like Antonides, he may have decided that his chances in Manila were better than aboard the *Maréchal Joffre*. He never got out.[38]

Lieutenant Gray had good reason to believe that the Japanese would sink the ship before it got out of the Philippines. The carrier *Ryujo* was still in the area, Cebu had been bombed on the 15th, the *Childs* had been bombed in Menado on the 17th, and there were reports of Japanese battleships, escorted by cruisers and destroyers, in the Celebes Sea, south of Mindanao. The rumors were largely true, though there were no battleships.

Even if the Japanese did not sink the ship, there was good reason to believe she would sink on her own. There were no charts aboard except those needed to operate her between Manila and Saigon, the chronometers had never been compared, and compass deviation had last been checked in 1939. But there were problems more serious than a lack of charts and navigation equipment.

> The ship was in a dilapidated and deteriorated condition. There were cracked cylinder liners and mainbearings in the diesel engines, and leakage of water from the stern tubes was such as to require pumping several times daily. The stern tube gland threads and valve operating equipment on the sea valves were rusted to the

1. W. D. Eddy, an NAP, 2. Edgar Palm, also an NAP, and 3. Hawk Barrett, photographed after the war at Alameda Naval Air Station. Palm was the NAP in Reid's plane the night that Reid and Neale flew General Brereton out of Manila. (Courtesy Edgar Palm)

point where operation was impossible. The auxiliary machinery was in a similar run-down condition, and badly in need of repairs. The evaporators did not work, making it impossible to make fresh water, and one third of the life boats could not be lowered.[39]

Despite the drawbacks "there was no hesitation about leaving Manila," and at 1530 the *Maréchal Joffre* got underway. Picking his way through the minefield, Warfield initially set course for Saigon to make any Japanese that saw the ship assume she was headed toward her home port. To complete the ruse the Vichy flag flew from the stern. After dark she turned south and hauled down the Vichy flag.

As the ship steamed south, the American flag flying at the gaff, Warfield entered in his diary, "Have to trust to luck on the weather and the compass. Have fuel for six days only, little water." As he wrote, Warfield noticed the ship rolling heavily. Low on fuel and unballasted, the *Maréchal Joffre* was very unstable.

Reviewing the problems facing him, Lieutenant Warfield recorded in his diary, "Only thirty-nine Frenchmen aboard, and no seagoing Americans. We were a motley crew, and about half the people didn't know which end of the ship was the bow and which was the stern—most of them were aviators."

The night passed uneventfully, but almost no one slept. By morning the whole crew was jumpy. Part of the problem was the clear day and the excellent visibility that went with it. "Our palms were sweating because of such beautiful visibility," recorded Warfield. Nervous lookouts repeatedly reported "islands, shoals, and rocks as ships" so that the crew was in a nearly constant state of agitation.

As the ship neared the southern tip of Mindoro, a radio message was picked up reporting Japanese battleships and two cruisers headed toward Panay. Warfield assumed they were coming from the southwest and could be seen from San Jose, because that was the source of the report. His plan was to run for Iloilo, and if the Japanese caught them, to run the ship "on the rocks rather than scuttle her."

Several hours later the ship was near the southern tip of Panay,

Left to right, Hawk Barrett, Jinna Barrett, Barbara Seaman, and Al Seaman. Seaman flew one of the utility squadron's small planes from Manila to Java. (Courtesy R. Barrett)

Left to right, Hawk Barrett, Marsha Ralston, Jinna Barrett, and Frank Ralston. (Courtesy R. Barrett)

and about to turn the corner toward Iloilo. Before the turn was made another radio message reported Japanese bombers headed toward Iloilo.

Warfield asked himself, "What do we do now?" and concluded, "Looks as if we are trapped."

Clearly, Iloilo was out since it was "foolish to head there if the Japs were headed there too." Warfield estimated he could run across the Panay Gulf to Negros in about three hours. He would then turn west running along the Negros coast until he could turn southwest and start across the Sulu Sea. He planned to enter the Sulu Sea just before dark. A few hours later Warfield decided he had made a "poor decision."

As planned, the *Maréchal Joffre* entered the Sulu Sea about a half hour before dark, when suddenly the masthead lookout reported a warship on the horizon. On the bridge all glasses trained in the direction of the sighting. The lookout was right, there was a cruiser out there, and it had to be Japanese.

The *Maréchal Joffre* was two hours away from the nearest land, so

running for cover was out. Studying the situation, Warfield noticed
that the Japanese ship was on the lighter side of the horizon, while
the *Maréchal Joffre* was hidden in the deepening gloom of the oncoming
night.

> The best course for us was south toward Zamboanga, and hope he
> hadn't seen us. Darkness came and with it those damn sparks from
> the diesels. Momentarily we expected to see a light or hear his guns
> and see their flash. An hour passed, two hours, then we began to
> believe he had not seen us.

The *Maréchal Joffre* had been lucky.

On the 19th, while the *Maréchal Joffre* was dodging the Japanese,
the *Childs* arrived in Balikpapan. She joined the ten PBYs from
Lake Lanao, the two tag-along J2F Ducks, and the *Heron* that had
brought her four OS2Us from Balabac Strait. Don Chay recorded
the event in his diary:

> Turned in at Balikpapan, in Borneo, to refuel. Our planes were
> there. Big reunion with the boys. Lost three Pesos at Poker.[40]

Before the war, PatWing-10 regularly practiced formation flying. After
they left Manila, they arrived over Surabaja and put on a "fine demonstration
of formation flying." But the Dutch did not know they were coming
and sounded the air-raid alarm. (Courtesy Gordon Ebbe)

The party over, the ships and planes headed south toward Surabaja. Hyland's plane stayed an extra day in Balikpapan to complete
an engine change before heading south on the 21st.

The main group arrived in Surabaja on 20 December, "unher-
alded, causing the Dutch to sound their first air-raid alarm of the
war."[41] Unaware of the panic they were causing on the ground, the
nine PBYs "made a great show of formation flying" as they passed
over the naval base.[42]

When the planes landed, the Americans' attempt to impress their
Dutch hosts took another unexpected turn. Unknown to the pilots,
the harbor at Surabaja was very shallow, a fact they learned when
five PBYs went aground in soft mud as soon as they came down off
the step. Looking back on the embarrassing experience, Charlie
Eisenbach commented, "We had very little knowledge about the
harbor, and the Dutch weren't much help."[43]

For the next two days PatWing-10 serviced and repaired its
planes. And the planes were in bad shape. None of them had been
out of the water since the war started, nor had they had much work
done on them. In that instance the Dutch were very generous, turning over to the Americans the excellent shops and facilities that
were available on the world's largest seaplane base.

Along with servicing and repairing the planes, the badly de-
pleted wing underwent a major reorganization. Because most of the
pilots had been brought out with the planes, there were many more
pilots than available planes. Many of the senior pilots, mostly lieutenants, were given assignments on Captain Wagner's staff. The reorganization also included merging VP-101 and VP-102 into one
squadron, VP-101. Peterson was named squadron commander with
Neale as his executive officer. It made sense. There were not even
enough planes for one squadron, much less two.

Surabaja was a pleasant break for the weary airmen. In fact, Don
Chay called it "quite a town." Girls, beer, and good restaurants
were available in generous amounts. The men were able to discard
their tattered uniforms for more complete outfits. In most cases the
result made them look more like an international brigade than U.S.
Navy men. But they looked better than they had.

On 23 and 24 December, eight of the PBYs left in two four-plane
groups for Ambon. Nick Keller led the first flight, followed the

The MS *Maréchal Joffre* was a French passenger ship, seized by the Americans in Manila. She transported many PatWing-10 pilots to Surabaja. She is shown here in her Navy warpaint after being renamed USS *Rochambeau*. (National Archives)

next day by Peterson's section. Captain Wagner established his headquarters in the Dutch naval base. All four tenders were still in Surabaja, but starting on Christmas day they would scatter to widely separated duty stations.

On Christmas day the *Maréchal Joffre* arrived in Surabaja and discharged her PatWing-10 "passengers." Two days later she steamed in convoy with the *Langley* and several other ships for Darwin, Australia, while the *Childs* departed to tend PBYs at Ambon. Only the *Preston* and the *Heron* remained in Surabaja, but the tiny *Heron* would soon steam north for the bloodiest encounter of her career.

When the flying part of PatWing-10 took up its new position in the Malay Barrier, morale had started to slip. The men were stunned by all that had happened in just sixteen days, by the fact that many friends had been left to an uncertain fate in the Philippines, and that their own futures did not look too bright. They were also deeply disturbed because they "still heard nothing from Washington."[44] The military situation was grim. The Japanese were on the move, and nothing the Allies did seemed to slow them down. It was an emaciated, troubled PatWing-10 that now turned to face the oncoming Japanese.

# 4

# Manila
# 24–25 December 1941

In the Philippines, the remnants of PatWing-10 were faced with a rapidly deteriorating situation. The Japanese were pushing inland, their advance covered by fighter and bomber swarms that subjected ground targets to virtually unopposed attacks. Much of the Philippine Army had proved ineffective, while the Americans and the tough Philippine scouts were too thinly spread to stop the Japanese advance.

With Cavite smashed, the Navy Yard's activities shifted to the seaplane base at Sangley Point. Though Sangley suffered little damage on 10 December, the situation there was grim. Personnel from the Navy Yard were quartered in the hospital area, while the airmen established temporary camps at Makanai and Caridad, where several Americans owned homes.

> Those houses were taken over, and the group was divided into sections to sleep in each yard. Watches were posted because it was known that many Jap sympathizers were in the area. One was caught within a hundred yards of Radio Highpower, jamming the combat frequencies with a transmitter of his own. There were reports of stabbings and attacks.[1]

While the surviving Navy Yard personnel salvaged what they

could from the Cavite ruins, the airmen were trying to restore their remaining six PBYs to flying condition. Two of the planes, P-14 and P-28, were on or near Sangley Point. P-14 was completing overhaul in hangar X-34, and McConnell's P-28 was a short distance away at the Pan American ramp.

The other four planes were on the south end of Laguna de Bay, near Los Baños. Two were ready to go, and Swenson's P-2 would complete its engine change in a few days. The fourth plane was Ogle's P-29 that sunk after hitting an obstruction on 16 December. The plane had since been raised and towed close to shore. Despite collision and submersion damage, P-29 was expected to be on line in about two weeks. Though working conditions at Los Baños were primitive, things were relatively quiet. The reverse was true at Sangley Point. Since 10 December when Cavite was destroyed, everyone expected Sangley Point to be the next target. Instead, the Japanese concentrated on finishing off the Far East Air Force. Understandably, with air raids going on all around them, the men were jumpy. Adding to their tension were the comings and goings of Lieutenant John D. Bulkeley's motor torpedo boats.

The Philippine troops shown here being reviewed by officers of Pat-Wing-10 did not measure up to MacArthur's prewar claims. (Courtesy Lowell Williamson)

Bulkeley's torpedo boats were having their troubles. They had no radio spare parts and no gas strainers to filter the water out of their gas. We were able to find some from our supplies to keep them going, but we would have readily been willing to sink them. Every time they started their engines someone sounded the air-raid alarm. Their engines sounded like a bombing formation.[2]

But on 19 December, the air-raid alarm was real.

Nine days after the Cavite raid, the Japanese got around to Sangley Point. The midday raid destroyed the gasoline dump, took out the high-powered radio station, and blasted hangar X-34 and the PBY inside into fragments. Surprisingly, the casualties were limited to "fifteen or twenty dead" and a few wounded. Though Sangley Point was out of commission as a seaplane base, there was still work being done there. Repairs continued on P-28 at the Pan American ramp, while anything salvageable was being dug out of the smoking ruins of the seaplane base. The biggest problem was feeding and housing the men.

The mess hall had been totally destroyed during the raid, and crude mess facilities were set up in the temporary camps. But meals continued to be a problem as supplies ran out and refugees started moving into the PatWing-10 area.

> We set up a galley on some bucks in the yard and cooked what food could be obtained from Sangley Point. The second night the Admiral sent word that some women were to be moved in. Someone has discovered them barricaded in a school house. They were scared and starved. Some were American wives of civil service employees at the Navy Yard, some Chinese, some Portuguese, and various mixtures. There were a number of youngsters.
>
> Several women had had no word of their husbands since the Navy Yard had been bombed, and there had been many attempts at molestation from the hands of the natives.[3]

On 22 December the Japanese landed 43,000 men at Lingayen Gulf, and two days later put 7,000 more ashore at Lamon Bay. Squarely between those two events, MacArthur reverted to War Plan Orange and started pulling his troops back onto the Bataan Peninsula and Corregidor. On the 25th he would declare Manila an open city.

Seen through the eyes of the men in PatWing-10, the war had taken a nasty turn. The army's resistance seemed ineffective, and there were reports that Philippine soldiers were deserting in large numbers. One account described them as "throwing away their uniforms and arms, and running around in skivvies so that Japs would think they were civilians."[4]

PatWing-10 still had a skeleton crew at Olongapo, as well as spare parts and supplies stored at the base. Clearly those men had to be brought in, along with the spare parts and supplies, before the Japanese overran them. The question was, was it still possible to get through along the highway? But when questioned, army intelligence "gave us no clue as to the extent of the advance. . . ."[5]

On the evening of 16 December, Tom Pollock "selected the best truck available and a reliable driver," and set out for Olongapo. Expecting the worst, Pollock armed himself with a Thompson submachine gun and a twelve-gauge, sawed-off shotgun. Though he and his driver did not know it, the Japanese were still two weeks away. As things worked out, the Filipinos were the biggest problem Pollock faced—and that was bad enough.

Their route took them north through Manila to San Fernando, and then west to Olongapo. The distance was about eighty miles, and the trip should have taken not more than four or five hours. It took over twelve.

The Home Guard was out in force, stationed at every bridge and crossroad. Around Manila there are bridges, or "over-grown culverts," about every half mile.

> The Home Guard had all been given whistles, and most were
> armed with shotguns, and occasionally rifles. At each crossing they
> would blow their whistles and yell halt.

Twenty miles of literally stop and go was getting on Pollock's nerves, but he expected clear sailing once he reached Manila. It was dark by the time he arrived just outside of town where he was told that the blackout was being strictly enforced, all lights were being fired on. Pollock proceeded cautiously— without lights.

> Shots could be heard around the town every few minutes. It wasn't
> safe for anyone to smoke a cigarette without the prospect of being
> shot. The casualties were much higher than from the Jap bombing.

Once through Manila there were fewer roadblocks and Pollock made much better time. The faster pace was achieved by driving with the lights on. But once through San Fernando, they again ran into road guards and Filipino troops. Driving without lights along the narrow road slowed their speed to five miles per hour. At one point, the truck nearly crashed into a huge boulder, and Pollock ordered the headlights turned on dim. They were immediately stopped by an angry Filipino soldier who told them, "in no uncertain terms," to shut off the lights. Pollock complied and asked where the front was. The soldier did not know, so Pollock went on hoping they did not run into the Japanese "around the next turn."

They arrived at the seaplane base after dawn, and found the place deserted. Driving along the road, aware of the "ghastly quiet," they passed a dead carabao near the still-smoldering ruins of a native shack. Bomb craters were spaced evenly along both sides of the road, but the base itself appeared in good shape.

When Pollock finally located the PatWing-10 detail, he learned that most of the food and supplies had been moved to Corregidor when the marine battalion was pulled out. Some of the airmen had gone along too. The remnants of the small detail were overjoyed to see Pollock, since they had been afraid they might be forgotten. Despite the lack of any word about what was happening, the men had faithfully maintained the gassing and repair facilities in case planes came in for service.

Loading all usable tools and spare parts into the truck, Pollock organized a convoy of commandeered automobiles. Only food that could be eaten without cooking was taken, and the convoy was ordered to keep together in case of breakdown. The trip back went much more quickly than had the trip up. Daylight made the difference, and the convoy reached Sangley Point by mid-afternoon.

Lieutenant Commander Neale greeted Pollock. "Am I glad to see you. The reports are that the Japs are moving down from Lingayen Gulf fast."

"We're glad to be back," answered Pollock, knowing that he spoke for all of them.

That evening Pollock was sent to Laguna de Bay to replace Roberts on P-5. Roberts had been sent to the hospital with a particularly severe, full-body skin rash, and there was no way to know when he would be released. Since P-5 had already been designated to fly army and navy brass to Java, an immediate replacement was needed. The flight was scheduled for Christmas Eve, and it looked to Pollock as though his ticket out of the Philippines had already been punched. He was wrong.

On 24 December the Japanese launched their heaviest raid against Manila. Concentrating on the waterfront, the bombers left Manila's port facilities a shambles of collapsed buildings, twisted rails, and cratered streets. In some sections the destruction was so complete that the streets were impassable to foot traffic. The rim of the bay from Manila to Cavite was blanketed by heavy black smoke. Fires burned out of control throughout the area, the air thick with dust from pulverized stone and cement.

In the midst of the destruction, military and government personnel were hurrying to evacuate the city. Their haste was largely due to MacArthur's intention to declare Manila an open city on the following day. But they were also spurred on by the speed of the Japanese advance.

The Japanese were coming from the north and south along first-class highways. The southern pincer had already been reinforced by a much smaller landing in Batangas Province that threatened to trap the Philippine troops in the Legaspi area. The result was that the Philippine troops were forced to fall back along Highways 1 and 21 toward Los Baños. Despite formidable difficulties, the retreat was accomplished in good order during the week following the Japanese landings, but on 24 December the front was just thirty miles east of the PBYs hidden in Laguna de Bay.

On the 24th the people in Manila who planned to use those PBYs were already packing their bags. Admiral Hart had set his departure date for the 25th, but was going to send key members of his staff out on the night of the 24th. Major General Lewis H. Brereton, Commander Far Eastern Air Force, had been ordered south by General MacArthur. Brereton would have liked to fly to Australia aboard an army B-17, but there were none in the Philippines on 24 December.[6] He had two alternatives. He could fly out in a Philippine airline transport or hitch a ride in a navy PBY. Brereton, an Annapolis graduate, chose the latter.

Just before dusk on the 24th, Utter and Pollock flew P-5 to Sangley Point to pick up their passengers. While waiting for their passengers to sort themselves out, they nervously watched the darkening sky for Japanese fighters. The passengers were still arriving at the ramp when the airmen heard the sound of a single-engine plane coming closer.

There was no doubt that the plane they heard was Japanese, and there was no doubt that as long as the plane hung around they would stay on the water. The problem was that it was getting dark very quickly, and a night takeoff across Manila's crowded bay was an unattractive proposition.

The PBY was crammed so full with army and navy brass, and their baggage, that it was nearly impossible to move forward or aft through the plane. The bothersome enemy plane prowled around until well after dark, then headed back toward its field.

At 2000 the PBY went down the ramp and taxied out into the bay.

> There were all kinds of barges anchored in the bay, and before we went over the ramp I saw a channel through them. I could just see a mountain through the smoke from the Cavite fires, and I used it as a reference point to take us through the barges. You couldn't really see the barges too well. They were just sort of lumps.[7]

P-5 was up on the step, charging full bore down the narrow channel when suddenly a boat loomed up ahead of them. The boat, a fifty-foot, steam-powered "680 boat," was steaming directly across their path from port to starboard.

Utter chopped both engines, kicking the rudder hard right. Pollock saw only the boat's masts flash past as P-5 swung violently to the right to avoid a head-on crash. The PBY waterlooped, her port wing tip and float smashing into the boat's bow. The PBY slewed around 180 degrees as her left wing tip dipped toward the water, submerging the damaged float. Quickly a crewman scrambled out on the right wing to counterbalance the dipping wing. The left wing tip rose, and on a reasonably even keel, Utter taxied carefully back to the ramp.

The twenty-one passengers and their baggage were put into automobiles and sent off to Lake Lanao to try their luck with another PBY. En route to the lake, General Brereton's car was sideswiped by an army truck, but the general was able to continue after a short delay. At that point the general must have wondered if the trip was really necessary.[8]

Meanwhile, at Los Baños, Swenson, Williamson, Reid, and Pew were gathered in the duty hut. Pew was the duty officer. They were discussing the massive Japanese landings at Lamon Bay and wondering how much longer they could stay where they were, when the phone rang.

"Aye aye sir," Pew said and hung up. "Reid, get your plane ready. Your passengers are coming."[9]

Reid had no idea what Pew was talking about, but he did not argue. Hurrying to his plane he set his crew to pulling off the branches that covered it. While that was being done, Pew came along and called for Don Kelly. Kelly was an NAP who had just recently joined Reid's crew.

"You're not going," Pew told Kelly. "You've got an SOC to fly."[10]

"That's wonderful," Kelly said sarcastically, " I never saw the inside of one. What are you talking about?"

But Pew knew as little about the last-minute order as Kelly, who grabbed his gear and headed down the road toward the SOC.

Kelly may have been pulled off the plane to make room for VP-102's CO, Lieutenant Commander Edgar Neale. Neale was at that moment en route to the lake with General Brereton's group. Neale did not normally fly with Reid, and Neale's presence aboard the plane put the young ensign in an awkward position.

Kelly was understandably unhappy about his new order, but Reid had mixed feelings about his. The Japanese landings were a serious matter, and since sundown everyone had been hearing night noises. Most of the men were convinced that they could hear tanks moving along Highway 21 toward Manila. Already they were discussing what to do if the order "every man for himself" were given. With those thoughts in his mind, the chance to get out of the Philippines looked awfully attractive. The thing that was bothering Andy Reid was a night takeoff from Laguna de Bay.

In addition to the usual hazards such as rocks, stumps, and floating debris, the lake was spotted with native fish traps. Those spade-shaped obstructions consisted of heavy bamboo poles driven firmly into the lake bed and lashed together with vines and hemp. In

Reid's words, "a trip into one of them in a PBY would have been a disaster."[11]

Reid's concern was well founded. But fortunately for him, AMM1c Edgar Palm, his NAP, had surveyed the area and had laid out takeoff headings through the traps.

While Reid waited, General Brereton and the other twenty passengers were stumbling down a narrow carabao path looking for the PBY. Their guide had led them on a wild-goose chase through the black night to the wrong plane. Weighted down with baggage that included several heavy boxes filled with army and navy documents, the men angrily retraced their steps, arriving at the right spot just before midnight.

By the time the passengers were aboard, Reid was concerned about the load he had to get off the water. In addition to 12,000 gallons of fuel, twenty-eight people and baggage, there were four 500-pound bombs slung under the wings. The plane was terribly overloaded and Reid wanted to do something to lighten the load.

"OK, Andy, let's go," Neale said.[12]

"How many do we have on board?" Reid asked.

"About thirty."

"My aching back!" groaned Reid.

"We won't say anything about it! Understand?" Neale snapped.

"Request permission to jettison the bombs, sir."

"Negative," Neale answered, and added, "Hell no. You're going to need them where you're going."

Reid knew better than to argue with Neale, who was well known for his bad temper. But there was still another problem bothering Reid. He did not know where they were going. As Reid signaled "start engines" he told Neale, "I don't have any charts on board."

"That's alright. I know where we're going."

"Sir, I don't have an octant, I don't have a . . . ."

"That's alright," Neale interrupted. He was getting angry now. "I know where we're going."

Reid dropped the subject and turned his attention to getting off. The plane had been tailed-up to the beach, and now heavily loaded, she stuck in the sand. Reid ran the engines up to half power, but the plane would not budge. He went to full power, and she still would not move. By now both engines were starting to overheat.

Reid throttled back and directed "as many people as possible to crowd into the bow and stand between the pilot and copilot." The rest of them were packed like sardines in the radio compartment. The purpose was to shift enough weight forward to break the tail loose from the bottom. With everyone jammed forward, Reid again ran the engines up and held them there for "a long ten count."

Painfully the plane shook and rocked while the engines strained to pull her forward. Suddenly she broke loose and slid off the sand into deep water. While Reid taxied in a slow circle, the human ballast was shifted aft and Reid moved out into the lake. Carefully following Edgar Palm's directions, the PBY moved between the fish traps and into deep water.

This was Reid's first heavy-load, night takeoff, and he intended to give the try his best effort. Reid quickly rechecked—cowl flaps wide open, elevator, rudder, and aileron tabs set for takeoff, propellers set for 2,700 revolutions per minute, mixture control in automatic position. It looked good.

"OK, Edgar, give me 33 inches." During peacetime, 28 inches of manifold pressure had been used for takeoff, to prolong engine life. But Reid had asked for more because of the load. He looked ahead as the plane started its run. In the right-hand seat Edgar Palm reached up for the throttles.

"Mr. Reid, this is no time to dillydally," Palm said, easing the throttles forward.

"OK, Edgar, full bore."

In the darkness Palm smoothly pushed the throttles forward driving the manifold pressure to 39 inches. As the PBY plowed forward, water rolled across the bow, crashed against the windshield, and was whipped up by the propellers. Reid and Palm could not see where they were going as the plane slowly gained speed on her dash across the lake.

The run seemed to go on forever. With agonizing slowness the heavy plane rose up on the step, but would not lift off. The plane continued forward, still on the step but lifting slowly. Then she was off the water by the thinnest margin.

"Mr. Reid. The cylinder head temperature is pegged." The voice in Reid's headphone was the mechanic in the tower.

Reid reached up, covering Palm's hand with his on the throttles, and slowly eased them back a fraction. The plane settled back on the water. Still on the step, Reid again went to full power. This time the PBY lifted cleanly off the water and began to climb slowly. Reid put the plane into a slow left turn starting a slow spiral ascent from the lake. The plane had made one 360 degree turn when Neale came forward.

"OK, Andy, where are we?"

"We're right over Laguna de Bay," Reid told him. At that point Neale exploded. "We're leaving the Philippines. Now get with it!"

Reid was having a hard time controlling his temper. His plane was barely in the air, he had no idea where he was going, and virtually no charts to get him there.

"Sir. The hills surrounding Laguna de Bay go up about 500 feet. Is there any particular direction you want me to head so we won't hit one?" Neale was not happy with the ensign's answer, and Reid recalls that "he blew up all over me again."

By the time Reid had completed another circuit over the lake, he was high enough to see Manila burning. He was then ordered to fly due west, over Corregidor, and then turn south. There was still no mention about their destination, but Reid had decided not to ask. It was probably a good decision.

For the next several hours the plane headed south with Reid in the left-hand seat, Neale in the right, and Palm in the navigator's compartment. The enlisted men were now suffering terribly from the cold. Most of them had on only a pair of shorts because it had been hot on the lake, and they had not had time to get dressed before takeoff.

After Neale replaced Palm in the right-hand seat, the NAP went aft to find his clothes. But there were so many people and so much baggage jammed into the limited space that he couldn't find them. Finally he borrowed a summer flight suit from one of the navy officers. The other enlisted men solved their problem in a similar way, but the solution was only a stop-gap measure.

Palm had been told to work out a route to the southeast corner of Borneo. He did not have charts that covered all the southern area, but he was confident that he could use a plotting board in the blank areas. At 0400 they flew over Tawitawi, which Palm recognized. His navigation to that point was flawless, but there was no chart for the area they were entering. Nevertheless, he calculated that they should stay on their present course until 0545 and then turn to 240 degrees true. He gave that information to Reid and Neale.

At 0545 they all saw an island below them, but lacking a chart, Palm could not identify it.

"God damn it. You're lost," Neale snorted.[13]

"I'm not lost," Palm argued. "I was right on time over Tawitawi and right on course. I don't know what that land is, but I know where I am."

There was no answer from Neale, and Reid was staying out of it. He had complete confidence in Palm, but did not want to cross Neale again. The plane continued on course, while Neale pondered what to do. Finally Palm spoke.

"What that hell you gonna do?" he prodded. Neale had no other choice, and told Reid to turn to 240 degrees true as Palm recommended. Not long after the course change had been made they reached the Borneo coast right on schedule. They turned and followed the coastline south.

"What time will we get to Balikpapan?" Neale asked.

Palm had a chart for that area and quickly answered, "We ought to be off Balikpapan at 0800."

Again Palm's navigation was right on the money as Balikpapan passed under the right wing. But he still did not know where they were headed, though he had a couple of pretty good ideas.

"What time are we going to get there?" Neale asked.

"What time are we going to get where?" Palm demanded, irritation creeping into his voice. "It's so goddamn secret you've never told me where we're going."

Surprisingly Neale ignored Palm's tone. "We're going to Surabaja."

"We oughta be there at noon," Palm said.

The PBY circled Surabaja, Neale in the left-hand seat, Palm on the right. Reid had gone aft. Neale and Palm watched a Dutch seaplane take off and decided to land there.

The badly overloaded PBY was still well above the water when the power was cut. The big plane dropped like a rock in a "nose-high belly flop," hit the water hard, and bounced back into the air. Knowing she wouldn't survive another hit like that, Palm rammed the throttles forward. The engines roared and the plane shook as she dropped toward the water, the big radials straining to keep her up. The second landing was also a hard one, but it was much easier than the first. But their troubles were not over.

Surabaja is a very shallow harbor. It is dotted with mud flats that bare at low water, and are just barely covered at high water. There was a deep channel leading to the Morokrembangan seaplane base that was usable by seaplanes at all times. But without charts or local knowledge, the channel was impossible to spot from the air. Reid, Neale, and Palm had neither charts or local knowledge.

As soon as the plane came down off the step, she ran aground, but the pilots were able to "blow her off" into deeper water. A short distance later she again ran on the mud. The stop-and-go progress across the harbor was getting on everyone's nerves, when Neale and Palm watched a Dutch PBY come in and land. The Dutch plane touched down, staying up on the step, and gracefully curved around a marker, proceeding up the channel toward the seaplane base.

"If he can do it, so can I," vowed Neale as he started to follow the plane.[14] The problem was that the American PBY was not on the step, and she did not curve around the marker. Instead she cut inside the marker, and got stuck.

This time it looked like she was on to stay, and no amount of engine power would budge her. After twenty or thirty minutes, several enlisted men got out to rock and push the plane. The engines roared, the men heaved, but the plane stayed where she was. Exhausted, the men climbed back inside while the engines were shut down to cool. Palm remained outside the plane, sitting on the port wing float. He was still there twenty minutes later when the engines were restarted.

Palm figured the other men would jump out any minute to push the plane off. Instead, he found himself pushing on the hull by himself. Suddenly, the plane lurched forward, leaving Palm standing waist deep in mud and water watching the plane taxi away. Alone, Palm started splashing toward the shore two miles away.[15]

Meanwhile, back at Laguna de Bay, Don Kelly was preparing to make his first solo flight in an SOC. At about the time Reid and Neale were changing course for Borneo, Kelly was going over the SOC's cockpit layout and instruments with a flashlight. In the rear seat was AMM2c Raymond F. ("Tom") Mix.

"Is your life insurance paid up?" Kelly asked his gunner. [16]
Mix nodded, "Let's go."
The takeoff was not as bad as Kelly had expected but it took him about ten minutes before he felt he really had the plane under control. Skimming along at treetop level the SOC drew fire from an antiaircraft unit near Manila. Streaking out over Manila Bay Kelly saw two submarines on the surface; when he looked again there was only one. Taking no chances the skipper had pulled the plug. But the incident gave Kelly something to worry about. Getting shot at by his own people, and making an American sub crash-dive meant that a lot of people figured he was the enemy. Since there were not many American planes in the air on 25 December that was a reasonable assumption.

> It was starting to get light as I came across Manila Bay. And I started to send recognition signals like mad because I didn't want Corregidor to open up on me. I guess they got my signals OK. At least they didn't shoot at me.

Kelly landed in Mariveles, taxied past a burning French ship, and anchored near the *Canopus*. A handful of SOCs, OS2Us, and J2Fs, the remnants of the utility squadron, were anchored near the shore. After anchoring his plane, Kelly and Mix swam ashore. Two weeks later all the planes were destroyed on the water.

Kelly had taken off at about the time that Utter and Pollock were returning to Laguna de Bay from Cavite. After their passengers had been sent off in cars, P-5's crew had worked all night to replace the damaged wing float. With their plane back in flying condition, they flew to Laguna de Bay and joined the two planes still there. Of the three, only the recently returned P-5 and Swenson's P-2 were flyable. P-29 was still about three days short of being ready. Within twelve hours all three planes would be destroyed.

Utter's and Swenson's PBYs were now earmarked to fly Admiral Hart and the remainder of his staff to Java. The PBYs were critical to Hart's plans because they were the only means of transportation that would keep to a minimum the time Hart would be out of touch with his command. Whether or not the required two planes would be available on the 25th had been questionable until just two days earlier, when Swenson's P-2 was reported back on line.

Swenson and his crew had worked seven days replacing the burned out engine. The job was particularly difficult due to the primitive conditions and lack of facilities on Laguna de Bay. Swenson overcame many of the difficulties by employing native labor for the "muscle jobs," and some of the surplus airmen as technical help. Unable to pay any of them, he enticed them to help by making them "honorary crew members in the 2-boat."[17] Many of the stranded airmen may have hoped that when P-2 headed south all her "crewmen" would go too.

The two flyable PBYs were anchored offshore, covered with blankets and branches. To a high-flying airplane, the two PBYs probably looked like clumps of land and vegetation that dotted the lake along the shore. But to a low flying airplane they probably looked like two camouflaged PBYs.

Though conditions on Laguna de Bay were primitive, Swenson's crew had made themselves as comfortable as possible. They had rented a native shack near the shore, complete with cooks and servants. And they had easy access to the famous hot springs of Los Baños. They had even commandeered a couple of cars to get around in. By contrast, Utter's crew was, according to Tom Pollock, "camping out." But regardless of the different living conditions they chose, the two crews had arranged to have Christmas dinner together.

On the afternoon of the 24th, Swenson and some of his crew went into Los Baños to buy a pig for the holiday meal. Finding several animals dressed out and hanging in the market place, they picked one that seemed to suit their need.

"We'll take that one," Swenson told the vendor, pointing to a fairly small animal hanging on the rack.[18]

"This one?" The vendor looked doubtful.

"Yea. That one. It's just the right size for our crew."

"Do you really want this one?" the vendor asked with disbelief.

"Sure." Swenson's answer was emphatic.

"But that's a dog," the vendor almost shouted, his tone a mixture of surprise and laughter.

The airmen quickly conferred, and decided that "if we couldn't tell the difference between a pig and a dog, we had better buy something else." They bought a turkey.

About mid-morning on Christmas day, Swenson, his NAP,

AMM1c John W. Clark, and the chief mechanic, AMM1c Robert E. Butterbaugh, were returning from Los Baños with the cooked turkey. Lowell Williamson, recently assigned as Swenson's copilot, was in the native shack. AMM2c Robert D. Foster was standing watch in their plane. Two hundred yards up the beach Utter and Pollock were in P-5, while their crew was ashore.

Suddenly, two twin-engine bombers roared low along the shore, machine-gunning everything in their path. Utter and Pollock went over the side, ducking beneath the surface as machine-gun bullets beat the water. In P-2, Foster opened up with the port .50-caliber waist gun. P-5 was already burning, and P-2 was riddled with holes, gasoline pouring from the wing tanks.

As Japanese planes flashed over, Foster scrambled through the plane to grab the .30-caliber bow gun. Utter and Pollock reached the beach, clawed their way up the steep bank, and took cover in the trees.[19]

Seeing the bombers wheeling around for another pass, Foster hurriedly returned to the waist gun. P-5 was burning furiously now, and the men on shore, fearing her four 500-pound bombs would explode, moved deeper into the trees. Inside P-2, Foster was only dimly aware of the water rising round his ankles and the fires that burned on the berths. He probably did not even notice the tracers that streaked through the hull around him. His attention was focused on the oncoming bombers as he adjusted his own stream of fire to lead them.

The water around the PBY foamed as machine-gun fire swept up to, and through, the PBY. Smoke from the burning berths was visible on the outside now. As the bombers passed over, Foster again shifted to the bow gun in an effort to nail them as they pulled away.

When the bombers were out of range, Foster turned his efforts to putting out the fires. Rigging the bilge pump, he used the water flowing into the bilge to deluge the burning mattresses. But his damage control efforts were cut short by the sound of the two bombers coming in again. Grabbing the port waist gun for the third time, Foster pumped a stream of tracers at the lead bomber. This time he was right on target. Heavy .50-caliber slugs stitched the belly of the Japanese plane, killing the belly gunner.

The volume of fire put up by Foster's tenacious defense drove the

Japanese off, but they had done their job well. Utter's plane had been reduced to flaming, sinking wreckage. Swenson's P-2 was afloat, but full of holes, gasoline leaking from the wings, oil from the engine. Farther down the beach P-29 had been sunk for the second time, and this time she stayed down. That left PatWing-10 with two PBYs on Luzon—Swenson's plane and P-28, still under repair at the Pan American ramp near Cavite.

There was now no reason to stay at Laguna de Bay, especially with the Japanese getting closer. It was time to pull out. Utter and his crew went to Cavite by car to join the withdrawal onto the Bataan Peninsula. A demolition crew led by Ensign Pew stayed behind to destroy everything at the camp, including the bombsight in P-29, and then join the others in Cavite. Swenson was told to fly his plane to Cavite or destroy it.

Flying P-2 to Cavite would take some doing, but Swenson sure did not want to abandon his plane, even though it was badly shot up. The port engine had been hit in the oil cooler, the fuel tanks leaked, water spurted through dozens of holes in the hull, some of the controls had been shot away, and the area around the waist gun looked like a sieve.

The holes in the hull were plugged with pencils, and the wings were patched with pieces cut from ammunition boxes. But there was nothing they could do about the cut-up controls or the leaky oil cooler. Swenson planned to fix those when he got to Cavite. While Swenson and his crew patched up their plane for the thirty-minute hop to Cavite, another patched up plane, already in Cavite, was about to leave on a much longer trip.

On 24 December, Joseph Antonides had told Commander Frank Bridget that P-28 was about ready to fly and should be ready the next day. That same day Ensign Roberts was released from the hospital and reported to Frank Bridget for assignment.

Bridget was glad to see Roberts and told him that he would be assigned to the first available plane. That sounded good to Roberts, who did not know there were only three flyable PBYs on Luzon, and two doubtfuls.[20] Roberts thanked Bridget and went outside where he ran into Bob Etnire.

Etnire was anxious to get to Manila to see his wife, who was staying in the Bay View Hotel. Frank Bridget told us we could take the barge to Manila for the night, but to be back at 0900—sober. I was told to be in shape to fly. I had Christmas Eve with the PanAm Group in the Manila Hotel while Bob spent it with his wife.[21]

Both men returned on time and Bridget told Roberts that there would be a plane available. He then told the ensign to stay "within hailing distance." At 1500 Roberts was again summoned to Bridget's office. This time there were several other, more senior, officers standing around "with long faces." By that time the word about the shoot-up at Laguna de Bay was out, but the condition of Swenson's plane was unknown. That meant that the only airplane that would be available was P-28, sitting on the Pan American ramp. Recognizing that their only hope of getting out of the Philippines lay in getting assigned to that plane, some of the more senior officers had tried hard to bump Roberts out of his spot. It did not work, and that was the cause of the long faces.

At that time he told me that one or two other pilots would arrive about 1800, and that we were to take off as soon as they were on board. He also said that Admiral Hart might fly out with us, so be prepared. I was told to pick six crewmen I wanted, if they volunteered to risk the flight.

Roberts hightailed it toward the plane, collecting two bottles of Scotch along the way.

In the meantime, Antonides was already at the ramp supervising the launching. Better than anyone, Antonides knew that the flight involved a substantial risk. Not only were the Japanese a threat, but the flight was also being made at night in a plane that had no instrument lights, no gyrocompass, no automatic pilot, and no radio. The engines had to be started by hand-cranking, and the wing tip floats had to be manually retracted. There was no navigation equipment aboard except two magnetic compasses that could not agree on any heading, and a chart that covered "everything from Australia to northern Japan."[22] But those problems were not Antonides' concern. He was not assigned to the flight.

When Bill Deam and Frank Bridget arrived at 1800, Antonides was sitting on the tractor preparing to launch the plane. Roberts was in the cockpit. As the last-minute pre-launching preparations were being made, Bridget walked over to Antonides and told him to go aboard the plane. With only two pilots assigned, and the plane lacking much-needed equipment, Bridget figured that a third pilot—especially one who was also an engineer—would be useful. Antonides lost no time in grabbing his gear and climbing aboard.

Roberts, Deam, and Bridget were standing beneath the waist hatch discussing the situation. Deam told Roberts that Admiral Hart had decided not to fly in P-28 because the risks were too great. Considering that the plane was little more than an airframe with two engines, the three officers agreed that the admiral had a point. The last good-byes said, Roberts and Deam climbed through the waist hatch, and P-28 started down the ramp.

It was dusk when the PBY lifted off the water and cut across the mainland at tree-top level. Twenty-five miles out they climbed to 10,000 feet and turned toward Palawan, guided by the fires they could see burning there.

From the start they were faced with fatigue, mechanical problems, and bad weather. Fatigue was the biggest problem. None of the pilots had gotten more than two hours' sleep the previous night, and they were already dead-tired. In order to keep going, they relieved each other at the controls every hour. According to Roberts, they were so tired that after an hour they "were letting the wings flop all over the place."

Antonides had relieved Deam, who had crawled into a berth, while Roberts slept in the right-hand seat. Lacking any electrical power, P-28 had no intercom and no instrument lights. Conversation had to be bellowed over the roar of the big radials mounted directly above the pilots. As the weather closed in, it became absolutely necessary to fly by instruments. The only way to read them was to illuminate them with a flashlight until their radium coating was energized. The radium would glow about fifteen minutes, and then the process had to be repeated. During the time the flashlight was switched on, the pilot kept his eyes shut to protect his night vision.

Two other problems had surfaced as soon as they were airborne. The first thing they had found out was that the plane would only go 90 knots. The second problem was more serious. The tab control cable to the elevator had been shot away, making it necessary to shift the crew around to trim the plane. What they did not know was that one elevator cable had also been shot away. They were making the trip with only one set of elevator cables hooked up.

As the weather deteriorated, the buffeting got worse, increasing the already formidable fatigue factor. Antonides was flying, Roberts was asleep in the right-hand seat, and Deam was asleep on a berth. At 2230, off Puerto Princesa, a signal light flashed upward from the black void below. A few seconds later a signal rocket exploded in the same area. Antonides woke Roberts and sent for Deam "in case of trouble." As Roberts woke, he saw exhaust flames from several planes ahead and above them, and realized they were between a group of Japanese airplanes and a Japanese fleet.

Throttling the engines back to quiet them, Antonides nosed the PBY over, heading for a layer of clouds 2,000 feet below. It was a scary situation, made scarier by the sudden explosion of a star shell overhead. Apparently the Japanese on the ships had heard the PBY's engines and had fired the rocket.

As Antonides leveled off, the Japanese planes answered the ships' challenge. Satisfied, the Japanese went back to doing whatever Japanese fleets did in those days. P-28 had made it safely through the most dangerous part of the trip south, but in Cavite, what had been the last flyable, or perhaps nearly flyable, PBY was already a burned-out wreck.

An hour after P-28 had taken off, Swenson and his crew taxied their battered wreck out onto the lake. It was already dark, and visibility was poor as they sat ready for takeoff. Swenson was in the left-hand seat, Clark in the right. Williamson stood in eighteen inches of water in the navigation compartment. Butterbaugh was in the tower, the rest of the crew manned stations at the guns and the radio. Cavite was notified to expect them.[23]

Butterbaugh told Swenson the engines were warmed up, ready for takeoff. Clark shoved the throttles all the way forward. As the plane moved forward, no one was really sure that they would get off the water, or stay in the air if they did. Early in the takeoff run, the increased water pressure blew out the pencils plugging the holes in the hull. Water sprayed the interior, "shooting in like a fountain." Despite the increased weight, P-2 slowly lifted off, Swenson staying close to the water "to see if our plan was going to work." It did, and P-2 climbed to 1,800 feet.

"Mr. Swenson, there's gasoline back here." Foster's voice was calm, but the warning was clear. A few seconds later Swenson heard another report that their plan might not be working.

"Port engine is losing oil," was Butterbaugh's report.

That was a more serious problem than Foster's report. In order to keep the damaged engine working they had to keep 30–33 inches of manifold pressure on it. The engine was already overheating, and no one was sure it would hold together. The flight to Cavite was only about thirty minutes, but it was obvious that the port engine would not make it. In fact, there was a strong possibility that the engine would burn. And if it did the gasoline-soaked airplane would burn with it.

As the plane limped through the darkening sky toward Cavite, Butterbaugh steadily reported the oil pressure falling.

"Oil pressure zero in the port engine."

"Shut her down."

The PBY could fly on one engine, but it was hard to control on the water, and Swenson was worried about how much room he would have when he got down. A few moments later, he added a new worry to his list when the starboard engine started to heat up and sputter.

Meanwhile, in Cavite the final evacuation to the Bataan Peninsula was in high gear. Utter and Pollock had already met with Admiral Hart informing him that there were no planes left to fly him out. The admiral had simply waited too long. The news distressed Hart, since it forced him to go by submarine to Java. He would be out of touch with his command for at least eight days.[24]

After Hart had left, Bridget turned his attention to getting his people over to Mariveles, on the east side of Bataan. Most of the men were being put aboard the USS *Quail* or onto a large barge for the trip across the bay. A smaller group had been organized into a truck and car convoy that would carry much-needed supplies and equipment.

At Sangley Point, and in the Cavite Navy Yard, Lieutenant Thomas K. Bowers was supervising the demolition of the remaining ammunition, powder, and fuel stores.

> Depth charges and TNT were placed at various places: fuel tanks, radio station and marine railway. Smokeless powder had been scattered throughout the ammunition depot.[25]

Despite efforts to move as much of the fuel and ammunition as possible to Bataan, there was still a lot left behind. The ammunition depot alone held 1,900 tons of smokeless powder, and there was another huge munitions dump on Sunset Beach. It was going to be quite a blast. But when the ammunition depot went off, the explosion was so violent that the order to blow Sunset Beach was canceled. The decision was "received with profound relief by those . . . who were about to set off Sunset Beach."[26]

While the sailors were still going aboard the *Quail* and the barge, and the convoy was loading up, Swenson landed off Cavite. The noise made by the wheezing wreck sent everyone ashore diving for cover, disrupting the evacuation for several minutes.

Dragging a sea anchor from one wing to counter the pull of the one good engine, P-2 struggled to a point near the Pan American ramp where she was beached in a sinking condition. Swenson and Williamson were already organizing a salvage and repair party to fix the damaged engine when Bridget drove up. Swenson told Bridget that he felt he could find enough parts in the abandoned seaplane base to repair the plane. It was then 2000 hours, and Swenson figured he could have the plane ready to fly in twelve hours.

Bridget told him "no" for several reasons. In the first place, the entire area was going up in smoke in about two and a half hours. Secondly, Bridget was under orders to transfer all his people to Mariveles that night. Those sound reasons were reinforced by Bridget's opinion that P-2 was, in practicality, unrepairable.

Swenson argued that he could locate the parts needed and taxi to Mariveles that night. Bridget turned him down and ordered him to take his men aboard the barge. Reluctantly, the men ran to the dock and leaped aboard as the barge was leaving the dock. Two hours later, P-2 was blown up in the blast and fire that engulfed Cavite.

As the *Quail* and the towed barge were moving slowly across the bay toward Mariveles, Tom Pollock, Harmon Utter, and a few others were lounging on the Pan American ramp. Bridget had told them to wait for Bowers and his small force to set their charges, and then escort them through Manila to Bataan. With nothing to do but wait for the fireworks, the men had dragged comfortable chairs outside and were waiting for the show. It started at 2230, and was described by Tom Pollock as "the biggest fireworks display, the likes of which I'd never seen and never will again."[27]

The Pan American ramp was located between the Cavite Navy Yard and Sangley Point. Tremendous explosions accompanied by rising fire balls and thick smoke erupted on both sides of the group. The earth shook with such violence that the watcher's vision was at times impaired. Everything was moving. Ammunition cans and oil drums spun high into the air and skipped across the water. The entire area was instantly set aflame, the roar of the fire and collapsing buildings filling the spaces between the deafening explosions. But nothing prepared the aviators for the grand finale.

When the fires reached the smokeless powder, it ignited and flash-burned with intense heat and light. As the airmen sat comfortably watching, the sky started to lighten as though the sun was rising from the earth. Steadily the light grew brighter, illuminating everything around them, casting sharp shadows.

Quickly the light reached the intensity of daylight and continued to grow stronger. The watchers, frightened by the "light, fire, and roar," leaped from their chairs and started to run. Not a word was said, no shout uttered. They were just six men running for safety.

> We suddenly realized the same thing—there was no place to go.
> All we could do was run a quarter mile, and hit the bay on the
> other side. Besides, if the whole thing was going to blow up, we'd
> had it anyway.

Sheepishly, they all returned to the ramp.

The explosions became farther apart, the light faded, but the peninsula continued to burn. Utter and the others waited an hour past the deadline for Bowers and his demolition crew to show up, before giving up. It was 0100 when they left the ramp to search for transportation to Bataan.

They joined a six-car convoy carrying supplies and equipment for the sailors at Mariveles. The trip through Manila was slow and dangerous. Shotgun-armed Filipinos guarded every bridge and crossroad, halting cars and demanding identification. The roads were choked with vehicles of every description, inching toward Bataan. Gasoline, stores, ammunition, and anything else they could carry was being moved around the bay. Hemmed in by the explosive mixture, unable to maneuver, the aviators prayed that the Japanese would not shell the road. It took nine hours to make the trip. At 1000 on 26 December 1941, while the last PatWing-10 group to leave Sangley Point reported to Frank Bridget, the last Pat-Wing-10 plane to leave the Philippines was approaching Surabaja.

After climbing above the mountains, Deam and his crew had flown down the east side of the Celebes almost to Kendari. They then turned, crossed the southern end of the Celebes, and headed across the Java Sea toward Surabaja.

Arriving unannounced over Surabaja, the three pilots made a quick survey of the harbor and started down. The last thing they wanted was to be shot down by the Dutch. As they neared the water Roberts took over to make the landing.

> Not knowing anything about the harbor, I figured to land straight off the base and then go right on in. All the water was the same dirty brown so I was going to do it like you do in deep water.

What Roberts did not know was the same thing that Peterson and his group had not known, and the same thing that Reid and Neale had found out the day before. Surabaja was about half mud flats. The PBY set down, planed across the water on her step, settled, and ran aground. A half hour later the Dutch came out in a boat to pick up the crew.

The last plane had arrived in Surabaja. In the Philippines there were fifteen wrecked PBYs, over half of the wing's aircraft. Trapped on Bataan were fourteen pilots and one hundred and forty enlisted men, more than half the wing's personnel.[28]

Admiral Hart wrote about all the navy men left behind:

> . . . Too many officers and men of the Navy were left on Manila Bay . . . This error in judgement probably came from the idea of not going too far in withdrawing the Navy from the defense of the Philippines. From Java, things looked different.[29]

Of the 154 PatWing-10 men still on Luzon, only eleven pilots would escape.

# 5
# Ambon, Part I
## 23–31 December 1941

PatWing-10 was now fighting two separate campaigns. Half the wing was on Bataan fighting a ground war, while the other half was at Ambon preparing to fight an air war. For the men at Ambon, action came more quickly than anyone had expected. The day after Christmas, PatWing-10 launched its heaviest bombing attack against the Japanese.

While the wing had been moving from Surabaja to Ambon, the Japanese had been moving south. The main Japanese landings had been made on Luzon during 22 to 24 December. But of far greater importance was the seizure of Davao, on Mindanao, where on 23 December the Japanese Eleventh Air Fleet began operations. At the same time 4,000 troops were en route to take Jolo, an island in the Sulu Archipelago. They accomplished their mission on Christmas Day.

Seizure of Davao and Jolo provided the Japanese with stepping-stone airfields along the route to the North Borneo oil fields. But it also played an additional role in the Japanese plan; by occupying airfields at those places, the Japanese effectively isolated the Philippines. Not only did this prevent any relief from being sent to the Philippines from the south, it also set up the Japanese twin drives—one across the Molucca Sea and one down the Makassar Strait.

Looking at the situation from the Dutch point of view, the loss of Davao, Jolo, and North Borneo brought the full weight of the Japanese attack down on the Netherlands East Indies. The speed with which the first two goals had been achieved alarmed the Dutch. They had good reason for alarm. The Japanese had already landed on Borneo's west coast.

It was at this point that Admiral Hart left the Philippines aboard the submarine USS *Shark*. He had hoped to be out of touch with his command for only twenty-four hours. Instead, he would not reach Surabaja until 2 January 1942—eight days later. In the meantime, PatWing-10 would make a valiant, but hopeless, attempt to smash the Japanese at Jolo.

On 26 December, Dutch headquarters in Surabaja received word that two Japanese cruisers, two destroyers, and three transports were at Jolo. Surabaja immediately ordered the Dutch commander in Ambon to attack "with all forces available." Since the Dutch had only two Brewster Buffaloes in Ambon, Surabaja obviously expected the local commander to enlist the help of their American and Australian allies.

Captain Wagner, who had arrived in Ambon the previous day, agreed to the Dutch request. But the Australians, though certainly willing, had to decline because their Hudsons simply did not have the necessary range. So, all the "forces available" were American PBYs.[1]

At 1400 hours, Lieutenant Commander Peterson was told to "attack Japanese forces known to consist of at least one light cruiser, two destroyers, and one large transport."[2] The location of the target was vaguely described as "in the vicinity of the island of Jolo."[3] While the second pilot and crews preflighted the planes, a "very general" briefing was given the PPCs.[4] The briefing was general because the planners had very little information about the situation at Jolo. They thought, for example, that the Japanese ships were in TuTu Bay on Jolo's south side. In fact, the ships were in Jolo Harbor on the north side. More important, the planners did not know that Jolo was protected by twenty-four Zero fighters.

The plan called for six PBYs, in two sections of three, to take off just before midnight, arrive over the target at dawn, and take the enemy by surprise. Total flight time to and from the target was estimated at fourteen hours.[5]

The attack leader was Lieutenant Burden Hastings in P-1. He also led the first section, filled out with Lieutenant (j.g.) Jack Dawley in P-6 and Ensign E. L. Christman in P-9. Lieutenant John Hyland led the second section in P-23, with Lieutenant (j.g.) Tom McCabe's P-25 in the second position and Leroy Deede flying P-11 in the third slot.

The planes took off in the final minutes of 26 December and formed up at 10,000 feet with Hastings's first section out in front. Satisfied that everyone was in place, Hastings ordered all navigation lights extinguished. Without navigation lights, the pilots had to maintain formation by picking out the planes in the moonlight or by watching for their exhaust flame.[6]

But two hours later the moon had set, the formation became ragged, and the two sections separated. Actually, they probably did not get too far apart and apparently arrived near the island at about the same time. In any event, both sections arrived off the island while it was still too dark to bomb.

Hastings took his section up to 12,000 feet, and circled thirty miles south of the island for about ten minutes, waiting for Hyland's section to show up. When Hyland's section did not appear, Hastings led his first section toward TuTu Bay. The sky was just starting to lighten.[7]

In the meantime, Hyland had led his group close enough to the island to make sure he was in the right place. While Hastings circled in a holding pattern thirty miles out, Hyland led his section back out to sea, at 10,000 feet and in an easterly direction. Ten minutes later the sky was lightening and Hastings section was still not in sight. Lacking a bombsight, Hyland turned the lead over to Tom McCabe in P-25 and ordered the second section toward TuTu Bay.[8] Both sections were now approaching Jolo independently, and at different altitudes.

The Japanese may have been alerted by the second section's close approach to the island in the predawn darkness. But the approaching bomb-laden PBYs may also have been spotted by the Japanese combat air patrol. In any event, the Japanese were ready.

The survivors of the raid are unsure which section went in first. But by comparing reports and interview statements, it seems certain that they came in very close together, with the second section leading. Both sections passed over TuTu Bay, found no ships, and continued on across the island. Heavy, accurate antiaircraft fire immediately rose up from Jolo Harbor to meet them. Adjusting their approach, P-25, 23, and 11 started their bombing run at 10,000 feet.

## P-25

Ensign Art Jacobson was crouched over the bombsight. Tracers streaked up at him, and flak exploded dead ahead, on altitude. If P-25 continued on her present run, they would fly right into the flak.

"Since they have seen us and seem to have the range, I suggest we turn around and make a new approach at a greater altitude." Jacobson's voice was calm and matter of fact in McCabe's headphones.[9]

McCabe turned right 90 degrees. Looking down, he saw what looked like three cruisers and two transports, all underway. Antiaircraft exploded all around his plane, shrapnel slashing the hull, the shock waves buffeting the plane. To escape the intense antiaircraft fire, McCabe again turned 90 degrees. At that moment the fighters jumped him.[10]

## P-23

Gordon Ebbe in the copilot's seat was awed by the volume of fire coming up from the Japanese ships. "God! You wouldn't believe the tracers going under us," he later recalled.[11]

In the left-hand seat John Hyland was listening to Tom McCabe announce that he was going around for another approach. As the section turned right, it appeared to Hyland that the enemy gunners "had the range."[12] Below he saw a transport anchored 1,000 yards off the Jolo dock. The antiaircraft fire was now very thick and very accurate as Hyland followed McCabe into a second 90-degree turn. Both pilots glimpsed three cruisers and two transports below. They also saw what looked like fighter planes on a dirt field near the harbor. They were right about the fighters on the field. What they had not seen were the eight Zeros coming in on their tail.

*P-11*

Deede and his copilot, Edgar Hazelton, heard McCabe say he was going to start another run, and followed the lead plane into the turn. P-11 was in the outside position as the three-plane Vee turned right. The antiaircraft fire, heavy and accurate, caught Deede's plane as it entered the turn. Like a boxer hit in the solar plexus, P-11 staggered as shrapnel slashed through the hull.[13] Recovering from the blow, Deede was checking for casualties when the port waist gun opened up.

"Let's haul ass." John Hyland's sharp command sent all three PBYs for a patch of distant clouds 7,000 feet below.[14]

From the port waist-gun position in Deede's plane, AMM1c John Cumberland watched a Zero make a diving pass on Hyland, plunge past the formation, and climb to attack P-11.

> He came in on me underneath the stabilizer. I stayed until he got in good range, and fanned my string on him. This was apparently ineffective.[15]

Cumberland was right. On 27 December, nearly three weeks into the war, PatWing-10 was still firing practice ammunition at the enemy.[16]

Fighters swarmed around Deede's plane, attacking from both sides. Deede jettisoned his bombs. Machine-gun fire chewed up his starboard engine, releasing a stream of oil. The oil pressure fell to zero, the engine shook violently, and died.[17]

One engine dead, Deede held a loose formation with Hyland and McCabe. Cumberland was frantically reloading his gun, while RM2c Glen Dockery fired at Japanese fighters with the starboard .50-caliber waist gun. Two Zeros came at Cumberland while another made a simultaneous attack on Dockery. The radioman went down as one fighter passed beneath P-11 and pulled up to attack P-25. Caught in a cross fire, the fighter rolled over and dove away.

Cumberland's gun was now reloaded, and the wounded Dockery was back on his feet, manning his gun. The PBY was just entering scattered cloud cover when the last attack was made on it. Machine-gun and cannon fire ripped open the gas tank. Fuel poured down through the tower, and streamed from the wings. Quickly, Deede shut down the remaining engine to reduce the fire hazard, as the plane headed for the sea 3,000 feet below.

Deede's plane had taken the brunt of the fighter attack made on the second section. Both McCabe and Hyland reached the cloud cover relatively unharmed and escaped back to Ambon. As they entered the cloud cover, both McCabe's waist gunners reported that P-11 was down safely.[18] John Hyland took a moment to look back toward Jolo.

> I looked back and saw the first section making a bombing run on one of the ships. They were being attacked by fighters, and were heading into severe antiaircraft fire.[19]

Hastings's section had crossed the south shore of Jolo Island at about the time McCabe was leading the second section in its first right turn. Watching the tracers and exploding rounds over the harbor, Dawley, in P-6, saw two groups of three aircraft over the harbor. He assumed that one group must be Hyland's second section and that the other three planes were Japanese fighters.[20] Actually all six were Zeros.

Hastings's section first ran into antiaircraft fire from batteries emplaced south of Jolo. The fire "was accurate, the range perfect." When they passed over the city at 12,000 feet, the antiaircraft fire became "extremely heavy . . . being directed very effectively at the planes, and as a barrage ahead of the planes."[21]

Dawley was concentrating on a cruiser, two destroyers, and a transport in the harbor ahead of him, when suddenly a stream of tracers poured from P-1's port waist gun, and arched over his plane. At the same moment rounds thudded into P-6 somewhere aft, tracers streaked down both sides of the cockpit, and waist gunners AMM2c Earle Hall and RM3c James Scribner died in the hail of fire from the Japanese fighters. Oil poured from the starboard engine nacelle. In the tower AMM2c Everen McLawhorn saw his instrument panel disintegrate in front of him, gasoline spurting from the shattered fuel gauges. Covered with oil and gasoline, McLawhorn retreated from the tower to the waist guns.[22]

An antiaircraft round exploded beneath the plane, punching holes in the hull and severing the rudder control cables. Grabbing the starboard waist gun, McLawhorn fired at another fighter closing in. The fighter fired back, slamming seven slugs and dozens of metal fragments into McLawhorn, knocking him down. Hit in both arms, both legs, and with metal splinters in one eye, McLawhorn crawled to the port waist gun. Swinging the gun aft, and sighting with his good eye, he opened up on a fighter attacking from the port quarter.

In the copilot's seat, Ira Brown ducked as the window next to his head exploded.[23] Ahead, P-1 was maneuvering wildly, trying to shake off three Zeros, and to the left, P-9 was falling back. As the formation fell apart, Dawley made a decision to attack independently.

> With my starboard engine damaged, my rear gunners out of action,
> . . . I dove out of formation and executed a dive-bombing attack,
> alone, on the nearest large ship in the harbor—the cruiser.[24]

P-6 was literally enveloped in antiaircraft fire as she dove at her target. Ignoring their own antiaircraft fire, the Japanese fighters followed the PBY down, pumping hundreds of rounds into her battered hull. Dawley was certain his plane would be destroyed before he could release the bombs.

At 10,500 feet AMM1c Dave Bounds, on Dawley's command, released the three 500-pound bombs. The bombs gone, Dawley continued to dive. Bounds manned the bow gun, and McLawhorn switched to the starboard waist gun to meet a new attack. RM1c N. T. Whitford felt bullets hitting the hull beneath him. His protective mattresses burst into flame, a round hit his wrist, another creased his back.[25]

Dawley leveled off among scattered cloud cover at 3,000 feet, flying south across the island. Scissoring left and right he tried to give McLawhorn a shot at the pursuing fighters. In the bow, Bounds blazed away with the little .30-caliber machine gun whenever a fighter came in range.[26] Gasoline streamed from the wings and sloshed into the bilge. With one engine out, control cables shot away, and over half the crew dead or wounded, P-9 did not have a chance.

> It became obvious that the plane would not continue long in flight.
> It was impossible to evade the enemy's fire. . . . I decided to land
> the plane while I still had aileron control to permit the surviving
> crew members to save their lives.[27]

*P-9*

Christman and his copilot, Ensign William Gough, were more concerned about the antiaircraft fire coming up from the island than the fire from the harbor. Christman described the shore-based batteries as "very accurate," but the "AA fire of surface vessels was ineffective."[28] Their interest in the shore-based batteries was abruptly interrupted by long bursts from both waist guns, and a shout, "Here comes a fighter."[29]

The burst of .50-caliber machine-gun fire from the port waist gun hit the Japanese fighter squarely in the engine. Thick, black smoke poured out, as the fighter rolled over, "going into a fatal spin." Pilot and plane smashed into the sea 12,000 feet below.[30]

The first fighter was immediately replaced by three more, and P-9 came under continuous attacks. The view from the pilots' compartment was a sky filled with exploding shells, tracers, and wheeling fighters. Christman saw Hastings's plane scissoring and making "quick zooms," one engine afire.[31] To the right he saw Dawley had also lost an engine. Suddenly Hastings turned and dove, followed by three fighters. Then Dawley nosed over.

It was obvious to Christman that they were not going to reach their target, and that Hastings and Dawley were attempting to dive-bomb. Selecting the largest ship in the group, Christman pushed the column forward.

Nosed down in a 60-degree dive, the air-speed indicator quickly jumped to 200 knots. Tracers raced directly at them, and a close antiaircraft burst felt like "a 1,000-pound slab of concrete" had hit the plane. Concentrating on the target, Christman failed to see Dawley's plane diving at the same ship. The planes were converging with P-9 on top. Suddenly seeing the danger, Gough, Christman's copilot, grabbed the controls. P-9 lifted slightly as P-6 hurtled past beneath them.

The miss had been close, but it had not interrupted Christman's power dive. He wanted to get as close to the target as possible, but it looked like his plane would fall apart first. The noise was tremendous, and the wings were starting to wrinkle and fold back. The whole plane shook like a "riveting hammer." At 5,000 feet Christman unloaded his three 500-pound bombs and pulled out.

Bullets peppered the cabin roof, smashing the instrument panel.

Christman scissored right. More bullets pounded the hull, as the starboard waist gun fell silent.

"I'm out of ammunition."

Christman kicked the rudder over and swung left to meet another Zero coming from that side. Machine-gun fire clattered along the hull, followed by a tremendous bang that rocked the plane.

"Gas tank punctured."

Gasoline pouring into the mechanic's compartment was soon six inches deep in the bilge. More gasoline was coming out of the top and rear of the tank. More machine-gun rounds raked the hull, cutting down AMM1c Andrew Waterman. A 20-millimeter cannon shell exploded in the radio compartment, and P-9 erupted in flame.

"Jesus Christ, we're afire."

Looking aft into the mechanic's compartment, Gough had the impression he was looking into a fire box. RM1c Robert Pettit, already badly burned, was dragged forward by RM2c Paul Landers and AMM2c Joseph Bangust. Christman had to get his plane down on the water before she blew up in the air.

They were at 1,000 feet when Christman started down. Landers and Bangust were clipping on their parachutes, Pettit lay on the deck between the pilots, and ACMM Donald Lurvey still manned the bow gun.

"What do you want us to do?" Bangust asked Christman.

"Do what you want. Jump, or stay and I'll try to get down."

Bangust and Landers jumped. The plane was just 300 feet above the water when the two men went out. Their chutes were seen to open moments before they hit the water.

P-9 literally came in "hot and fast." Completely afire from wings aft, and traveling at over 100 knots, the PBY hit hard, "water looping both ways, swinging crazily."

*P-1*

No one really knows what happened to the lead plane. Witnesses said a Zero followed the plane through its dive and shot it down. There were just two survivors.[32]

The raid on Jolo had been a failure. More important, the raid had demonstrated that the PBY was completely unsuited as a daytime, horizontal bomber. Inadequately armed, poorly armored, lacking self-sealing gas tanks, and much too slow, the plane was easy meat for a Zero fighter. John Hyland and Tom McCabe landed at Ambon at 1415 with an account that stunned their squadron mates. Sixty-six percent of the attacking force had been lost, and so far as Hyland and McCabe knew, no hits had been scored on any enemy ship. The losses reduced PatWing-10's strength to just eight planes. But the loss of the planes seemed small compared to the loss of twenty-eight comrades. Though the casualty rate was high, sixteen of the missing men would return.

*P-6*

Dawley, having decided to land, "cut the ignition switches to prevent the leaking gasoline from igniting."[33] When he hit the water he still had a Japanese fighter on his tail. P-6 went down 200 yards off the beach, on Jolo's south shore, lost way, settled, and exploded into flame. The five living crewmen went over the side, swimming hard to clear the burning plane as the Zero again dove to strafe.

> The fighter pilot made no attempt to fire on the swimming survivors. The plane began to sink immediately; within three minutes the hull was completely submerged. . . . There was no sufficient time to remove from the plane the bodies of Hall and Scribner, nor to get out the confidential publications.

Dawley's crew was quickly picked up by villagers who had watched the spectacular show from the beach. At first the Moros seemed friendly, but within a short time Dawley began to have doubts about their sincerity. There was little he could do about it. In fact, there may have been some indecision among the Moro leaders about what to do with the five Americans. Jolo is not a very big island, and it would not take long for the Japanese to learn that the village was harboring the Americans. Inasmuch as the Japanese were firmly in control of the island, the best policy might have been to turn the Americans over to them. Instead, and fortunately, arrangements were made to send the five airmen to the island of Siasi that night.

Though he did not know it, Dawley had good reason to question the Moros' intentions. On the other side of the island, the two survivors from Hastings's P-1 were similarly rescued by Moros at about the same time. Apparently there was some indecision about what to do with the two men, but the indecision was resolved when they were turned over to the Japanese. Both were publicly executed.

## *P-9*

While Dawley was worrying about what the Moros might do, Christman and his crew were in a much worse situation. Their burning plane had crashed west of Jolo, and north of Siasi Island. Christman, Gough, Lurvey, and Pettit had barely escaped before it sank. When they were just fifty feet away, P-9 broke in two, the starboard wing fell off, and an engine crashed into the navigation compartment.[34]

They were about fifteen or twenty miles from shore without a life raft, and only three life jackets between them. Gough's Mae West had been punctured and was useless. In the two or three minutes before the plane went under, Lurvey swam back, boarded the flaming hulk, and retrieved a life ring, which he gave to Gough.

Christman took stock of their situation. He, Gough, and Lurvey were uninjured, but Pettit was badly burned and nearly blind. Somewhere behind them were Landers and Bangust who had parachuted from the plane. Christman had no idea if they were even alive, since they had jumped from so low an altitude. In fact, both men were alive, though Bangust was badly burned.

Thus, in two groups—four and two—the survivors of P-9 struck out for the nearest land. Bangust lasted about five hours before shedding his Mae West and sinking beneath the waves. Landers went on alone.

By 1500 Christman's group was showing signs of fatigue and despair. It took two men to keep Pettit moving, and at their slow rate, there was no hope of ever reaching the shore. All the men were badly sunburned, thirsty beyond description, and nauseated from swallowing sea water. Gough, the strongest swimmer, was sent on alone in the hope that he would reach the island and send back help. Slowly Gough outdistanced his three companions, until he was completely alone. At sunset Pettit died, and Christman and Lurvey prayed that Gough would reach help in time.

During the night of 27–28 December 1941, Dawley's crew, escaping from Jolo, sailed in a native vinta toward the island of Siasi. Unknown to them, they passed through the area where P-9's crew was struggling toward the same goal.

At 1000 on 28 December, after twenty-seven hours in the water, Landers waded ashore on the island of Lugos. Two hours later, an exhausted Christman and Lurvey were plucked from the water by natives in a vinta. Three hours later, and five hours after Landers had gone ashore, Gough was picked up by natives between Lugos and Siasi. Fortunately, by that time Christman, Lurvey, and Landers were already rescued, but of course Gough did not know that. When he asked his rescuers to send a boat back to find his friends, the natives refused.

## P-11

Deede's plane, the only one lost in the second section, went down sixty-five miles due south of Jolo. Unlike P-6 and P-9, Deede's plane did not burn and did not sink. But as soon as the plane hit the water the crew started getting ready to leave. To their surprise there were no Japanese fighters in sight, and Deede immediately decided "to stay with the plane, as it could be more easily seen if a rescue plane was sent."[35]

The crew plugged bullet holes below the waterline and pumped out the bilge, while Dockery tried to raise Ambon on the radio. His attempts throughout the day, and that night, were unsuccessful due to interference. To pass the time, they drank Heineken beer from a case they had aboard, and read to each other from a book titled *Young Love.*[36]

At 0820 on 28 December, Dockery made contact with Ambon. His weak signal was also copied by RM2c Arthur Dermott, in P-3 fifty miles south of Menado. Dermott's plane, piloted by Duke Campbell, was about three hours away from Deede's reported position. But Campbell was not sure the weak distress call was genuine.

> We knew it was up near Jolo, and at first we thought it was the Japs trying to trap us, that it wasn't Deede at all. They were just trying to get us to home in to where they could shoot us down.[37]

Campbell sent a message to Deede asking the name of a girl they both had known in Manila. Deede gave the correct name, and Campbell's suspicions were set aside. Still, Campbell was cautious and directed Deede to send MOs only on request. He did not want the Japanese to home in on the downed PBY's signals and be there waiting for him.

The USS *Peary* was spotted by Duke Campbell as she ran south toward Java. Misidentified as a Japanese cruiser, she was attacked by RAAF Hudsons. She was sunk at Darwin on 19 February 1942.

Three hours and ten minutes later P-3 landed alongside the drifting P-11, while Deede's crew waved and shouted. P-11's crew had already thrown the bombsight and confidential material overboard and had their raft inflated by the time Campbell was ready to take them aboard.

Deede's crew brought what was left of their case of beer with them, and "had a hell of a celebration on the way home."[38] In recognition of P-3's efforts on their behalf, Deede's crew promised to save some of their beer to share in Ambon.

On the five-hour flight home Campbell was feeling great, and three hours after picking up Deede's crew he saw something that made him feel even better. About twenty miles away he saw a ship headed toward Menado that he identified as a Japanese cruiser. He sent a sighting report to ComPatWing-10.

UNKNOWN SHIP BELIEVED TO BE JAPANESE CRUISER-LOCATION-COURSE-SPEED. Upon receiving the message at 1515 Captain Wagner conferred with the Dutch and Australian commanders. Based on what they knew, the three commanders agreed that Campbell was correct and ordered three Lockheed Hudsons of Number 2 Squadron, RAAF, to attack the ship.[39]

The three-plane flight, led by Flight Lieutenant R. B. Cumming, expected to be over the target at about 1745, and his estimate was pretty close.[40] To everyone concerned, Campbell's sighting seemed to have presented a great opportunity to strike back at the enemy. The target was, however, not what it appeared to be. The ship about to be attacked by the RAAF Hudsons was the American destroyer USS *Peary* (DD 226).

The *Peary* had already taken some hard knocks. She had been badly damaged during the 10 December raid on Cavite and been attacked by Japanese planes regularly since her departure from Cavite the day before.

The RAAF attack was short and violent. After first appearing to have recognized the ship as American, the Hudsons made six runs on the destroyer, killing two men and injuring three. A near miss just thirty feet from her port propeller guard knocked out the *Peary*'s steering engine, peppered the depth charges with shrapnel, and started a fire in the after, 4-inch ready racks. One of the Hudsons, badly damaged by antiaircraft fire, made it back to Ambon by the narrowest margin.[41]

Realization that a terrible mistake had been made came the next day, when Captain Wagner received word from the Dutch on Ternate about an American destroyer that had been bombed by "British planes." As the report unfolded, a shocked Wagner realized that "at our urging, the Australians had bombed one of our own destroyers." Duke Campbell felt "terrible about it," and the Australians were quick to defend their role in the tragedy.[42]

> No blame for this incident was held against the attacking flight as the destroyer had been sighted and shadowed by a US Catalina and . . . a senior American naval officer had decided on the reports made that the destroyer was hostile and had ordered the attack.[43]

Though unfortunate, the incident was the result of an honest mistake. Campbell had no way of knowing that the *Peary* was in the area. In fact, so far as he knew any ship that far north had to be Japanese. Campbell certainly was not the only person who mistook an old four-piper for a cruiser.

Captain Wagner's decision was correct, based on the information he had. He had been told that two American destroyers were running south from the Philippines. But according to his information they would be coming down the Makassar Strait together.[44] Thus, the *Peary* alone, and in the "wrong place," was logically assumed to be an enemy ship. How the Australians missed the American flag flying from the main mast is not clear, but they did.

Once he had learned of the mistake, Wagner made repeated attempts to raise the *Peary* by radio.

> We sent dispatch after dispatch telling her to work her way south as far as she could with the fuel she had remaining. But we could not reach her by radio.[45]

The *Peary*'s silence caused alarm in PatWing-10 headquarters. The extent of the destroyer's damage was not known, but it now appeared that her radios had been knocked out. Actually, the *Peary*'s radios were fine, but her skipper, Lieutenant Commander John M. Birmingham, was maintaining radio silence to prevent the Japanese from finding his ship. He also was not sure that Wagner's repeated messages were genuine. On 29 December Lieutenant Commander Birmingham knew who his enemies were, but he was not too sure about his "friends."

Fully expecting another attack, the *Peary* was hiding along the shore of Maitare Island, near Ternate. So close to shore that she appeared to be beached, covered with foliage, and most of her crew ashore under cover, the *Peary* waited to make her next move.

Unable to raise the battered destroyer, Captain Wagner dispatched the *Heron* to Ternate to locate the *Peary*, "and if necessary, take the *Peary* in tow." While the *Heron* moved north, ComPatWing-10 continued to send unanswered messages to the *Peary*.

On the day that the *Heron* set out to find the *Peary*, Ensign Reid returned to Ambon from Balikpapan. Reid had spent the night in the oil port after searching all day for the men who had been lost on the Jolo Raid. Reid's search for survivors was unsuccessful, but he located 6,000 rounds of "welcomed, armor-piercing machine-gun ammunition."[46] When Reid landed in Ambon and delivered his find, it was the first time since the war started that PatWing-10 had something other than practice ammunition to shoot.

On 30 December more search planes combed the sea south of

Jolo looking for survivors. Near Sangi Island, north of the Molucca Passage, Earl McConnell and John Sloatman in P-27 were jumped by four Zeros out of Jolo or Davao. Luckily, there were plenty of clouds, and the PBY escaped undamaged.

In the meantime, Tom McCabe and Gordon Ebbe in P-8 had also been looking for survivors. They were headed home when they received a radio message to look for the *Peary* in the vicinity of Ternate. They were to land, talk to the skipper, and tell him to "come on down to Ambon." P-8 circled the area twice without seeing the destroyer. On the third pass Gordon Ebbe spotted her "broadside to the beach, all covered with palm fronds."[47]

McCabe landed and taxied to smoother water while the second radioman sent a blinker message to the *Peary*. Soon a launch left the ship and came alongside the PBY.

> The skipper came out by boat and we talked. I told him that Pat-Wing-10 thought he should come to Ambon. He told me what had already happened to his ship since the war started. He didn't know if he wanted to come down. He said, "I've been bombed by everyone else, and I'm not about to let you guys have a shot at me too!"[48]

There was no arguing with Birmingham's logic, and McCabe did not try. But clearly, the *Peary* could not remain holed up forever, so at dusk the destroyer shed her camouflage and limped south toward Ambon.

As so often happened during the first months of the war in the southwest Pacific, there was a breakdown in communication. As the *Peary* started south at dusk, the *Heron* was approaching Ternate. No one told the *Heron* that the *Peary* had already been located, and ComPatWing-10 may or may not have known that the destroyer left its hiding place at dusk. In any event, the *Heron* was told nothing, not even the *Peary*'s last known position. The oversight very nearly cost Lieutenant William L. Kabler his ship and her crew.

The *Heron* entered the small harbor at Ternate at 2215 and anchored at 2255.[49] According to one source, Kabler was subjected to "four hours of bickering with [Dutch] authorities who did not believe that the *Peary* and *Heron* were American ships."[50] Finally, Kabler was told by the Dutch commander at Ternate that the *Peary* had already sailed. At 0212 the *Heron* "got underway . . . in obedience to dispatch orders of ComPatWing-10."[51]

At 0930 the *Heron* was about seventy miles south of Ternate, steaming at 10 knots, using only one of her two boilers, when an unidentified plane was sighted. The general quarters alarm was still ringing when the plane was recognized as a four-engine, Kawanishi, H6K "Mavis," flying boat. On its first run the big flying boat flew right into the *Heron*'s antiaircraft fire, taking several hits from the .50-caliber machine guns. No bombs were dropped.[52]

"0940 lighted fires under number 2 boiler."[53]

"0947 cut in boiler number 2 on main stream line. Went ahead at full speed, 12.2 knots."

Between 1015 and 1042 the Mavis made two more runs on the *Heron*, dropping two 100-pound bombs on each run. The heavy antiaircraft fire received on the initial pass had convinced the Japanese pilot to make his later runs from "high altitude." The results were misses by 300 to 1,500 yards.

At 1042 the *Heron* entered a heavy rain squall and remained hidden for thirty-eight minutes. When she came back out, the plane was still there, but quickly retired to a respectful "station about 15 miles distant." For the next three hours and forty-three minutes the *Heron* ran south at maximum speed, shadowed by the Japanese flying boat.

At 1500 Kabler slowed to standard speed, and three minutes later let the fires die out under boiler number 2. Seventeen minutes later he realized that the shutdown had been premature. Three Mavis flying boats were "attacking at high altitude from the port bow." Again the general quarters alarm sounded, followed closely by the order to commence firing.

"1521, lighted fires under boiler number 2."

"1523, cut in boiler number 2 on main steam line, and went ahead full speed."[54]

For the next hour and forty minutes the *Heron* was subjected to attacks by at least fourteen planes that dropped a total of 4,200 pounds of bombs and launched three torpedoes. The first run was made by three Mavises that released twelve 100-pound bombs in salvo. All exploded 200 yards astern. Then three more flying boats showed up and unloaded six 100-pound bombs that hit the water 200 yards off the *Heron*'s starboard beam. One of those planes took a 3-inch round in an engine, fell out of formation, and was last seen headed away trailing dense black smoke. The two remaining partners wheeled around and dumped four more 100-pounders that were wide of the mark.

The Japanese were not doing too well. They were finding out, along with the other warring nations, that horizontal bombing attacks on moving ships were not very successful. And the *Heron* was definitely moving.

At 1600, five twin-engine, land-based, Mitsubishi G3M Nells joined the attack. At medium altitude, the bombers raced in on the *Heron*'s starboard beam; Kabler turned into the attack, and the planes passed over without dropping. Machine-gun fire from the tender splattered the planes' bellies as they roared over. Banking around, they came in for a second run on the port beam.

At 1615 the five tightly packed Nells dropped twenty 100-pound bombs in salvo from 5,000 feet. The salvo straddled the small tender, but one bomb hit the top of the mainmast. For an instant the ship all but disappeared between two walls of water. Shrapnel punched through the port side from waterline to deck, destroying the degaussing circuit, smashing fresh-water tanks, and slashing powder bags. The aircraft boom was completely destroyed. The ship's boats were riddled with holes, their engines damaged. A stubborn fire was started in a forward storeroom, and the port 3-inch gun was momentarily knocked out. But the worst damage was caused by the single bomb that hit the top of the mainmast.

MM1c Ted Wachter was manning the starboard .50-caliber machine gun when the bomb exploded almost directly above him. Shrapnel sprayed downward, cutting down the exposed crewmen. Stunned, Wachter realized he had been hit. Around him the deck was littered with wounded men, and blood was actually starting to flow out the scuppers. Chief Bosun's Mate W. E. Bates staggered up to Wachter and shoved his mutilated hand out for Wachter to see. Most of the fingers were gone.

"Look here, Ted, I won't be able to play poker any more."[55]

For the next half hour the Japanese left the ship alone. The pause gave Kabler a chance to see to his wounded and get the less seriously injured back on their feet. The damaged port 3-inch gun was partially repaired, and all guns were reported manned and ready. Half of Kabler's crew was injured, and two were dead. But there was still plenty of fight left in the *Heron*.

At 1645 three torpedo-laden flying boats made an "anvil attack, from each bow and the port quarter." Firing their machine guns as they bore in, they launched their torpedoes at the same time.

Antiaircraft fire spewed from the *Heron*, pounding the onrushing bombers and knocking one down. Backing one engine and going all ahead on the other, Kabler literally did a "right face" movement, laying his ship parallel between the oncoming torpedo tracks.

Going all ahead on both engines, the *Heron* surged forward and swung left. The damaged Mavis had landed so close to the *Heron's* port bow that Kabler could clearly read her squadron identification number, 0-53. The Japanese airmen were already going over the side when *Heron's* port 3-inch gun blew the downed plane to pieces. While the Heron was destroying 0-53, the remaining two flying boats made a strafing run and then pulled away. The sky was soon empty, and the *Heron's* crew gave a general sigh of relief.

> 1700: Ship maneuvered to pick up eight survivors from 0-53. Survivors refused to pick up life lines. All Japanese planes observed to be retiring to northward.[56]

Their offer of rescue refused, the *Heron* "resumed base course" and headed toward Ambon.

On 31 December, while the *Heron* was being attacked, nine survivors of the Jolo Raid alternately drifted and paddled on the smooth, windless sea. After having been shot down on the 26th, they had all come together in Siasi on the 29th, where, working with a school globe, maps, and geography books, they had sketched a map of the Sulu Islands and the east Borneo coast. The wounded had received some medical treatment, but there was nothing that could be done about McLawhorn's injured eye. A metal sliver imbedded in the eye was clearly visible, but the local doctor had no anesthesia for its removal.[57]

After spending two uneasy days at Siasi wondering if the natives were going to help them, murder them, or turn them over to the Japanese, a boat, paddlers, and provisions were obtained for the trip south. At dusk on 30 December the nine airmen set out on an uncertain journey.

New Year's Eve found them miles at sea, in little more than an outrigger canoe, surrounded by the enemy. Though wounded, suffering from exposure, and with McLawhorn enduring terrible pain, they still remained optimistic. They had aboard four bottles of brandy that Dawley described as "more poison than potent," with which they intended to celebrate the new year.

> Having no way to tell time exactly, it was agreed that when the moon could be seen by sighting up the sail mast, it would, arbitrarily, be midnight. At "midnight" then, with toasts to loved ones, to our shipmates, to ourselves, and to the hope that we would all be able to toast again in 1943, and with the time-honored custom of singing *Auld Lang Syne*, we dropped the hook for 1941 and weighed anchor on 1942.[58]

# 6

# Ambon, Part II
## 1 – 11 January 1942

On 1 January 1942, ABDACOM (American, British, Dutch, Australian Command) had not yet been established, but a cooperative working relationship had already been set up between the Americans, Australians, and Dutch. One of the resulting arrangements in late December had been the assignment of PatWing-10 to Ambon, where the Dutch had been basing several PBYs. But as soon as the Americans arrived, the Dutch pulled their planes back to Surabaja.[1] The Dutch did leave their base operations personnel, and the Americans were teamed up with an Australian Hudson squadron for patrol duty out of Ambon. The American-Australian joint effort was very successful, and relations between the two units were very friendly. Unfortunately, the same relationship did not exist in regard to American-Dutch relations.

Generally speaking, men who were assigned to staff positions thought the Dutch were pretty good fellows. But most of the men who flew the patrol missions considered the Dutch as little more than "haughty-taughty Krauts."[2] Don Chay summed up the feelings of most of the flight crews when he wrote:

> The Dutch are sore at us if we help them, and they have to feed us. And they gripe if we don't help them. To hell with the stingy louses![3]

Hawk Barrett felt the same way, but he had a better understanding of the problem.

> The Dutch seem to think we have let them down, and they are right. Their blocking back (the Philippine Islands) is lost, and now the Dutch are open to attack.[4]

Nick Keller reported in an official interview:

> I hope no Dutchmen hears this record because all the Dutchmen that I ever came into contact with had the attitude that everything you did for them was just doing yourself a favor to do it for them. They had the attitude that it was just your duty to do these things for them, and you were honored to do it.[5]

The language barrier probably contributed substantially to the problem, but the biggest complaint was that the Dutch were unappreciative of what the Americans were doing. The Americans felt they were fighting, literally, to defend Dutch interests in the Pacific. The Dutch, on the other hand, seemed to believe that the Americans had let them down. In such a situation, it was inevitable that friction would develop between the two allies. Unfortunately, the mutual ill will became worse as the military situation deteriorated.

But fortunately, the military situation remained, insofar as Pat-Wing-10 was concerned, relatively stable during the first week in January. Except for the loss of a J2F Duck and an OS2U Kingfisher in accidents, the wing suffered no losses between 27 December 1941 and 11 January 1942.[6] However, engines were starting to wear out because of inadequate maintenance and hard use, and there were numerous instances in which planes were forced back from patrols with one engine dead. There were also a couple of close calls when P-7 and P-28 tangled with two four-engine Mavis flying boats. The five-minute battle ended in a draw, which was a good thing, since PatWing-10 was down to eight PBYs.[7]

The faster, more heavily armed Japanese flying boats were a real threat to the PBYs, even though the Americans were flying in pairs. To counter the threat, the Americans got help from the RAAF Hudson squadron stationed on the island. Starting in January, an Australian Hudson flew escort for the vulnerable PBYs. The idea

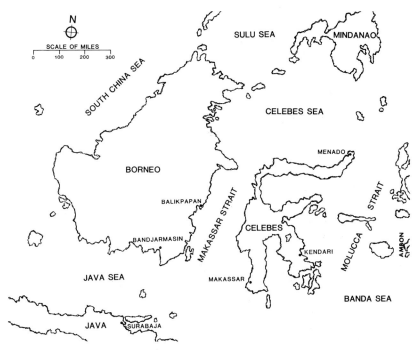

N

SCALE OF MILES
0    100    200    300

SULU SEA    MINDANAO

SOUTH CHINA SEA

CELEBES SEA

MENADO

BORNEO

BALIKPAPAN

MAKASSAR STRAIT

STRAIT

BANDJARMASIN

CELEBES

KENDARI

MOLUCCA

AMBON

JAVA SEA    MAKASSAR

BANDA SEA

JAVA    SURABAJA

PatWing-10's area of operations 25 January 1941–16 January 1942.

was that the PBY would act as bait to lure the big Mavis flying boats in close enough for the Hudsons to put them away. There was reason to believe the plan would work. The Hudson was not only faster and more maneuverable than the PBY, but also had a revolving top turret. But the plan failed for a lot of reasons, mostly due to the Hudson's short range and the refusal by the Japanese to take the bait.[8]

In addition to the RAAF squadron, there was a Dutch naval detachment at the seaplane base. Apparently few, if any, Dutch aircraft operated there, however. The seaplane facilities were completed, but the quarters were only partly ready. The Dutch occupied the completed buildings, turning over the unfinished quarters to the Australians and the Americans.

Most of the Americans were housed in a collection of buildings situated on a small hill overlooking the bay. The more senior officers were housed at the top of the hill.

We were living in the Dutch quarters that were unfinished. They didn't have any water, just bare walls, and no windows. We slept on canvas cots under mosquito netting.[9]

The lack of water in the quarters was a major problem that angered everyone. The Dutch ran a water line up the hill, but the results were not satisfactory. In fact, the best that was accomplished was "a trickle of water, but usually not."[10]

In addition to the uncomfortable quarters, the men had a hard time with the food. The Dutch officers' mess was too full, so the Americans ate with the Australians. Socially it was the best arrangement, but the mess hall was similar to the quarters. There was, however, a difference of opinion about the officers' mess.

In his official report, Captain Wagner described the officers' mess in Ambon.

> The officers' mess was extremely pleasant. The mess was located inside a concrete building whose walls and floors had been completed, nothing else was finished. Meals were taken at tables made of planks on sawhorses. Everything was very rough and ready, but extremely pleasant, and all of us looked back on our stay at Ambon with pleasant memories. . .[11]

In contrast to the captain's glowing remarks, his subordinates were considerably less enthusiastic.

> Our chow hall is an open affair with plenty of flies and cracked pewterware. The food is frugal—stew, bread or rice, no butter, beans once in a while and terrible coffee.[12] Food seems to be a major problem. It is not varied and what there is of it is scarcely enough. For breakfast, tinned corned beef and coffee. For lunch, beans and sauce. For dinner stew, rice, and canned peaches, with butter but no bread.[13]

The major problem was that Ambon had been built by the Dutch to serve as an advance seaplane base for the Dutch navy. The influx of Australians and Americans created a demand for supplies that exceeded what the Dutch had on hand. There was no resupply during the 23 December 1941–16 January 1942 period, so that toward the end food was in very short supply. Many Americans resorted to eating wild bananas and other fruit to supplement the increasingly meager rations.[14]

In many cases, they made the eight-mile trip to the town of Ambon to buy food, "mostly canned juice and chocolate."[15] Fortunately, Heineken beer was plentiful, and a bottle was served with every meal. It at least took the edge off of some of their hunger and made things look a little less grim.

Social life in Ambon was pretty well limited to card playing and beer drinking, but Americans who made contact with Dutch families in Ambon enjoyed an occasional taste of home life. In an effort to entertain the Americans, the Australians staged a bare-knuckle fight that turned out to be one of the bloodiest events ever witnessed by a sporting crowd.[16]

But the Australians were at their best when they threw a party. The Americans enjoyed these affairs enormously because the Australians' uninhibited character was much like that of the Americans. A feature at the parties was the seemingly endless stream of jokes the Australians told, nearly all of them terribly foul.

There was, however, a problem at the parties, and the problem's name was Captain Wagner.

> Wagner was so proper you wouldn't even want to swear in front of him—just like you wouldn't swear in front of your mother or your aunt. So his presence at those parties, when we told those horribly filthy jokes, put a damper on the proceedings.[17]

Among the most popular joke tellers was the Australian commanding officer, Wing Commander Dallas ("Scotty") Scott. He told a joke that was so foul that when Wagner heard it for the first time, he left the party. The Americans immediately saw the solution to their problem.

> After that, on several occasions we would see Wagner coming to join our party. As soon as we did, someone would grab Scotty and say, "Now, Scotty, don't forget when he gets here, you tell that joke and he'll leave." It always worked.[18]

Though the housing and food were poor, and social life limited, operating conditions for seaplanes in Ambon were excellent. The small harbor was surrounded by hills about 800 feet high, and the narrow harbor entrance was closed with a log boom. There were mines sown outside the boom, and, apparently, some just inside. Those mines very nearly got the *Peary*.

Having been bombed and harried by the Japanese and attacked by her allies, the ship's crew was badly rattled and exhausted. After he had been contacted by Tom McCabe, Lieutenant Commander Birmingham had reluctantly left his hiding place and steamed toward Ambon, arriving there at night on 31 December. As the battered destroyer entered the harbor, the *Childs* was just moving to a new anchorage.

"Ship entering harbor."

The lookout's report caused the skipper, Doc Pratt, to raise his glasses to look at the new ship.

> And a strange looking ship it was. We finally recognized her to be the *Peary*, a destroyer we had last seen in Cavite—badly damaged during the bombing of the Navy Yard. Much altered in appearance, but still the *Peary*.[19]

As Pratt watched, he realized the destroyer was heading directly toward the inner mine field.

"Man the signal searchlight" he shouted as the *Peary* continued unerringly toward the mines.

STOP STOP STOP MINES MINES MINES

The signal was repeatedly flashed without any apparent effect, until the last moment. The destroyer stopped.

Calling away his gig, Doc Pratt went across to the *Peary*, climbed to the bridge, and offered to act as pilot through the mine field. The offer was quickly accepted. As he conned the destroyer to a safe anchorage, Pratt noticed that the bridge crew was "very shaky." He knew why, since there was evidence all around him of the terrible beating the ship had taken.

With the *Peary* safely anchored, Pratt returned to the *Childs*. During the trip across Ambon Harbor, the tender's skipper wondered to himself if the *Peary* was a lucky ship, or an unlucky ship—unlucky to have been so badly battered, but lucky to have survived. One thing was certain; she had been lucky that night. If she had hit one of those mines she would have gone down like a rock.

The mine fields that had nearly claimed the *Peary* were no threat to the PBYs, since there was plenty of room inside the boom for takeoffs, unless the plane was heavily overloaded. A few pilots worried about hitting the boom, especially during predawn takeoffs when it was still dark and the boom was hard to see.[20]

Most of the takeoffs were made before dawn, since the planes were making very long patrol flights. They were looking for the Japanese, and for any of the men that had disappeared on the Jolo raid. They also picked up downed allied aviators, an activity for which the PBY became famous later in the war. On 1 January 1942, John Hyland, in P-23, performed such a rescue.

ComPatWing-10 broadcast the plain-language message at 1430 with the hope that someone, near enough to act, would hear it. An Australian Lockheed Hudson had ditched about sixty miles north of Ambon. The plane's last known position was pretty accurate, but there was no way of knowing if there were any survivors. There was also no information about what had put the plane down, enemy fighters or engine trouble.[21]

John Hyland's radio operator picked up the message when P-23 was just thirty miles north of Ambon. He acknowledged receipt of the message and told PatWing-10 headquarters that they were headed toward the area to look for survivors. By the time the PBY was over the Hudson's reported position, the plane had already sunk, but a large oil slick marked the spot.

Circling, Hyland saw a man in the water, waving. There was no sign of anyone else. From 1,000 feet, the sea looked smooth and Hyland dropped down to land. It may have been that Hyland was fooled by the natural flattening effect of viewing the sea from above, or the effect of the oil on the surface. Whatever it was, the sea was not smooth, it was rough.

> I learned from that experience to fly low over the water before I tried to land. But I didn't know all that then, and besides, I was anxious to get down and get that guy. We hit like a ton of bricks, bounced about ten feet back up, and hit with a hell of a thud. I was amazed that the airplane would take a whack like that.[22]

Once down, Hyland's next problem was coming alongside the downed airman. The PBY pitched heavily in the swells—so much so that Hyland was afraid that the propellers would nick the water and the man they were trying to rescue. While the PBY approached

This view of 21-P-3 shows the sliding waist hatch and sea ladder of the PBY-4. Chief Schnitzer fell from the ladder while trying to rescue a downed Australian airman. The photo also shows the tower and the mechanic's window just below the wing. (Courtesy Gordon Ebbe)

carefully from down wind, the plane captain ACMM Charles E. Schnitzer crawled out the starboard waist hatch to stand on the boarding ladder. As the PBY taxied slowly past the Australian, Schnitzer grabbed him, and with the help of other men leaning through the hatch, struggled to pull the Australian aboard.

In the cockpit, Hyland, worried about the pounding his plane was taking, was anxious to take off.

"How about it, you got him yet?" Hyland asked through the intercom.

"He's hurt and he's heavy," was the reply.

Hyland worked to keep his plane's bow into the steep waves as the time dragged on.

"We got him."

"OK, close the hatch, and let's get out of here." Hyland's elation was only momentary. Instead of hearing that the hatch was closed he got a chilling report.

"Sir, Schnitzer is gone."

"What?"

"Yea. He lost his hold on the ladder and he's back aft."

"Can you see him?"

"No. We can't. By the time we got this guy in a bunk, and then got back to get Schnitzer, he was gone."

Hyland felt his stomach knot, and his mouth go dry. He thought to himself:

I'll be goddamned! I've done it this time. I've landed, when it probably wasn't the best judgment in the first place, to pick up a guy who probably won't live long enough for us to get him back. And now I lost my plane captain. Now isn't that going to be just great when I get back.

"Get someone up on the top of the wing to watch for him," Hyland ordered, swinging the PBY around sharply. For five minutes P-23 taxied dead down wind, six crewmen anxiously looking for the lost plane captain. It was, possibly, the longest five minutes in Hyland's life—not to mention Schnitzer's.

"There he is."

Schnitzer was dead ahead, "riding up and down in the swells." As the PBY taxied past, Schnitzer grabbed the ladder and heaved himself aboard. The hatch slid shut, Hyland turned into the wind and took off.

When Hyland landed at Ambon, the battered *Heron* was anchored in the inner harbor. Ashore, a funeral service was being held for CQM D. Allmond and Cox. M. Borodenko, the two crewmen killed in the attack by the Japanese Nells. Many of the men attending the service thought about the twenty-one men who had not come back from Jolo and wondered what kind of a service, if any, they might have.

At that moment nine Jolo survivors were ashore on Tawitawi where, aided by a catholic priest, Father C. B. Billman, the wounded were being treated in the small local hospital. The priest was also helping to find paddlers and boats to take the Americans farther south.[23]

The airmen were joined by the provincial governor of Sulu, Major Alejandro Suarez, Philippines Constabulary, who had been on Jolo during the raid. He gave Dawley detailed information about the Japanese and said that he had seen one transport sunk and a warship left burning. The news encouraged Dawley and made it even more important that he get back to Surabaja as quickly as possible.

The Americans spent two days on Tawitawi, resting and looking for transportation south. But none of the natives were willing to act as paddlers, and no boats were made available to the Americans. Father Billman sent a messenger to another island to seek a boat and paddlers. While the messenger was gone, a boat-load of Moros came along, and Suarez was able to hire them to take the airmen to Sitangkai on the south end of Sibutu Island. Dawley was told about the "good news," and went down to the beach to have a look at the boat. What he saw was a small vinta and "five evil looking Moros."

> It was smaller than the two small vintas we had been using thus far
> . . . Despite the sorry condition of the boat, it was still transportation and transportation was hard to find. None of the Moros could speak English, they were armed, and out-numbered the able-bodied men in our crew. Father Billman and two constabulary officers said they were the unreliable type, and the boat was not too seaworthy. So, considering everything, including the uncertainty that another boat could be secured for days, I took a chance and told the governor I couldn't risk taking the boat.

Dawley's decision proved to be a good one. The next day a boat, pilot, and paddlers arrived from the neighboring island. Leaving at night on 3 January, they made a five-hour passage through heavy seas to the island of Sibutu, arriving on the morning of 4 January 1942 at the village of Sitangkai.

In Sitangkai, they were told by Deputy Governor Amirhamja Japal that they could have the customs launch, a fifty-foot, diesel-powered cabin cruiser. But the offer sounded better than it was. The boat had been condemned several years earlier by the Philippine Maritime Commission after a survey revealed that the hull was 75 percent rotten. The boat was still there because Japal had not yet received the order to destroy it. Despite the apparent drawback, Dawley said, "It looked good to us."

But Dawley's optimism quickly faded when his crew told him that the air tank had five holes in it. Because the engine was started with compressed air, and was too big to hand start, the air tank was an absolute necessity.

Undaunted, the Americans put their heads together to figure a way to plug the holes. The plugs would have to be strong enough to hold against 150 pounds per square inch (psi), the pressure required to start the engine. To accomplish the job, they had brass tacks, some screws, solder, and a blow torch. Not much to work with, and made less so when it was discovered that the tank was so rusty that the solder would not stick. Things were going down hill. But men who toast New Year's Eve while drifting at sea are not easily discouraged. By noon on 5 January they had come up with a better idea. It was an example of American ingenuity at its best.

Wooden pegs were driven into the holes and covered with white lead. Then small rubber patches, made from shoe soles, were placed over the lead-coated pegs. Next, wooden blocks were placed on top of the rubber patches and held in place with metal straps that were wrapped around the tank. In order to press the blocks down on the patches and pegs with maximum pressure, wedges were driven between the tank and the straps.

The job complete, the next step was to find out if the jury-rigged patches would hold. The compressor was fired up and the pressure gauge started to climb. At 80 psi the needle stopped, air hissing from the patches. More wedges were driven under the straps, and the needle started to climb again. Anxiously, the men watched the needle. 100, 120, 130, 140 psi were registered before the needle stopped at 146. Though four pounds short, it was "good enough for government work," and the pressure held. Dawley and his men had a boat.

That night they set course for Tawau in British North Borneo. From there they would sail down the Borneo coast to Tarakan. The direct route to Tawau across the Alice Channel was chosen in order to spend as few daylight hours as possible on the open sea.

Their stop in Tawau was just long enough to have the dressing on McLawhorn's eye changed, and to get directions for the trip to Tarakan. While they were in Tawau, they were warned that the Japanese were expected any moment. They were also warned that Tarakan was mined, and they should not attempt to enter the port before daylight. Accepting the advice, Dawley calculated that they would have to anchor some place to use up about four hours of excess time.

The first leg of the trip down the coast was no problem. They had picked up a good chart in Tawau, and there was plenty of light to take bearings on the shore. But after dark things began to go wrong.

Dawley planned to be off Boenjoe Island at 2200, as far south as he could go without entering the Tarakan mine fields. But those plans were upset by a strong current that pushed them southward faster than expected. By 1900 Dawley was not sure where he was or how much farther he ought to go, so at 1900 he put into shore to anchor.

There was no moon to help pick out the shoreline, and the chart showed many reefs in the area that Dawley estimated to be their position. But he was not even sure about that.

> As a matter of fact, I didn't know how far off shore we were when we changed course. Without any navigational aids, and with tidal and river currents drifting us in what direction was anybody's guess, there was no way to establish our position.

An hour later soundings showed they were in shallow water and a shoreline could be seen. At 2030 on 6 January 1942, Dawley anchored, planning to get underway again at 0300.

Dawley stood the first watch until 2400 when he was relieved by a native crewman. Planning to take just a short nap, Dawley told the men to wake him in half an hour. Three hours later Dawley woke up, found the native asleep, and the boat firmly aground. There was nothing to do about it, except wait for the tide to rise and hope that the rotten planks would hold. Either the Maritime Commission's survey was wrong or Dawley was lucky. Despite being grounded, and having worked on the coral, the planks held. The sun was well up when the boat finally floated free and the anchor was hauled up. By 1100 they were alongside the Dutch lightship at the entrance to Tarakan Harbor, asking for directions from the startled lightship master.

> If Barnum and Bailey's talent scouts had been . . . looking for the wild men from Borneo, I am sure they would have taken us in preference to any of the local gents who popularized that phrase. I

doubt if Borneo ever produced any wilder looking men than the nine of us wearing Moro clothes, scraggly eleven day old beards, and with patched up bullet holes . . .

Three hours later they were in Tarakan, and arrangements were made to fly them to Balikpapan on the 8th. From Balikpapan, seven of them were sent to Surabaja aboard the SS *Valentyn*, while Dawley and the badly wounded McLawhorn were flown there in a Dornier.

> Our plane landed at Surabaja, Java, at 1100. By noon McLawhorn was in the hands of doctors in a hospital. At 1230 on the fifteenth day after leaving the naval base at Ambon, on what was to have been a routine fourteen-hour bombing flight, I walked into the headquarters of US Naval Forces in Surabaja and reported.

The officers and men of PatWing-10 were overjoyed at the return of their missing comrades, and at the same time sobered by the loss of the others. The returnees had a lot of news to catch up on, and little of it was good.

While the Jolo survivors had been repairing the customs launch in Sitangkai, the Japanese had bombed Ambon. The bombers unloaded over Ambon at 0230 on 5 January, in what was the first of a series of nightly raids. The first raid caught the Ambon defenders completely by surprise.[24]

The Dutch had an air-raid alarm system that they touted as "unbeatable." It consisted of a jungle telegraph spread out across the western tip of Ceram, and the small islands of Kelang and Boano. The idea was that as the Japanese formations were spotted, the native drummers would pound out the alarm. The drum alarm would then be picked up by the next station down the line and passed on. Since sound traveled faster than Japanese bombers it was expected that Ambon would have at least a ten- to fifteen-minute warning before the bombers were overhead.[25]

The Dutch tested the system regularly, and the Americans became accustomed to hearing the sound of drums faintly in the distance, drawing closer and closer. The system seemed to work, and many Americans had "quite a bit of confidence in it."[26] The system must have been designed to work during the day because it sure did not work at night.

It was very hot in Ambon and most of the Americans slept with little or nothing on. Some could not sleep at all. Gordon Ebbe was sitting naked on the concrete steps outside his hut when he heard engine sounds. He did not hear drums, but he knew the airplanes overhead had to be Japanese.

The bombs were already exploding when Ebbe ran inside to rouse the others. Hawk Barrett was awakened by the "thud of bombs" and Ebbe shouting, "Here they come. Get in the shelter." Barrett leaped out of bed, "did not tarry to dress," and streaked toward the shelter. Al Armbruster was right behind him.

The grounds around the quarters were filled with naked and nearly naked men all running for the air-raid shelter. The sounds of bare, fast-moving feet were covered by the thundering blasts of exploding bombs. The route to safety lay through a two-foot wide opening between a fence and a garage. And several dozen men were converging on the narrow gap. Gordon Ebbe was leading the pack.

> We were all trying to hit that space at once, trying to get through. Just this side of the fence was a concrete drainage ditch. About that time a Dutch gunner, up on the hill, cut loose with his .50-caliber, and tracers were going right over our heads. We all hit the drainage ditch. Then we saw it was full of women and kids. I had a pillow I'd grabbed, but a lot of guys didn't have any clothes [on] at all.[27]

The nightly raids did little damage, though the base radio was temporarily knocked out and the RAAF airfield runway was chewed up. In fact, the night raids were so ineffective that most of the men stayed in their cots rather than go to the shelter.[28] Nevertheless, the raids were definitely a nuisance that increased the men's fatigue. The raids also made it clear that the war was coming closer to Ambon.

> The Japs were only a few hundred miles north, massing in the Sulu Sea and off Sarawak, readying for the capture of resources . . . Oil in abundance, rice for their soldiers, manganese for their steel mills, rubber and tin.[29]

For the Philippines veterans, visions of Olongapo and Laguna de Bay became more frequent, and some made preparations to get out. Andy Reid knew what it was like to be left in an exposed position with the enemy breathing down your neck. If it had not been for the fact that he flew General Brereton out of Manila on 24 December, Reid would have been caught on Laguna de Bay with Pollock, Swenson, Utter, and the others. That same possibility was again starting to look stronger and stronger as the Japanese increased the pressure on Ambon. Reid was without an airplane, and if anything happened to the *Childs* and the few PBYs, he and a lot of other people were going to be stuck.

> Most of us were expecting to receive an order at any moment of every man for himself. That would let us have a chance at survival in other than a Japanese prisoner-of-war camp. Earl McConnell and I had discussed this several times.[30]

Both Reid and McConnell were experienced small-boat sailors. Reid had been on the Pensacola sailing team, and McConnell had made several blue-water passages, including a San Pedro–Hawaii trip before the war. They therefore decided that their best bet was to obtain a native sailing craft to escape to Australia, if the need arose.

> On the road between our base and the small town of Ambon were groups of fishing outriggers pulled up on the beach. All we had to do was walk this road one afternoon, late, and locate a fisherman willing to sell his boat. We took the walk and found that once our mission became clear we were hip deep in a buyer's market. We could have purchased fifty outrigger canoes that evening. Using a Netherlands Navy officer as our interpreter, we purchased the one that appeared in best condition, with particular attention to the sail, mast, spars, and rigging. We added about 10 percent to the asking price as inducement for the seller to keep watch on our vessel until we claimed it. Our total investment was less than twenty U.S. dollars.

At the same time they obtained native costumes, to fool the Japanese pilots who might spot them, and collected a supply of hooks, line, and sinkers. They solved their water problem by purchasing several bamboo water poles. Each hollow section of those large-diameter poles was filled with water. The filler holes were plugged with wood pegs, the poles to be towed in the water behind the outrigger canoe.

The Japanese Mavis flying boat was a formidable opponent for the PBYs. Faster and more heavily armed than the American planes, the Mavis was highly respected by PatWing-10 aircrews. (National Archives)

Fortunately, Reid and McConnell never had to use their native outrigger. On 9 January, the *Childs* took aboard the excess aircrews, upped anchor, and sailed for Surabaja.[31]

The men in Ambon were not the only people who saw signs that the war was moving south. By early January the Dutch East Indies had become the focal point of the allied defense, and a unified command, ABDACOM, had finally been organized. It was not yet in place, but its creation caused changes in PatWing-10's organization—at least on paper.

Captain Wagner had, up to now, held two posts. He was Commander Aircraft Asiatic Fleet, and Commander, PatWing-10. On 6 January 1942 he turned the wing over to Lieutenant Commander Peterson, who became ComPatWing-10. Wagner retained the post as Commander Aircraft Asiatic Fleet and picked up an additional post on the ABDA staff. Lieutenant Commander Neale took over VP-101. Actually, there was no change, except that three men traded titles. Wagner retained control of the wing, and Peterson, effectively, remained a squadron commanding officer.[32]

The change did prompt hope among the rank and file that sending PBYs on daylight missions would stop.[33] There was also a rumor going around that pilots with dive-bomber experience were going to form a special attack squadron equipped with army A-24s. On 9 January, Peterson even asked for the names of pilots who had flown dive-bombers.[34] That rumor proved to be false, but another one turned out to be true.

Admiral Hart had been negotiating with the Dutch for the transfer of some of their PBY-5s to PatWing-10. The Dutch had more planes than they had qualified pilots, and their PBYs were not only newer, but also in much better shape than PatWing-10's worn out PBY-4s. At first the Dutch refused to go along with the idea, but were finally persuaded to part with five of the newer planes.[35] Hawk Barrett recorded the news in his diary:

> Heard today that we are getting five PBY-5s from the Dutch . . . it will give us some decent engines. The Dutch planes are in Surabaja, and some of the lads will be fortunate enough to go down to bring them back. Perhaps John will go and I'll get a crack at it with him.[36]

Barrett and Hyland did not get to pick up one of the new planes, and Barrett's plans for liberty in Surabaja fell through. Instead, they went to Menado, demonstrating that the rumor about no more daylight bombing missions was just a rumor.

On 10 January 1942, two Japanese assault groups were moving toward Tarakan, North Borneo, and Menado on the northern tip of the Celebes. Seizure of those two ports would put them astride the Makassar Strait and allow them to start their parallel drives south through the Makassar Strait and across the Molucca Sea. As the fleets steamed south, a Dutch patrol plane reported three Japanese cruisers shelling Sangi Island, midway between Mindanao and Menado. The information was passed on to PatWing-10 in Ambon.

Hawk Barrett, the duty officer, had spent the morning supervising the moving of planes to remote buoys, making a buoy chart, and drawing stores. He had three PBYs ready, fueled, and bombed up, when the message arrived. He did not like the sound of it.[37]

Sangi Island was just 220 miles south of Davao, well within range of the Japanese fighters based there. The PBYs, on the other hand, would have to fly more than twice that distance to reach the target, and would be without fighter escort. The Jolo raid had been a powerful lesson to the PatWing-10 aircrews, and the proposition of sending three PBYs to attack at Sangi was not well received.

Like it or not, at 1400 three bomb-laden PBYs took off. Though the three planes were going to attack a target north of Menado, they were flying on the first of what later became known as the Menado Missions. It was a pitiful gesture. Three slow, lightly armed planes with a total of nine 500-pound bombs were being sent to "stem or stop the menace."[38]

Four hours out of Ambon, and fifty miles south of the objective, they spotted a large Japanese formation steaming south. Three transports, six destroyers, and three cruisers were spread out on the water, 15,000 feet below.

Lieutenant Marcy led the group up to 17,000 feet and started a run on the largest cruiser. The sun was just going behind the horizon when the airmen spotted two more enemy groups steaming south. They could hardly believe their eyes. There were now eighteen destroyers, six cruisers, and ten transports.[39]

As the PBYs started their bombing run, a four-engine Mavis cruised above them, prepared to spot antiaircraft bursts for the gunners below. In the lead PBY George Webber, Marcy's NAP, sighted through his Norden bombsight. In Hyland's plane, Hawk Barrett had crawled into the bow to release their bombs on command. In the other arm of the "V," Robbie Robinson and his copilot, Andrew Burgess, were also ready.

A wall of antiaircraft fire rose up to meet them. Peering downward through the bomb window, Barrett was awed by the intensity of the antiaircraft fire. The flashes from the gun barrels were so close together that the ships appeared to be afire. Despite the heavy flak, Barrett had "a half feeling" that they would score a hit.[40]

The Mavis was doing its job well. The antiaircraft fire found the altitude, bursting ahead and around the rock-steady PBYs. Robinson's plane was hit in the starboard wing, but maintained formation. To Barrett, the last seconds of the run seemed to go on forever until, in Marcy's plane, Webber pulled the release levers. Seeing the bombs tumble away from the lead plane, both Hyland and Robinson shouted, "drop." Four thousand five hundred pounds of explosives plunged down toward the target. They all missed.[41]

The three PBYs dove in formation to gain speed, and turned south. The sun disappeared, the sky turned black, and the planes became separated. Hyland and Robinson returned to Ambon before midnight, but had to wait for the moon to rise before landing. Marcy's plane came in an hour later, much to everyone's relief.

By now the entire base was in an uproar. The size of the enemy fleet reported was much larger than had been expected, and a joint allied raid was hastily put together. Composed of four American and three Dutch PBYs and five Australian Hudsons, the scratch force was sent off to bomb the Japanese Fleet.[42] On paper, the attacking force looked pretty good, but by January 1942 the realities of war had reduced the force to a polyglot suicide squad.

John Hyland, later to become a full admiral and Commander United States Pacific Fleet, observed that:

> By that time in the war, people in ships realized that you could actually look up at high-altitude bombers, and you could see the bombs when they were released. If you then just made a radical turn off in one direction or another you were going to make them miss; unless they guessed that you were going to do that, and they were bombing where you were headed. But most times that wasn't the case.[43]

PatWing-10's aircrews also understood that, and were, therefore, not enthusiastic about being sent on missions that had small hope for success. One would have thought that after his Philippines experience, and the outcome of the Jolo mission, Wagner would have reconsidered sending so inadequate a force against the Japanese Fleet. Maybe he did.

But Wagner was an aggressive commander who believed that the best way to hurt the enemy was to attack. He may also have been slow to recognize the failure of prewar bombing theory. But he certainly could not just sit and do nothing. So he did what he thought best, and ordered PatWing-10 to join the allied attack force. He shared a bum decision with his Australian and Dutch counterparts.

The Dutch planes took off first, followed by the American PBYs at 0255 on 11 January. The faster Lockheed Hudsons were the last away. The American section was made up of four PBYs, numbers 3, 7, 25, and 28, led by Lieutenant Bill Deam. The other PPCs were Ensigns Tom Collins, Jack Grayson, and John Sloatman. Grayson and his copilot, Frank Ralston, were flying P-28, the same wreck that Antonides, Deam, and Roberts had flown south.[44]

The fleet they were about to attack was actually two groups. One group was en route to seize Menado, and the other was headed toward Tarakan, on the Borneo east coast. Both boded ill for PatWing-10. The seizure of Menado was the first step toward taking Timor and Bali, and sealing off Java from Australia. The second step in that process was the taking of Ambon.

Like a replay of the Jolo raid, planes P-3 and P-15 became separated from P-7 and P-28 shortly after takeoff. Sometime later P-7 and P-28 became separated, but joined up again south of Menado. There was no sign of the other two American PBYs. As Ralston and Grayson approached Menado, they could see the Japanese Fleet standing offshore. Ahead of them three Dutch PBYs were starting their bombing run against heavy antiaircraft fire.

Before P-7 and P-28 could even get organized, they were jumped by two Japanese float-plane fighters. As both planes dove for cloud cover, Ralston noted the airspeed indicator climbed past 180 knots. In the distance a Dutch PBY fell, burning, toward the water.

The safety of the clouds seemed a million miles away. Both PBYs were still in formation as they headed down, Japanese fighters attacking aft, from both sides. The waist guns in P-28 kept jamming, allowing the fighters to make virtually unopposed runs on the fleeing PBY.

Still in formation, both planes entered the clouds, hotly pursued by the fighters. As the cloud cover thickened, the attacks ended, and both American planes parted company. Grayson was spiraling down through the cloud intending to come out low on the water, and scoot for home at minimum altitude. But age, hard service, and lack of proper maintenance had taken its toll on P-28.

P-28 was still buried in the cloud when the port engine abruptly stopped with a resounding crack and thud. A camshaft had snapped. Moments later P-28 popped out beneath the clouds and into the waiting fighters.

One engine short, and still loaded with three 500-pound bombs, P-28 became one of the early "cold turkeys" for the Japanese. Grayson jettisoned his bombs, the waist guns jammed, and his starboard engine was shot to pieces. Powerless, streaming fuel from both wings, and surrounded by fighters, P-28 headed for the sea. South of the stricken plane, P-7 was headed due south at wave-top level.

Grayson and Ralston put P-28 down fast and hard. With fighters already starting to strafe, the seven crewmen hastily abandoned the doomed plane. Swimming as hard as they could, diving beneath the surface every time a strafer came in, the crewmen distanced themselves from P-28. After five runs the fighters pulled off and headed back toward Menado to chew up the Australian Hudsons that were now arriving. There now occurred one of the finest examples of teamwork and mutual support ever performed by a naval aircrew.

Though shot full of holes and sinking, P-28 was still afloat, and drifting away from the swimming men. AAM1c A. A. Eherman and RM1c R. W. Preece were in serious trouble, about to drown. They either did not have their Mae Wests on, or they were not working, because the two men were being dragged down by their heavy flying suits. Quickly swimming to Eherman, Grayson kept the man afloat while helping him shed the soggy coveralls. AMM2c C. Betts did the same thing for Preece. Both Eherman and Preece were saved by their comrades' quick action.

While the dual life-and-death dramas were going on, Ralston shed his Mae West and started swimming toward the drifting plane. If the crew was to survive, he had to get the life raft, which had been left inside. While Ralston was making his effort, CRM R. A. Palenga swam from man to man, gathering them into one tightly packed group. In the meantime, Ralston had recovered the raft, and soon everyone was aboard.

The P-28 was low in the water, but still afloat, and the men decided to paddle back to the plane and salvage what they could. While they were in the plane, a Lockheed Hudson on its way home from the raid flew over. Palenga tried to raise the Australian on the radio, while Preece signaled him with an Aldis Lamp. Both attempts failed. As Grayson, Ralston, and RM1c Delwood C. Westfall were destroying or jettisoning all confidential gear, Eherman and Betts threw ten gallons of canned water and some emergency rations into the raft. By now the plane was going down fast, and Grayson ordered everyone into the raft. Before going through the waist hatch, Grayson took one last look around and counted heads. He did not want anyone left behind. Satisfied that the plane was empty, he stepped into the raft and shoved off. They had paddled about 500 yards when P-28 sank.

The Menado raid had been a failure, just as Jolo had been a failure. The unfortunate fact is that Menado had been a predictable failure. Today the tally is inaccurate. Australian and Dutch records were later destroyed, and postwar accounts are often hazy reconstructions. But we know that PatWing-10 lost one plane. The Dutch lost one, maybe two, and had another one badly shot up with two dead and two seriously wounded. The Australians lost four Hudsons. At least half the attack force was lost, without having accomplished a thing.[45]

The Menado raid marked the last time that PatWing-10 aircrews were sent on high-level daylight bombing missions. Captain Wagner finally accepted what his pilots had been telling him for several days. In the future, PatWing-10 planes would fly only reconnaissance and rescue missions. But those missions were not going to be mere pieces of cake, especially when they were flown up the Makassar Strait. PatWing-10 aircrews would soon rename Makassar Strait, "Cold Turkey Alley."

# 7

# Ambon, Part III
## 11 – 16 January 1942

In early January 1942, VP-22 flew out from Hawaii in twelve PBY-5s to reinforce PatWing-10. The flight was made in two groups of six planes each. The first group, led by VP-22's squadron commander, Lieutenant Commander Frank O'Beirne, took off from Pearl Harbor on 3 January. Flying along an island-hopping route, O'Beirne's group reached Townsville on 8 January. Two days later they reached Darwin and went aboard the USS *Langley*. The second group, led by the squadron's executive officer, Lieutenant Doyle ("Ducky") Donaho, reached Darwin on 11 January after following the same route.[1]

By the time VP-22's second section reached Australia, the situation had become so desperate that the squadron was immediately broken up and scattered throughout the Dutch East Indies area. In fact, VP-22 never functioned as a squadron during its assignment to PatWing-10, and Lieutenant Commander O'Beirne essentially became a detachment commander in charge of two or three planes. It is amazing that, though broken up and scattered, the squadron never lost its identity, and its morale remained unusually high.

After a short layover in Darwin to complete engine checks, the first group took off before dawn on 11 January. O'Beirne, in 22-P-1, and Ensign Robert ("Buzz") LeFever, in 22-P-2, went to Surabaja. The other four planes, 22-P-3, -10, -11, and -12, flown respectively by Lieutenant (j.g.) Charles ("Grabba") Holt, Lieutenant (j.g.) F. R. ("Fuzzy") Drake, Ensign C. C. Hoffman, and Ensign Guy Howard, went to Ambon. A few hours after the first group left, Donaho landed in Darwin with his six-plane group. The dispersal of VP-22 was so complete that O'Beirne and Donaho would not see each other again for several weeks.[2] And by that time only two VP-22 planes would still be in commission.

The men in VP-22 were no strangers to combat. All their planes had either been destroyed or damaged at Pearl Harbor on 7 December, but patching together what they could, they continued to fly patrols for three weeks after the attack.[3] They were a well-trained, highly motivated squadron led by exceptionally able officers. It was because of those factors that VP-22 performed as well as it did in the chaotic conditions that existed in the southwest Pacific. Unfortunately, those qualities were not immediately appreciated by Admiral Thomas C. Hart.

When O'Beirne landed in Surabaja, he reported immediately to Captain Wagner, who took him to see the admiral. O'Beirne and Hart discussed VP-22's flight west and the conditions at Pearl Harbor. Up to that point things were going well. Then Hart told O'Beirne:

> . . . that he was specially glad to have VP-22 join PatWing-10, for he had a special mission in mind for us. His staff had brought thirty-four aircraft torpedoes down from the Philippines. He wanted them loaded on our twelve planes so that, in conjunction with an attack by our surface forces, we could deliver a squadron torpedo attack against the Jap Fleet as it passed southward.[4]

O'Beirne was taken aback by Hart's statement. Such a mission would be sheer suicide, and Hart should have known that. After all, experience so far had repeatedly shown the PBY to be too slow and vulnerable for use in daylight attacks. Surely Admiral Hart knew about the situation.

But when O'Beirne told the admiral that VP-22's planes were unequipped to carry and launch torpedoes, Hart became angry. He demanded to know why there were no torpedo racks on the planes. O'Beirne explained that they had carried bombs out from Pearl

Harbor, plus spare engine parts, and essential ground personnel. Already overloaded, the planes had been stripped of all "unessential" equipment, including torpedo racks.

> Not knowing he had a supply of aircraft torpedoes, and being well aware of the fact that a PBY was not a good airplane for dropping torpedoes, we left our torpedo racks in Pearl Harbor. I informed him that it was my personal decision, that I had not requested permission from any higher authority. I added that even if we . . . attempted to launch a torpedo attack against Jap warships, it would be a futile gesture. A PBY had to fly a straight and level course for at least 30 seconds at a speed of about 100 knots, and at an altitude of less than 100 feet, before being able to drop a torpedo successfully. During that period of steady flight the Japs would have no trouble shooting us down. . . . We would have lost all our planes without torpedoing a single Jap ship.[5]

Furious, Hart threatened to court-martial O'Beirne for "improper performance of duty." Fortunately, Hart's threat was never carried out. Either he finally realized that O'Beirne was right or he "was just too busy with war operations."

While O'Beirne was butting heads with Admiral Hart, the new arrivals were settling in at Ambon. The arrival of the four VP-22 aircrews in Ambon gave the VP-101 veterans a shot in the arm and reunited many old friends. But it was a reunion under a dark cloud. The morale of the Philippine veterans was slipping badly. Ensign Harvey Hop recalled that the "Philippines-based officers were there to greet us, but they were not a very enthusiastic lot."[6]

There were several reasons for the morale slump. In the first place, the VP-101 and VP-102 people felt like refugees; having lost all their personal belongings in Luzon, they were dressed in bits and pieces of clothing scrounged from the Dutch and Australians.[7] They also knew firsthand how badly the war was going, and they felt their government had let them down. Hawk Barrett summed up the general feeling when he recorded in his diary:

> We have not been paid for nearly a month. The men have not been able to obtain uniforms, nor have we as yet. Perhaps we will lose our name as "Peterson's Irregulars" and emerge fully and properly clad before too many more days. Things are serious. The Japs have taken Davao, troops in Malaya and Singapore are being driven

back. Danang has been taken. Still we hear nothing from
Washington.[8]

The VP-101 people were also depressed over the PBY's vulnerability. It was not just the Zeros and the floatplane fighters that
preyed on the PBY, but also the twin-engine land-based bombers
and four-engine Mavis flying boats. By the time VP-22 arrived in
Ambon, VP-101 was down to just eight planes, and only five of
those were in Ambon. The general attitude of the pilots was recalled by Andy Reid:

> Once we had retreated, perhaps faster and farther than any mili-
> tary force in history, we were stationed on Ambon Island in the
> Netherlands East Indies. We created a new word for "boxing" the
> compass, east-west-south and scrag. A PBY ordered to fly to the
> north was almost certain to engage the Japanese "Zero" fighter air-
> craft. If the PBY was enjoying heavy clouds, the PBY had a chance
> to survive. If the weather was clear and sunny, the PBY would be
> scragged.
>
> In order to be scragged, a pilot had first to be placed on the flight
> schedule. All of us were nervous while the daily flight schedule
> was being posted. The scheduler knew this, and one day as he was
> walking to the schedule board he passed me. He said to me, "Don't
> worry, Andy, you don't get scragged until tomorrow."[9]

Closely related to the PBYs' vulnerability was the poor condition
of the old PBY-4s that had been without proper maintenance since
the start of the war. Typical of their condition was the list of problems that plagued P-23. The plane had 130 loose rivets, no bombsight, inter-telephone troubles, faulty magnetos, and starter problems. In fact, she was literally falling apart, but she was the best
they had.[10]

The darkening war situation did not help matters either. On the
day that VP-22 arrived in Ambon, the base was fast becoming untenable. The first evidence of that fact came when Commander
Peterson shifted PatWing-10 headquarters from Ambon to Surabaja
on 12 January, leaving Lieutenant Commander Neale in command
of the Ambon group.

In the face of increasing Japanese pressure, and the need to cover a
wider patrol area, PatWing-10 prepared to disperse its planes to

widely scattered advance bases. Ambon would still be used for a short time, but Surabaja and frequently relocated, tender-supported bases became the focus of operations.

The scattered deployment program was launched on 12 January when Lieutenant Commander O'Beirne was sent to Kendari to establish a base there. The *Preston* had been sent ahead to act as the detachment's tender. During the meetings with Captain Wagner on 11 and 12 January, Frank O'Beirne kept notes. He recorded:

> I was designated as "Base Commander," with instructions from Captain Wagner to forget that I was a squadron leader. Henceforth I am to organize and run my detachment of planes.[11]

At first glance, it would appear that the PatWing-10 reorganization would create an unwieldly, fragmented organization without a clearly defined chain of command. Captain Wagner held the post of Commander, Aircraft Asiatic Fleet and was on the newly formed ABDA staff. Commander Peterson had moved up to command the wing, including VP-22, with Neale and O'Beirne as the squadron leaders. But Wagner actually retained control of the wing, and both squadron commanders would have little authority beyond their own three- or four-plane detachments. And there were several other detachment commanders. But according to Frank O'Beirne, the setup was logical and efficient.

On the morning of 12 January, O'Beirne in 22-P-1 and Buzz LeFever in 22-P-2 took off for Kendari, a small harbor on the Celebes east coast, almost due west of Ambon. The *Preston* was already in Kendari Bay, camouflaged with shrubbery and tree branches, when 22-P-1 and 22-P-2 arrived. As the two PBYs approached the bay, a lone Japanese scout plane was spotted. Lookouts on the *Preston* had also seen the plane, and warned the PBYs to "circle away and return later."

After the enemy scout plane had flown north, the PBYs landed and O'Beirne conferred with the *Preston*'s skipper, Lieutenant Commander Etheridge Grant. Both men were certain that the Japanese pilot had spotted them and that Japanese bombers would soon pay Kendari Bay a visit. There is little doubt that the pilot had seen the bush-covered tender anchored near the beach, since the camouflage attempt was not very effective. Remarking on the *Preston*'s camou-

The PBY-5 was a slightly better plane than the PBY-4. VP-22 flew west in PBY-5s such as this one. The most noticeable difference is the addition of blisters that replaced the sliding waist hatch on the PBY-4. (National Archives)

flage attempt, O'Beirne wrote, "The only known effect was that the *Preston* became infested with bugs and insects of every description."

Despite the fact that Kendari offered a number of services, including a repair shop, the two officers rejected the bay for use as an advance base. Inasmuch as they had certainly been spotted, it was a sound decision. In fact, the harbor was bombed three days later.

With the arrival of VP-22, PatWing-10 looked pretty healthy—it now had twenty-five PBYs more or less on line. There was hope that the arrival of VP-22's twelve newer PBY-5s and the addition of the five PBY-5s acquired from the Dutch would make it possible to get the older PBY-4s back into shape. With that goal in mind, Peterson had taken three of the old planes with him to Surabaja when he moved his headquarters there. But it did not work out that way, and things started going wrong on the 15th.

On 15 January the Japanese hit Ambon with a daylight raid, aimed at knocking out the RAAF field. Twenty-seven Nell bombers, escorted by nine Zero fighters, arrived over the target, while the Zeros went down to strafe targets of opportunity. Two of those targets were at that moment arriving from Darwin and a third was tied to a buoy.

Ducky Donaho and Ensign Doug Davis in 22-P-7 were nearly on the water, wing floats down and engines throttled back. Behind them, off to one side, Ensigns Al Barthes and M. L. Butler were about to land 22-P-8. Not a soul in either plane had the slightest inkling that the Japanese were anywhere near Ambon.[12]

Donaho's first warning came when AMM3c F. Farragut's waist gun opened up. Rounds from the diving Zeros splattered 22-P-7 and rows of gysers sprang up from the water's surface.

"Ducky, what is that?" Davis shouted as he saw a huge hole suddenly appear in the starboard float.[13] Almost at once the starboard wing caught fire.

Donaho and Davis put 22-P-7 down fast. Luckily for them the fighters had pulled off and were going after 22-P-10, which was moored to a buoy. With the starboard wing aflame, Donaho headed for the shore to beach the plane.

22-P-8 had also been caught flat-footed. AMM1c Ed Aeschliman was looking out the tower port when he saw splashes on the water. In the next moment 22-P-8 was hit by a fusillade of machine-gun fire that "sounded like marbles" hitting the hull.

"Hey! We're under attack" Aeschliman shouted, then thought to himself, "My God, we sure didn't last long."[14]

CRM Herb Casey's first warning was "when the bullets started whizzing through the plane—in one side and out the other."[15] AMM1c Don Burham saw dozens of holes suddenly appearing overhead, accompanied by a "rattling sound." In the bow AMM1c Curtis M. Richardson, the NAP, was hit in the hand and elbow.[16] As Barthes put P-8 on the water he glimpsed P-7, wing afire, headed toward the beach.

22-P-7 was still being attacked as she raced for the shoreline and the cover of overhanging trees. It looked like a question of which would get her first, the Zeros or the fire, until Farragut climbed out on the wing with a fire extinguisher. As a result of his quick thinking, he had the fire out by the time Donaho had gotten the plane under the trees.[17] As soon as 22-P-7 was beached, the crew abandoned her, running for cover ashore.

Out on the water 22-P-10 was already sinking at her mooring, and Barthes was going "hell bent for election" toward the far shore.[18] Dropping out of the tower, Aeschliman joined the other crewmen preparing to get out. They were still under attack when the plane beached and Barthes cut the engines.

Despite the later recollections that they had made a "speedy, mass exodus" from the plane, the crew's departure was actually orderly.[19] While still under attack, Barthes and Butler detailed men to get the injured Richardson ashore, and others to strip the guns from the plane. Aeschliman grabbed a .50-caliber gun from the waist hatch and jumped into chest-deep water. The crew was splashing ashore, under heavy enemy fire, when Barthes and Butler jumped clear. They were the last men out of the plane.

In the town of Ambon, Ensigns Guy Howard and Harvey Hop had just ordered a beer. Their plane, 22-P-12, had been moored next to 22-P-10, but a premature air-raid alarm had caused Olongapo veteran Ensign Edward Bergstrom to fly their plane to a scatter base thirty miles away. He had taken the two regular crewmen who were standing watch in the plane with him. The crewmen, AMM2c Ted Shuler and RM1c Charles Fraser, may have survived because of Bergstrom's quick action.[20]

While Hop and Howard were waiting for their beer, the real air-raid alarm sounded. They walked outside just in time to see two Dutch Brewster Buffaloes climbing to intercept the incoming Japanese.

> We saw nine fighters at 9,000 feet . . . They had just disappeared into a cloud bank when off to our right we saw two Brewsters climbing to engage them. They were in a climbing turn at about 8,000 feet when two Jap fighters returned to engage them. Pop, pop, pop, went the cannon of one diving Jap, and one Brewster started falling out of control. The pilot bailed out and promptly opened his chute. The other Dutchman made a futile attempt to

maneuver when we again heard the pop, pop. The second plane started to make a flaming arc across the sky.[21]

The bombers were now pasting the RAAF base using the same precise formation and method that they had used over Cavite. There was no more fighter opposition—the two Dutch Brewsters had been the total allied fighter strength.[22]

Grabbing an Australian staff car, Hop and Howard raced toward the harbor. Behind them the RAAF base was burning fiercely, while four or five Zeros criss-crossed the field shooting up anything that moved.

In the meantime, the crews from 22-P-7 and -8 were also under heavy fire from the strafing Zeros. The men had taken cover among the trees, and Barthes's crew was trying to set up their machine guns. But lacking proper mounts, and exposed to heavy fire, they were driven away from the guns and took cover. Herb Casey was hiding behind a four-inch-diameter tree when a cannon round narrowly grazed his exposed rear end. Though only nicked, Casey was knocked twenty feet, and when he stood up his pants fell off.[23] Surprisingly the only other casualty was AOM1c L. H. Rohren, who was hit in the elbow.[24]

But the biggest loss to many of the men, particularly the Philippine veterans, was 900 pounds of fresh beef in Barthes's plane. The beef, the first fresh meat to arrive in Ambon in several weeks, was soaked in gasoline from the punctured wing tanks. The lack of self-sealing tanks in the PBY-4s and -5s was roundly damned by the airmen.[25]

The loss of the beef was, of course, little compared to what the Ambon raid portended. For the Philippine veterans it was a replay of a show they had already seen; Japanese planes wheeling overhead unopposed by fighters or antiaircraft fire. For the newly arrived VP-22 crews, the raid was a preview of things to come. That night, Don Chay wrote in his diary:

> . . . they bombed and strafed hell out of us today, and sank three PBYs. One unhappy day. No fighters or anything to stop them. Those damned deadheads in Washington better move.[26]

The Japanese raid underscored the need to disperse the wing. Two PBYs were total losses, 22-P-8 and 10. Donaho's plane was badly damaged, but appeared to be salvageable. The fire had burned away the fabric on the starboard aileron, and the plane was full of holes, but everything else seemed intact. Fortunately, the other Pat-Wing-10 planes were either in Surabaja or on patrol, and 22-P-12 had been saved by Ed Bergstrom's quick action.

More importantly, none of the tenders had been in Ambon during the air raid. The *Preston* was already en route to Alor to set up an advance base there, the *Heron* and the *Childs* were in Surabaja, and the *Langley* was still in Darwin.[27] For the remainder of the campaign around the Malay Barrier, the tenders would become the most important pieces of equipment in the PatWing-10 inventory. Without the tenders, the PBYs would be unable to operate for any period of time away from a fixed base. Loss of the tenders would cause curtailment of Wagner's dispersal system, making it impossible for the PBYs to cover ABDA's center and right wing.

In effect, only three tenders could be deployed in the forward area, the *Childs*, *Heron*, and *Preston*. The *Childs* and *Preston* enjoyed speed and size, while the *Heron*, though much smaller and slower than the ex-destroyers, had the advantage of shallow draught.

Under better conditions, the *Langley*, with her great size and large working spaces, would have been PatWing-10's premier tender. But she was wholly unsuited to operate, literally, under the enemy's nose, and was left in Darwin to act as a radio relay station and stores ship. Ironically, she was the only one of the four tenders lost to enemy action.

The day following the raid, PatWing-10 pulled out of Ambon, going first to Surabaja. The evacuation was accomplished with four PBYs, twenty-seven men in each plane.[28] Three of the planes had been based in Ambon, and the fourth, flown by Lieutenant Thomas Moorer, was sent over from Surabaja. Donaho was flying 22-P-12 with Howard as copilot and Hop in the bow. The overloaded plane had such a tough time getting off that she nearly ended up in the mined area at the harbor entrance.[29] The other three had less trouble, but all four got a scare as they climbed away. Just outside the harbor entrance, a patrolling Lockheed Hudson was misidentified as a Japanese bomber. Once the scare was over everyone settled down, and the rest of the flight was uneventful.

Don Chay led the wing's remaining J2Fs out of Ambon, but be-

When operating at advance bases, PatWing-10's tenders often had to resort to drastic measures to avoid detection. The camouflage technique used here by the *William B. Preston* is a typical example. (Courtesy J. L. Pratt)

cause of the lack of refueling stations on the way to Surabaja, Chay's group was sent to Darwin. His flight was more eventful.

> They told me to gas at Tanimar Island or at a town on another island. Then, while on the way, they radioed me to go to a town that my map didn't show. Finally we landed at a small town, and the natives headed for the trees. We finally coaxed them back with signs and gestures, and found the location of the town we wanted.
>
> We went there, caused an air-raid alarm, and were fired at. We finally landed . . . and gassed up. We made it to Darwin by night and were hoisted aboard the thrice-accursed ship, USS *Langley* "Maru."[30]

PatWing-10's evacuation from Ambon was carried out none too soon. Though there was no practical reason for the Dutch and Australians to stay, they did, and were subjected to almost daily air raids. The Dutch had pulled the wrecked 22-P-7 into the only hangar, which surprisingly survived the repeated bombings, but the Australians were not so lucky. Hudsons flown in to replace those already destroyed were themselves blown to pieces. The situation in Ambon was grim. In fact, the situation in all of the Netherlands East Indies "looked pretty grim." [31]

The Japanese three-pronged attack against Java was underway. The Central Force and Eastern Force were actually one big force, split in two by the Celebes. The Central Force had taken Tarakan on the 11th and was prepared to push down the Makassar Strait to seize Balikpapan. The Eastern Force had taken Menado on the 11th and was now headed down the Celebes east coast toward Kendari, and across the Molucca Sea toward Ambon.

From the 16th onward, PatWing-10 operated from its headquarters in Surabaja to patrol up the Makassar Strait. An overnight harbor was established at Makassar on the Celebes west coast, at the south end of the strait. The three tenders, operating from any small harbor that would hide them and their broods, covered the Molucca Sea, across which the Eastern Force was driving. The principal harbors they used were on the islands Alor, Timor, the Tanimbar Group, Soemba, Flores, and Boeton. In fact, it was from Baubay on Boeton that 22-P-3 took off on her last flight on 16 January 1942.

The plane, returning from a patrol to the Gulf of Tomini, was flying at about 11,000 feet. The sky was cloudless, visibility unlimited. The patrol was a dangerous one, since it took 22-P-3 close to the airfields at Menado and Tarakan. It also followed the flight path used by Japanese bombers headed to and from targets along the Celebes east coast. It was in that air corridor, near Salabangka Island, that 22-P-3 ran head on into twelve twin-engine Japanese bombers, probably Nells. The events that followed were sudden and chaotic.

The bombers attacked the PBY with cannon and machine-gun fire. Lacking cloud cover, the pilot nosed the PBY into a violent, turning dive. In the bow, the NAP, AMM1c Clarence Bannowsky, had not seen the Japanese. The first warning he had was when the plane suddenly rolled over and dove. [32]

"What the hell is going on?" Bannowsky shouted. [33] In the radio compartment, RM1c Murl Benefiel saw " a hell of a commotion for-

Clarence Bannowsky was an NAP when he
saved the crewmen that were trapped in his
PBY. Bannowsky landed the plane after both
officer pilots had bailed out. He was later
commissioned. (Courtesy C. Bannowsky)

ward" just as the plane started into a steep dive, and a waist gun
opened up.[34]

22-P-3 was hit in the wing and the nose as she plunged down
7,000 feet, shedding fabric from both wings. At 4,000 feet the pilots leveled off, jettisoned the bombs, and "full-feathered the pro-

pellers."[35] The plane was now headed toward a small island, in a powerless glide, and "without lateral control."[36]

Bannowsky scrambled into the cockpit in time to see both pilots clipping on parachutes.[37] Assuming he had missed the bail-out order, the NAP clipped on his parachute. After a short discussion between Bannowsky and the two officers about how to use the parachute, the pilot stepped up onto the navigation table, crawled out to the navigator's hatch, launching himself headfirst out of the plane. He was followed immediately by the second pilot.[38] Two other crewmen jumped from the waist hatch.

The plane was again diving, making movement inside the plane difficult. In the radio compartment Benefiel watched Bannowsky struggle through the navigator's hatch and stop. The enlisted pilot was half way out of the plane, looking aft, when he saw another man still inside the port blister. Figuring there was a crewman trapped in the plane, he dropped back inside. Bannowsky was stunned to see not just one, but three men still in the plane, and not one of them had a parachute on.

> I figured I'd better try to land her because we were already down
> to a thousand feet, and those guys weren't going to get out.[39]

Sliding into the left seat, Bannowsky took a quick look around. The plane was traveling at 130 knots, and so much fabric had come off the wings that Bannowsky could see through them. Pulling back on the column he got a response, "but she shuddered like she was going to stall."[40] Easing the column forward, he turned into the wind guiding the fast-moving plane toward the water.

The landing was a gem, and Benefiel said that Bannowsky "greased the plane onto the water."[41] Unable to lower the wing floats, Bannowsky used all his skill to keep the wings level until the last moment. When that time came, "she just sort of settled on one wing, and floated on the wing tip."[42] They were safely down, but their problems were far from over.

The Japanese started strafing the plane the moment she hit the water. Behind him Bannowsky heard the waist guns, now manned by Benefiel and RM3c E. B. Haynes, hammering back at the attackers. But the firing ended abruptly when the .50-caliber waist guns ran out of ammunition.[43] In the meantime Bannowsky and

AMM2c M. G. Armstrong had inflated the rubber boat and thrown it over the side. Turning to go forward, Bannowsky had just shouted to the others to abandon the plane, when a chunk of shrapnel slammed into his back, knocking him down.

By now the plane was filling fast with water, and one engine was afire, the flames spreading to the wing. Benefiel and Haynes hurriedly stripped off Bannowsky's heavy flying jacket, put a Mae West on him, and pitched him out the hatch into the water.[44]

Without inflating their life jackets, the four men swam to the rubber boat, and were trying to turn it right side up when the Japanese came after them. As the machine-gun fire stitched a path across the water toward them, the men ducked beneath the surface.

> The water was so clear that we could see the bullets lose velocity after they hit the water. They sort of went "splut" when they hit, and just trickled down trailing bubbles. The strafers came in nose to tail so we had plenty of time to catch our breath between runs. But we were getting tired because, even uninflated the Mae West had some buoyancy, and it was hard to push under. After about twenty minutes we just gave up and watched.[45]

About that time the Japanese also gave up. 22-P-3 was deep in the water and still burning when the last bomber disappeared. While Benefiel and Haynes turned the raft over, Armstrong tried to shed his heavy flying boots. For some reason he could not, and attempted to cut them off with a huge Bowie knife he carried. He got the boot off alright, but he nearly cut off a big toe in the process. Blood from Armstrong's nearly severed toe spread quickly, raising the fear of sharks.[46] Hastily, the men clambered aboard the raft, dragging Bannowsky with them.

The raft had taken several hits, but was still afloat. The holes were soon patched and the raft reinflated. Bannowsky, laid out on the bottom of the raft, was bleeding badly and going into shock. Armstrong's injury, though bloody, did not affect him badly. The bright spot in an otherwise dim picture was that they were close to a small island. After a few hours paddling they were picked up by native boatmen and taken to their village.

Amazingly, the crew was reunited on the island. During the next four days friendly natives provided them with food, shelter, and transportation down the coast to the same harbor from which their ill-fated flight had started.[47]

On 17 January 1942, the day after Bannowsky had landed 22-P-3 off the Celebes east coast, P-28's crew went ashore about 220 nautical miles to the northeast, on the island of Mangoli. After being shot down off Menado on 11 January, Grayson and his crew had drifted for six days in their rubber boat. During those six days they had paddled, or rigged a parachute sail, in fruitless efforts to reach distant islands. To avoid being strafed or captured at sea, they had covered themselves with their dungarees as camouflage against prowling Japanese patrol planes. They had tightly rationed their meager water supply and tried vainly to add to it by catching water during a passing storm.[48]

The storm itself almost killed them when their boat was nearly upended in the twenty-foot waves. Grayson was suffering from sunstroke, and all of them were blistered to the point of illness. During the day they baked, at night they froze. By the evening of the 16th their water was gone, their morale was shot, they were very weak, and none believed they would survive.

But on the 17th they saw land, and it was close. Frank Ralston had kept a daily diary on the back of their only chart. The 17 January entry reads:

> Dawn found us ten miles offshore—the closest we've been to land since we started. It renewed all of our morale, and we paddled with renewed vigor. Finally made land around 2400. Upon stepping on land everyone so weak that they could hardly stand for more than ten minutes. Everyone immediately went down on his knees and thanked God for bringing us safely to shore.

They were ashore, but their ordeal was not entirely over.

Grayson and Ralston left the others on the beach and headed inland looking for help. Grayson wore his .45 automatic. They had not gone far when they rounded a bend in the trail and came face to face with a native youth. The boy, startled at the appearance of the two foreigners, leaped back, raising his machete-like blade to strike. Grayson and Ralston stopped dead in their tracks and shouted, "We're Americans."[49]

The fact that the two men made no aggressive move, and that Grayson completely forgot about his pistol, probably kept both of them from being carved up. The boy certainly did not understand English.

After a few tense moments, the boy's shouts brought more natives who acted curious, but friendly. With gestures, the Americans bargained for food and water that was delivered to the beach. Then, through an interpreter who spoke broken English, they arranged for transportation to Sanana Island, where there was a Dutch government official.

By that time it was too late to start across the island to the village where they could get a boat. So they made themselves as comfortable as possible under the trees and spent the night. During the night it rained and the mosquitoes ate them alive. No one slept. The following morning, 18 January 1942, seven tired, weakened airmen set out to cross Mangoli Island. It was not easy.

> Started out at approximately 0600 . . . to cross the island of Mangoli, a distance of about ten miles that became twenty miles because we had to climb a mountain about 5,000 feet tall. . . . In company with several native men, we walked at a killing pace in order to reach the other side of the island by dusk. . . . Only four members of the crew had shoes so we made shoes for the others by cutting up flight and life jackets, and wrapping them around their feet. . . . Still the feet of all hands were cut, bruised, and so sore we could hardly walk. We reached a small native village by 1600, so tired we almost had to be carried.[50]

At last Grayson and his crew had paid their dues, and their ordeal was over. They were heartily welcomed by the natives who treated them "royally," and the next day they were in Dutch hands. But the experience had taken its toll. Grayson was in such bad physical shape that it took months for him to recover. Ralston developed blood poisoning after his lacerated feet became infected, and saw only limited duty before Java fell. RM1c Westfall, Grayson's NAP, was so badly burned that he ended up in the hospital next to Clarence Bannowsky. The rest of the crewmen suffered similar disabilities.

Both the crews from 22-P-3 and P-28 were picked up and taken to the *Preston* before being sent to Surabaja. The safe recovery of downed aircrews was always a joyous event. But it was also a reminder that operating PBYs in an area controlled by the Japanese was hazardous. VP-22 had only been in the theater a few days, and already a third of its planes had been lost.

Despite the unequal struggle and the danger, a surprisingly high percentage of missing PatWing-10 aircrews were making it back to the allied lines. Throughout the Java campaign that remained the case, and may have given them something to hope for. Unfortunately, the men of PatWing-10 who were still on Bataan had no similar hope. For them escape was out of the question.

# 8

# Mariveles
# 26 December 1941 –
# 29 January 1942

Mariveles, on Bataan's southern tip, was a small harbor about two miles long, and a mile wide. At the top of the harbor was the town of Mariveles bounded on the right by the Mariveles River, and on the left by a steep, jungle-covered ridge that formed a spur on the tip of the Bataan Peninsula. About half the spur formed the west side of the harbor. The high ridge, or spur, was dominated by Pucot Hill at the upper end and Mt. Mauankis at the lower end. On the China Sea side, the spur was deeply indented in five places forming six points: Lapiay, Longoskawyan, Naiklec, Hornos, Talaga, and Chochinos.

Other than having some limited naval facilities, Mariveles's primary importance was the airfield being built there. Pacific Naval Air Base Constructors, a civilian company, had started construction before the war and continued working even after MacArthur had ordered everyone onto Bataan. They were still working steadily when the remnants of PatWing-10 came to Mariveles and established their base of operations at the construction camp on the harbor's east shore.[1]

At the same time American and Filipino troops, and Filipino

Mariveles was at the lower end of the Bataan Peninsula. PatWing-10 occupied the area shown here after Manila was evacuated. The air field was being constructed in the bare space on the right side of the picture. (Courtesy Tom Pollock)

refugee civilians, were pouring into the Bataan Peninsula north of PatWing-10's location. The Japanese were still several miles north of the peninsula, but were rapidly converging on Manila. Bridget and his men were, at that moment, free of any immediate threat from the Japanese, but they were nonetheless faced with serious problems.

The airfield construction camp was not equipped nor provisioned to handle the sailors who now occupied it. In addition to PatWing-10's people, Bridget had already picked up several stragglers from other units, and his force would soon swell as more men arrived. Housing was adequate, but sanitation facilities, a water supply, a power station, a base radio, and a galley/mess hall had to be provided. The most serious problem was the almost total absence of food to feed the men.[2]

Lieutenant Commander Bridget called an officers' meeting to discuss resolving their problems and organizing the camp. During the meeting it was reported that there were probably enough food and supplies still at Sangley Point to last at least sixty days, at full rations. The supplies had been left behind for lack of transportation during the hasty evacuation.[3]

As a result of the meeting, Tom Pollock was ordered to Sangley to recover the supplies. It was not an easy assignment. There were now plenty of trucks available, but there was only one road north along the peninsula's east side. That road was already choked with southbound traffic.

The route would also take Pollock and his men dangerously close to the Japanese lines. The convoy would have to drive north to San Fernando, then turn south, crossing the Pampango River at Calumpit, and pass through Manila and Cavite before reaching Sangley Point. It was about a 200-mile round trip, complicated by poor roads, heavy traffic, and the constant threat of air attack. The last problem was partially eliminated by driving north at night, but that just made the first two problems worse.

There was a fourth problem. If the Japanese seized the bridges at Calumpit while the convoy was still in the Manila area, Pollock and his men would be trapped.

Two round trips were made between 27 and 31 December, with no break between trips except to load and unload the supplies. Driving only during the late afternoon and at night, Pollock's men delivered twenty truckloads of supplies to the men at Mariveles.

The supplies having priority were nonperishable foods, blankets, medicine, and cigarettes. After four days of shuttling back and forth between Mariveles and Sangley Point, "they had pretty well cleaned out most of the items of use."[4]

Though Sangley had been cleaned out, there were still supplies at Cavite and in Manila. Lieutenant Hugh McGowan, an intelligence officer, knew Manila well and knew where a large number of truck tires were stored. Someone else mentioned seven .50-caliber machine guns hidden at Sangley, and Pollock recalled a complete radio setup in San Rogue. Stores of clothing and additional food were also reported to be at various places. On the afternoon of 31 December, Pollock and McGowan decided to make one more trip. For some of them it would be one trip too many.

> Prior to the last convoy trip, Lt. Hugh McGowan and I went to Army Intelligence to find out where the enemy lines were. We could find out nothing except that Jap patrols had been as far as the Manila-Bataan road.[5]

In fact, the situation was a lot worse than that. The Japanese were pushing steadily south along Highway 5 toward the vital Calumpit bridges. At noon on 31 December, while Pollock and McGowan were asking about the enemy's location, Japanese troops were already in Baliuag—just nine road-miles from the Calumpit bridges.

Ignorant of the true situation, Pollock, McGowan, and fifteen enlisted men, all volunteers, headed for Manila. The convoy was made up of five trucks and a station wagon, each truck carrying two BAR-armed sailors. Throughout the afternoon on 31 December 1941 and into the early morning hours of 1 January 1942, the small convoy crept toward Manila. The major problem was the frequent identification checks made by Filipino guards, who apparently did not recognize the Navy.

> Volunteer guards were on the job stopping all cars at every small bridge, and there were plenty of bridges. Those guards who weren't able to find some sort of gun had managed to get whistles. They were sure exercising their lungs that night, because we didn't miss a one. After a few miles this monotonous procedure became irksome, so when we were challenged by the guards we just yelled

"Army convoy" to them and kept on going. When the guards were armed with only a shotgun we weren't too worried, because we figured the shot would not come through the truck. But if they had a rifle, we usually stopped.

In Manila the convoy separated into two groups. Pollock, the station wagon, and a nearly new Reo truck drove to Sangley Point. McGowan kept the other four trucks, since the tires and the food supplies amounted to the largest loads.

Pollock's mission was twofold. He intended to destroy some radio equipment in San Roque, salvaging those parts that he could use. Then he was going on to Sangley Point in search of anything else of value, and to pick up the seven machine guns. He quickly located the radio equipment, destroyed one transmitter, and loaded one aboard the Reo. At the Naval Air Station, he found a cache of abandoned medical supplies, clothing, more food, and spare aircraft parts. All that was loaded into the Reo and the station wagon, leaving just enough room in the truck for the seven machine guns.

It was daylight by the time he arrived at the warehouse where the machine guns were reportedly hidden. But instead of finding seven, he found fifty-five brand new Brownings, and all their spare parts, still in crates. It was a treasure trove discovery, and Pollock saw at once the value those guns would have on Bataan. The problem was he did not have room in either the station wagon or the Reo to carry them. And he sure did not want to give up the stuff he already had loaded on the truck.

To resolve the problem, they drove back to San Roque and hunted until they found an abandoned truck. It was not much of a find, being a "clunker with two speeds forward, and essentially no brakes." But it was, at least, a truck.

By now it was late in the morning, and Pollock had to hurry to meet McGowan and the others in Manila. Working like stevedores, the men transferred the radio, clothing, medical supplies, spare engine parts, and food from the Reo to the clunker. They then loaded the Reo with the fifty-five heavy machine guns and spare parts, and headed toward Manila.

Throughout the morning they had been working in an atmosphere of impending danger. As the day wore on, the feeling of danger grew. There was good cause for the feeling. The men had seen no signs of life since reaching Manila before dawn. Smashed buildings, burned out trucks and cars, the twisted remains of the Navy Yard, and the smashed air station were the only signs that this place had once been inhabited. Fires still burned, and heavy black smoke hung over the area like lowering storm clouds.

Having returned to Manila, Pollock went directly to the meeting place he and McGowan had selected. But instead of finding the rest of the convoy ready to go, he found disaster. Quickly as he talked to McGowan, the feeling of danger became a reality. The Calumpit bridges had been blown up by army engineers five hours ahead of schedule. They were trapped in Manila.

McGowan, justifiably concerned about Pollock's delayed return had already sent the four trucks, plus another he had commandeered, back toward Bataan. After the trucks were gone he found out about the blown bridges, and there was no way he could call back the trucks. Fortunately, the men who had "ridden shotgun" on the trip up from Mariveles had stayed with McGowan because there was no room for them in the loaded trucks. As McGowan and Pollock were talking, the five trucks were being shot to pieces by a Japanese tank column, one mile outside Manila. Only one of the drivers survived.[6]

The two officers did not know that the convoy had been wiped out, but they did know that they could not get back to Mariveles by road.

> We put in a call to Corregidor to see if there was a chance of any boat transportation. We were informed that a 680 boat would be over that night to pick us up. So we relaxed to a much-needed rest . . . But, as it got dusk, we began to get uneasy, and called the "rock" again. The answer was that the boat had been canceled.

The boat had been canceled because Manila had been declared an open city on 25 December, and there were not supposed to be any military personnel in the city. It was the first any of the stranded sailors had heard about MacArthur's open city declaration. The decision not to send a boat was a setback, but not a knock-out blow. They might be in a trap, but they were not caught yet. If Corregidor would not send a boat, they would find their own.

The fifty-five machine guns were unloaded from the Reo and

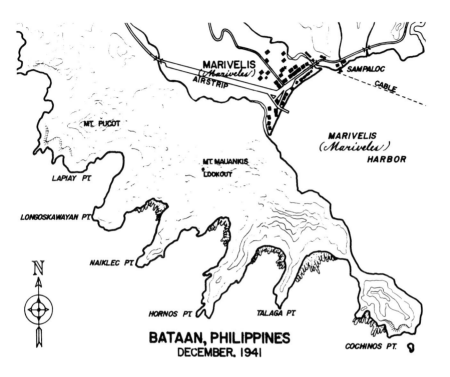

**BATAAN, PHILIPPINES**
DECEMBER. 1941

stacked on the Army-Navy Club landing. The two trucks were then driven out on the lawn and burned. While the men rested, Pollock, McGowan, and CRM Burton C. Fuller drove the station wagon along the waterfront, looking for a boat. By nightfall their search appeared to be a lost cause, and they were beginning to believe that "every boat over twelve feet long was burning in Manila Bay." At the point when their search seemed fruitless their luck changed.

Tied up to Pier One were a tug and a barge. The barge was stacked high with 3-inch ammunition, atop which sat a lone marine guard.

"What are you doing?" Pollock shouted to the marine. The marine had to think about the question a minute. After all, it was pretty obvious that he was sitting on top of a barge-load of ammunition. But it was no time for sarcastic humor.

"I'm trying to get to Bataan, but I'm not having a hell of a lot of luck." He gestured toward two Filipinos who were loading tires and camouflage nets onto the tug.

Propaganda leaflet that was dropped on Philippine troops on Bataan.
(Courtesy Tom Pollock)

For Pollock and McGowan the tug and barge were a golden opportunity to accomplish more than they had hoped for. The combination would not only get them across the bay, but would make it possible to take the machine guns too. On top of that, the marine battery at Mariveles desperately needed 3-inch ammunition, and there was a whole barge-full ready to be delivered.

Before they could act a tremendous explosion erupted at the head of the pier. A powerful shock wave and a wall of hot air rushed through them as huge, orange balls of flame rolled skyward. Someone had blown up the fuel and oil storage. Black smoke smothered the area, making an already dark night black. But there was enough light to see that the tug had been hurriedly cast off and was pulling away from the pier.

"Take a flashlight and signal me from the Army-Navy landing." Pollock was running toward the tug, Fuller right behind him. Both men jumped across the widening gap between the dock and the tug, as McGowan, shifting the station wagon into second gear, headed for the Army-Navy landing.

Hurrying to the pilothouse, the two Americans stepped inside.

"Go to midstream and cast off the barge."

The Filipino tug captain ignored Pollock's order. "Corregidor," he snapped, steering the tug and its barge toward the "Rock."

"We're going to the Army-Navy landing. Move to mid-stream and cast off the barge." Pollock was beginning to realize that the Filipino did not "speak much English."

"Corregidor." The Filipino focused his attention on the water ahead.

Fuller pushed past Pollock, shoved the barrel of his service .45 into the Filipino's side, and snarled, "Get that barge cast off. Now!"

The Filipino looked down at the .45, looked at Fuller, and nodded his head. He got the message.

The barge was soon cast off and anchored in mid-channel. The marine guard, still sitting atop the stacked ammunition, was given a flashlight, and told to signal the tug when it returned. Satisfied that they would be able to relocate the barge, Pollock and Fuller pushed off for the Army-Navy landing. With Fuller at the helm, the tug crept forward "at a snail's pace" through floating wreckage, and around half-submerged, burned-out hulks that littered the bay.

Thick smoke pouring from the burning fuel and oil dump made it almost impossible to see. Through the pollution, Pollock saw a dim spot of light. The light flashed rhythmically two dashes and three dashes, MO, MO, MO. It was Hugh McGowan on the Army-Navy Club landing.

After three attempts, a line was finally passed ashore, and the tug was warped alongside the landing. At that point Pollock got another surprise. Instead of just McGowan, ten enlisted men, and a stack of machine guns, Pollock found a large crowd waiting to go aboard. Many were civilians and Filipino soldiers. There were also an army nurse with two wounded airmen, a very drunk army captain, and a man who claimed to be a Swiss national. The Swiss was also very drunk, and together with the army captain, gave Pollock a headache from the start. Before the trip was over, Pollock gave serious thought to throwing them both overboard.

When this picture was taken, Tom Pollock would never have believed that in a few months he would be doing the real thing. At least half of Pat-Wing-10's enlisted personnel and a handful of officers were left on Luzon. They all fought as infantry until Corregidor surrendered. (Courtesy Tom Pollock)

The big building on the left is the Army-Navy Club in Manila. Pollock's trucks were burned on the lawn in front of this building, and Pollock and Fuller brought the tug and bargeload of ammunition to the landing in the lower left corner. (Courtesy Tom Pollock)

With so much extra manpower, the machine guns were quickly put aboard. As the tug pulled away from the dock, several American sailors burst out of the dark, sprinted across the dock, and leaped aboard the tug. One of them was Art Burkholder, the man who had "done something really stupid on 13 December" by volunteering to deliver a new engine to Laguna de Bay. On that occasion he had been left behind when PatWing-10 headquarters headed south aboard the *Childs*. Moments before he had jumped aboard the tug, it had appeared that he might be left behind a second time.

Burkholder and several others had volunteered to take a whaleboat across Manila Bay on the night of 31 December and blow up the remaining fuel and oil stores. That had been the tremendous explosion that caused the tug's hurried departure from Pier One. After the blast Burkholder and several others had become separated from the main group, and through sheer luck arrived at the Army-Navy Club landing just in time to catch the tug.[7]

Proceeding cautiously back the way they had come, Fuller and

Pollock searched for the barge. An hour later they found it, but were unable to come alongside and make fast to it. The two Filipino crewmen were no help, and after several time-consuming tries, Pollock gave up. Instead of taking the barge alongside, a line was passed from the stern, and the barge was taken in tow.

At 2230 on 1 January 1942, the tug and its tow cleared the breakwater, and started across Manila Bay at just 2 knots. Automatic riflemen were stationed in the bow, stern, and atop the barge. On deck, Pollock was having increasing problems with the army captain, the Swiss national, and several civilians who had gotten roaring drunk on liquor they had brought aboard. Dog tired, with the Japanese literally snapping at their heels, and with unidentified patrol boats prowling around in the dark, Pollock and his PatWing-10 crew were in no mood to be bothered by a bunch of drunks. When the problem reached a certain point "it was taken care of." How that was accomplished has never been made clear, but a number of the revelers probably had "knuckle sandwich headaches" the next day.

At 0230 on 2 January 1942, they reached the mine field. Pollock saw what he thought was a torpedo boat, and signaled for direction. There was no reply. After a period of waiting to decide the next move, one of the PatWing-10 airmen said that he had once seen a chart of the mine field, and thought he knew how to get through. Pollock, McGowan, and Fuller discussed the problem, and decided that if they "stayed put," Japanese planes would surely get them in the morning. Figuring that "with a shallow draft, the odds were better in the mine field than with the Jap strafers," they headed through.

They were well underway when they "received a red signal from the Rock." Obviously they were in real danger, and now had no choice but to "stay put." For the rest of the night, the tug and barge circled slowly in one place—or so they hoped. At first light a patrol boat came out, led them through the mine field, and sent them on their way to Mariveles.

It was a swell reunion. Bridget had heard of our plight, but wasn't worried. He said he had every confidence that we would make it. His confidence was certainly stronger than ours had been at times. There was a marine working party swarming over the barge within a few minutes of our arrival, unloading the precious ammunition.

Pollock, McGowan, and the others had been on the road without a break for six days. During that time a lot had happened. On 27 December the 153 men of PatWing-10 were joined by fifty men from the Naval Ammunition Depot (NAD).[8] Those men, plus stragglers from several other units, increased the camp's population to nearly 250 men. Because of their exposed position, and the inadequate facilities, Bridget had given three tasks equal priority for preparing the camp as quickly as possible. He wanted a galley set up, a head built, and foxholes dug.[9]

George Gaboury, who had built the decoy PBYs at Olongapo, was given the task of building the head. Bridget told Gaboury to build a "big one," and assigned ACMM Robert Davis to help. The two men approached the task with the zeal of builders about to produce an architectural masterpiece. The first building was a sturdy "eight cylinder, four holes on each side" design, enclosed in four walls, but without a roof. The open-top feature "provided better ventilation and made it easier to hear the bombers coming.[10]

But their best effort was a huge "twelve-holer, over a four-foot deep pit." It featured hand-crafted, lifting seat rings and lids, and had that edifice belonged to the army it most certainly would have been designated the Officers' Latrine. But Gaboury's masterpiece was never used. On the day he installed the last seat lid, a Japanese 500-pound bomb blew it to pieces.

Digging foxholes was done with considerably less enthusiasm—at least at first. Bob Swenson said that after the first Japanese attack on 29 December, "we had no trouble whatsoever getting them to dig foxholes."[11] Initially the men had to be pushed, and the holes they dug were much too shallow. But after the first salvo of 500-pounders had blasted the construction camp, "the digging was done voluntarily, and the holes became too deep."[12]

At first the men dug their holes close to the barracks, but they soon learned that the airfield and the buildings were the prime targets. As the raids went on, holes were dug farther and farther away from the buildings, until some were as far away as a hundred yards. The NAD personnel decided that the whole area had gotten too hot, and moved their quarters to a small stream a half mile away.[13]

The first air raids caught them by surprise, because of a totally inadequate air-raid warning system. There were several casualties during the early raids, men dying in their bunks, or caught in the open. PatWing-10 solved the problem by setting up their own warning system. It was no small task.

From the marines, they scrounged several old World War I field telephones and reels of wire. Observation posts were set up on the ridge above Cochinos Point, Longoskawayan Point, and atop Pucot Hill, and a line was run to the USS *Canopus* (A59). The submarine tender, heavily camouflaged and moored beneath a towering cliff, was acting as the service ship for the sailors and marines in and around Mariveles.[14]

The man responsible for laying more than twenty miles of wire, and hooking the whole thing up, was EM1c Earl H. Stockdale. He was "a quiet, unassuming man," with enormous energy and courage. After the system had been installed, Stockdale almost single-handedly maintained and repaired it himself. Even after PatWing-10 became engaged in ground action against Japanese troops, Stockdale, alone and unarmed, laid new wire through the enemy-infested jungle.[15]

The new warning system was a life-saving success that gave the men up to twenty-five minutes advance warning. There were, however, a couple of gaps in the system. One could be closed, but there was nothing to be done about the other.

The first gap showed up when it was found that the civilian construction workers could not hear the alarm over the din of their heavy equipment. But the armed guards, provided by PatWing-10 as defense against fifth-column activity, could hear the alarm, though their shouts and arm waving were no more noticeable to the construction workers than was the air-raid alarm. The solution was simple, effective, and probably disconcerting to the heavy-equipment operators. When the alarm sounded, the guards fired at the heavy equipment, aiming at a blade or other heavy steel surface. The sound made by the round hitting the steel got the operator's attention.[16]

The other gap became apparent on 10 January 1942. Recall that on 24 December, Don Kelly had flown an SOC from Laguna de Bay to Mariveles harbor. There his plane joined four others, another SOC, two OS2Us, and a J2F. There had been some plans kicked around about using them for bombing missions, and serious consideration had been given to a night attack. The whole idea was

scrapped because only two or three of the pilots were really qualified to fly the planes, making any hope for success remote. The decision was welcomed by the pilots.

> It's probably just as well . . . we are big boat men. It's easy to play
> ball with a winning team, but it takes solid men . . . when there is
> no question as to the possible outcome.[17]

The planes were anchored in a semicircle near the beach—at
least partially camouflaged, but clearly visible from the air. At dawn
on 10 January, five Zeros swept in at wave-top level and sank all five
planes. The early hour and low altitude combined to defeat the
warning system.

But low-level strafing attacks were rare, while the high-altitude
bombing raids were a regular daily event. Casualties were fairly
low, but the constant routine was hard on nerves. Oddly, it was hardest on the men who had the most substantial shelters—tunnels.

The tunnels had been started before the war, but were not completed by the time MacArthur's troops had retreated to Bataan.
They were intended to be bomb and artillery shelters for hospitals,
supplies, and headquarters. In some cases they served those purposes, but they had also become living quarters. Some men lived in
the tunnels rather than stay in the construction barracks and use the
foxholes. Apparently, living in the tunnels had a very bad psycho-
logical effect on those people, causing what Bridget termed "tunnelitis." Their condition was characterized by "a loss of all senses
except fright, and a constant glassy stare." They were almost unable to talk, and never got more than two jumps away from the
mouth of a tunnel.[18]

Bridget took action as soon as he spotted the problem. He had a
small rest camp built in the mountains, on the bank of the Mariveles River, and sent all "tunnelitis" cases there to recover. Then he
put a stop to going in the tunnels and moved everyone back into the
barracks. There were still cases of "bomb jitters," but nothing so
serious as "tunnelitis." And morale went up when the men found
out "they could take all the Japs could dish out."

There were good reasons for a man getting "bomb jitters." The
bombings were punishing, earth-jarring affairs against which there
was almost no resistance. The few marine antiaircraft guns could

not reach the bombers, and the men who fired machine guns, rifles, and pistols at the bombers were only venting frustration. All a man could do was crouch in his hole and hope a bomb did not land on his head, or hit so close that his hole caved in on him. There were plenty of close calls, and several men were buried alive.

George Gaboury and another man, recalled only as Dixon, were putting the finishing touches on another "twelve-cylinder master-piece" when the alarm sounded. Their first impulse was to jump into the as yet unused outhouse pit. It was, after all, four feet deep, topped by a heavy wooden structure, and looked pretty safe. Bombs or none, there was something unattractive about jumping into an outhouse pit, even if it had never been used, and the two men headed for their foxholes.

Crouched in their holes they saw the bombs drop from the formation several thousand feet overhead. Dixon counted, marking the time before impact. Gaboury watched the bombs.

> I looked up and saw a silver bomb. It must have hit about five feet from my hole, because there was a big bang. My hole collapsed and water started to gurgle in. It took ten minutes for smoke and dust to clear, and for me to dig myself out.[19]

Gaboury's latest twelve-hole sanitation palace had taken a direct hit, and nothing remained except a huge hole in the ground, considerably deeper than the original four-foot pit.

A man did not have to be in a foxhole to be buried alive. Bob Swenson and his NAP, John Clark, were going to pick up a truck when the alarm sounded. Since the alarm did not always mean the bombs would fall in their area, the two pilots continued walking. They were walking up a road toward the truck when the bombers came over. Both men looked up in time to see the release.

"So this is the way people get killed. I'm going to watch the whole thing and enjoy it, because this is the biggest event in my life." The thought flashed in Swenson's mind.[20]

"Oh Jesus Christ! The strike is going right into the camp." Clark's concern for his friends' fate was apparent in his voice. Then his concern became more immediate. "God damn! Here's one for us." His warning erased Swenson's fatalism and sent both men diving into a shallow ditch.

The entire stick exploded around them. The earth heaved, dust clogged their eyes, noses, and throats as their bodies were successively lifted and then slammed back down. Rocks and clods rained down on them, and Swenson felt his entire body being pushed down. He was being buried.

Instinctively he tried to push himself upward, to relieve the weight and to gain some breathing room. He told himself to remain calm. Something hit the back of his head, and he felt an equally sharp blow on his forehead. At last everything stopped moving, and Swenson, still pushing himself upward, felt the weight on his back lessen. Putting all his strength into the effort, he broke free.

In the middle of the road was a crater "over seven feet deep and ten feet wide."[21] The bomb had hit so close to them that from where they had been lying, they could reach out and touch the edge of the crater. Clark had also been covered by the overspill, but emerged unharmed. Swenson had a nasty gash across his forehead and a lump on the back of his head, but was otherwise unhurt. The truck was demolished.

A day or two later the Japanese delivered a particularly heavy raid on Mariveles City that started a raging fire. The flames swept through the lightly constructed buildings and shacks with alarming speed, and soon threatened to spread to the huge ammunition dump.

A call to fight fire was answered by several PatWing-10 men led by Lieutenant Tom Pollock. But by the time they reached the scene, the ammunition dump was already burning, and exploding ammunition forced them to take cover. At that point, a new and more serious threat developed. The fire was burning toward a bridge that crossed the Mariveles River. If the bridge burned, the supply line to the troops holding the Maubau-Abucay line would be cut. The Japanese were at that moment attacking along the entire front, and the line was starting to weaken.[22]

Leaving cover, the airmen set to work clearing a block of bamboo huts to create a fire break. One group went for dynamite, while another group tried to knock the houses down with axes and their bare hands. But the airmen made little headway because the houses turned out to be more strongly built than they looked.

The fire was gaining, igniting buildings that were in the block being cleared. In desperation, the men gave up trying to build a fire break, turning instead to plastering the wooden bridge with mud from the river. They had been working for an hour when a fire truck showed up with the dynamite. Setting the dynamite aside, they laid a line to the river, and started pumping water onto the fire.

> It was about even for an hour or so, and then things started to go our way. We saved the bridge, and about a quarter of the town.[23]

As the fire was being brought under control, a Filipino ran to their group shouting that some wounded men were about to be burned alive on the other side of town. ACMM Herbert Foulkes, ACMM Earl Dee, and AMM1c Raymond Tysinger volunteered to go get the men, but to get there they had to run past the exploding ammunition dump.

Alternately running in a crouch and hitting the dirt when a really big explosion went off, they dashed through the still-burning portion of Mariveles. Reaching the other side, they found several wounded men in a building directly in the fire's path. Most of the men were not badly wounded, but one man lay on the floor with a compound fracture of the thigh. The less seriously wounded were moved to safety first. The badly wounded man needed medical aid right away, and the only way to accomplish that was to take him back through the burning town, past the ammunition dump, to the fire line.

Using a door for a stretcher, the three airmen made the perilous return trip. This time there could be no running and no hitting the dirt when something blew up in the dump. Bent over as low as possible, they walked slowly through the fire and shrapnel to the fire line, and delivered their charge to a waiting ambulance.

The Mariveles fire was the first large ground action the men had taken part in, even though the enemy had been fire instead of Japanese soldiers. But the characteristics of a scratch organization fighting with courage and dogged determination were revealed in that episode. In that sense, the Mariveles fire was a preview of things to come. The fire also marked a change in the camp routine.

Despite the daily bombing raids, the period up to 20 January was generally uneventful. The fighting was still several miles north, allowing the sailors to spend much of their time improving their living conditions. Among other things they built a power plant, an ice plant that produced up to four blocks of ice per day for the hospital, and they published a widely distributed daily newspaper.

But because of the worsening situation at the front, orders were given on 15 January to establish the Naval Battalion Mariveles.[24] The battalion was formed from PatWing-10, miscellaneous naval units, two companies of the 4th Marines, and a draft from the *Canopus*. Overall command was assigned to Commander Bridget, with Lieutenant Commander H. W. ("Hap") Goodall the executive officer.

Two marine antiaircraft batteries, Battery A and Battery C, 3rd Battalion, 4th Marines, were the nucleus of the naval battalion. Battery A, equipped with .50-caliber, water-cooled machine guns was commanded by First Lieutenant William F. Hogaboom. Battery C, equipped with four 3-inch guns, was commanded by First Lieutenant Wilfred D. Holdridge.

About 150 bluejackets were drawn from the naval personnel on Bataan and added to the two marine units. The bulk of the draft came from PatWing-10 and the *Canopus*. The marines now had two responsibilities; they had to man their guns and train the sailors in infantry tactics. In fact, nearly all the marines stayed on the guns and only a few marine NCOs were assigned to the newly formed bluejacket platoons. With one exception, the four platoon leaders were PatWing-10 pilots, Ensigns Les Pew, George Trudell, and Lowell Williamson. The fourth platoon leader is recorded only as Gunner Carlson, and probably came from the *Canopus*. The small infantry force was supported by an attached Philippine Army howitzer battery.[25]

But that was by no means the extent of the naval battalion. In fact, it was only the beginning, since Bridget planned to use that initial draft as cadre, after they had trained. Around them he planned to build two full companies of naval infantry. At one time or another, during the defense of Bataan, all naval personnel in the Mariveles area took part in naval battalion operations in one capacity or another.

The next few days were spent giving the sailors basic infantry training and scrounging weapons and field equipment to supply them. Most were given the M1903 Springfield, a few received BARs, and a few had pistols. But equipment shortages in other areas were impossible to eliminate. Canteens, for example, were very hard to find, and most of the men had to make do with a jury-rigged tin can, or share with someone.[26]

Spurred on by reports of heavy fighting to the north, and rumors of Japanese infiltrators, the newly formed naval battalion trained enthusiastically. Those not assigned to the battalion continued to develop the camp area and stand guard. The battle reports and the rumors made everyone jumpy, resulting in at least one injury when a chief machinist's mate shot one of his own men by mistake.[27] Being jumpy also confirmed the rumors about infiltrators, and resulted in the capture of three Japanese soldiers.

Bob Swenson was driving a jeep along the west perimeter road when he was hailed by three Filipinos. The men were dressed in what appeared to be hospital uniforms, and one asked Swenson for a lift. Swenson told them to climb in, drove them a couple of miles up the road to a point where the leader said they wanted out, and stopped.[28]

There were no signs of a hospital, and no one around. But Swenson figured that wherever his passengers were going must be off the road, out of sight. After they had disappeared into the bush, Swenson drove on. About a mile up the road, he became suspicious and drove back to where he had dropped them. They were nowhere to be found, and a quick inspection of the area off the road showed no signs of any sort of military post.

Two days later, Swenson was again driving north when three Filipino soldiers—an officer and two privates—hailed him. Again he picked them up, but this time he was suspicious from the start. The uniforms looked good, but the men just did not look like Filipinos to Swenson. He became more suspicious when the officer asked to be taken to the local Philippine Army headquarters, but was unable to give directions to get there.

Instead, Swenson drove them to an army outpost, ostensibly to get directions. Stopping inside the perimeter, he got out, telling his passengers to wait in the jeep. Swenson walked quickly into the headquarters office and grabbed a sergeant by the arm.

"I think those three guys out there in my jeep are Japs."

"What makes you think that?" The sergeant was looking out the window at the three men.

"They just don't look right. See if you can get your men to disarm them. If I'm wrong, I don't want to cause a stink and get someone shot."

"We'll take care of it," the sergeant said as he picked up a phone. After speaking briefly, he next called Army Intelligence and asked for a Japanese speaking officer to come over.

Outside, Swenson watched a corporal walk over to the jeep as two or three other soldiers walked up behind it. Something was said, and the three Filipino soldiers handed their weapons to the corporal. Swenson was beginning to think he made a mistake, it was all going so smoothly. Suddenly the corporal pointed his Thompson submachine gun at the three men. Three pairs of hands went up. Through the open door Swenson could hear the "Filipino" officer speaking loudly, with obvious authority, to the two privates. The language was Japanese.

Swenson's capture was hard proof that the enemy was getting close. The next day, 23 January 1942, the enemy arrived. There is some difference of opinion over why the Japanese landed so far south of the main battle line. Some believe they were a raiding party sent to cut the supply road at Mariveles. Others believe they were part of a much larger landing force that had been broken up and scattered by American PT boats during the night of 22 January.[29] Whatever the circumstances were, about 350 fully equipped, combat-hardened Japanese troops were ashore in the Mariveles area. And their only opposition was the rag-tag gang called Naval Battalion Mariveles.

Standing on the airfield construction site, looking south, there were two prominent peaks: Pucot Hill on the right and Mt. Mauankis on the left. Battery C was roughly in line with Pucot Hill, and Battery A was roughly in line with Mt. Mauankis. The peaks were connected by a ridge, or saddle, that gave a commanding view of both the Mariveles harbor on one side and Lapiay Point, Longoskawayan Point, and Naiklec Point on the other.

There were lookout posts on both peaks, about a mile apart. The distance between the marines' position, near the airfield, and the lookout posts was even shorter. But the terrain was extremely rugged—broken, steep, and covered by thick jungle.

The Japanese came ashore between Longoskawayan Point and Naiklec Point sometime during the night of 22–23 January. Being well-trained combat infantrymen, they quickly pushed inland to seize the high ground—Pucot Hill and Mt. Mauankis. At about 0800 on 23 January they overran the Pucot Hill lookout post.

"Longoskawayan, Lapiay, and Naiklec Points are crawling with

Japs. We're getting the hell out of here, right now." PFC McKenzie, one of four men assigned to the Pucot Hill post, dropped the phone and "joined the exodus from the hill."[30]

Bridget could hear gunfire over the telephone, but no one answered his repeated question, "What's the situation there?" He then called Lieutenant Holdridge at Battery C and told him to investigate and secure Mt. Mauankis and Pucot Hill. A few minutes later he gave the same instructions to Lieutenant Hogaboom at Battery A. The problem was that he failed to tell either lieutenant that he had given the same order to both units. It was a tactical mistake that could have had serious consequences, but instead turned out to be a blessing.

While Hogaboom and Holdridge were moving out, Bridget set up a command post in the switchboard center at the west end of the runway. From there he sent out a call for all available able-bodied men to form a reserve.

From that point forward the Battle of Longoskawayan Point, as it became known, was very confused. There was no radio or telephone communication between Bridget and his commanders in the field. And there was none between the several platoons that were struggling up the steep slopes, through dense jungle. All communication was accomplished with runners, a time-consuming process. Napoleon's tactical dictum, "March toward the sound of the guns" was adopted by Hogaboom and Holdridge.

Hogaboom quickly secured Mt. Mauankis on the left, without resistance. Leaving a squad to hold the position, he turned right, moving along the ridge toward Pucot Hill. At the same time Lieutenant (j.g.) Pew was moving toward Pucot from Battery A's base camp with a bluejacket platoon. While Hogaboom and Pew were moving across the front, Holdridge had split his force into three platoons and had sent them off in a three-pronged assault, the right prong aimed at Pucot Hill, the middle prong over the center of the ridge, and the left prong toward Mt. Mauankis.

The lines of advance were hopelessly interwined, but by some miracle none of the platoons mistakenly fired on each other. In fact, the apparently helter-skelter deployment allowed the Americans to reinforce hot spots with superior numbers in a very short time. The first instance occurred when Ensign Trudell's platoon arrived atop Pucot Hill.

There had been no opposition until the platoon started down the other side, toward Lapiay Point. Suddenly the Japanese opened up, cutting down Trudell and his marine NCO. Rattled, Trudell's platoon hit the dirt, firing wildly into the dense bush. What they did not know was that they also had Japanese behind them. Hogaboom, hearing the firing as he moved along the saddle toward Pucot, "immediately cut down the hill to get behind the Japanese."[31] At the same time, Pew was nearing the top of Pucot Hill when the firing broke out. Pew swept up the hill, ran into the Japanese who were behind Trudell, driving them back. The weight of Pew's attack, supported by Hogaboom's arrival on the enemy's flank, drove the Japanese off Pucot Hill. While Hogaboom's platoon gave chase, Pew joined up with Trudell, and both platoons dug in.

In the meantime, Holdridge, leading the center prong, arrived on the saddle between Pucot and Mauankis where he set up a defensive position. To his left, on Mauankis, his left prong joined up with the squad Hogaboom had left there. The naval battalion now held the high ground. Considering their lack of training, poor communications, and the quality of the enemy, it was quite an accomplishment.

Hogaboom returned to Pucot Hill after a short thrust onto Lapiay Point, during which he had seen Japanese troops at long range, but had not been able to engage them. At dusk he returned to Pucot and held an officers' meeting. All agreed they had accomplished their mission, and a defensive line was set up for the night. Then Hogaboom and Holdridge reported to Bridget.

The two marine officers estimated the enemy strength at about a platoon. Bridget disagreed. The main line of resistance was just twenty miles north, and Major General Naoki Kimura was pushing toward Bagac. It made sense to Bridget that Kimura might be trying to secure his right flank by cutting the Mariveles-Bagac road. If that were the case, then the landing party would be considerably stronger than one platoon. He had already organized a new platoon made up of thirty sailors and five marine NCOs. Hogaboom and Holdridge added more beef to their forces by squeezing a few more marines from their batteries.

Bridget, figuring that most of the Japanese were on Longoskawayan Point, planned an attack for the next day to clean them out. His new plan was a good one. Hogaboom and Pew would move down

Lapiay Point while Holdridge and Williamson took Longoskawayan. The reinforced platoon on Mt. Mauankis would move onto Naiklec Point, and the newly formed platoon would be the tactical reserve.

Just after dawn on 24 January, the naval battalion moved out. On the right, Hogaboom's section was formed up in two platoons, one led by Pew. They ran into Japanese almost at once, but no shots were exchanged. At the neck of the point, Hogaboom left a BAR man to cover the only exit, and started down onto the point.

A short distance down they ran into a well-protected Japanese machine gun that quickly pinned them down. Hogaboom had hardly pinpointed the machine gun when he found his platoon under fire from the flanks. Pew's platoon pushed into the ambush, reinforcing Hogaboom, and a vicious fire fight developed. Grenades thrown at the Japanese position bounced off the thick, tangled foliage "that was as effective as barbed wire."[32] Holdridge and Pew could not advance, and were unable to disengage.

George Gaboury recalled:

> We were all on our bellies about three feet apart, facing the Japs. I saw Wagner clutch his stomach and keel over dead. We kept banging away with everything we had, which was mostly Springfield rifles and .45 autos.[33]

To their left, on Longoskawayan Point, Holdridge and Williamson had also run head on into the Japanese. They had stumbled onto a Japanese light artillery battery being set up in the clearing. Hitting the dirt, the marines and sailors opened up with BARs and rifles, cutting down at least a dozen Japanese.

It suddenly dawned on Holdridge that they were in the Japanese rear area, which meant they were probably cut off. At that point someone shouted, "Let's get the hell out of here!" It was good advice, and everyone heeded it.

Fully alerted, the Japanese moved to cut off the Americans' retreat. A series of short, sharp actions followed as the Americans fought their way back toward the high ground. Reaching the Pucot-Mauankis Ridge, Holdridge reestablished a defensive line, and sent a runner to tell Hogaboom to pull back.

In the meantime, Hogaboom had dug in for the night thinking

he could hold his position. But he changed his mind when a second machine gun raked his left flank and Japanese artillery pounded his position from Longoskawayan Point.

"It was then that I started getting a good idea of the force we were up against."[34] Hogaboom's reassessment of the situation agreed with Holdridge's new estimate that the enemy was battalion strength. As night fell, Hogaboom and Pew attempted to disengage and fall back to the ridge. The Japanese hotly pursued the Americans until firing from Holdridge's defensive line stopped them. As the cut-up platoons gained the ridge, the firing slackened and quit.

During the night, a marine 81-mm mortar section arrived, and set up on the northwest of Pucot. Throughout the morning the mortars pounded Lapiay and Longoskawayan. The fire was accurate and effective, causing heavy casualties among the Japanese, and forcing them to abandon Lapiay. When the battalion again moved onto the points that afternoon, Hogaboom found his assigned area abandoned, but Holdridge and Williamson walked into a meat grinder.

The two platoons were moving down a narrow, jungle-covered trail. Holdridge was in the lead followed by a platoon of marines, with Williamson following at the head of his thirty-man platoon.[35] About half way down the point, the trail widened and crossed an open area. At the edge of the clearing the column halted, and word was passed back for Williamson to come forward.

> Holdridge was squatted down, drawing a map on the ground when the Japs opened up. There were fifteen of us around Holdridge when the machine gun started firing, and thirteen were hit. Everybody hit the deck and scuttled to the other side of the ridge.[36]

Among the injured was Holdridge, and command devolved on Williamson. Quickly Williamson spread the men out and placed a BAR at the ridge overlooking the clearing. As soon as the shooting stopped, Williamson organized stretcher bearers to carry the wounded back. There was a delay getting things moving due to a lack of stretchers. The deficiency was corrected when someone suggested using marine ponchos and freshly cut poles. It took two hours to complete the evacuation of the wounded and organize his reduced attack force.

As the wounded were moved out, the others opened fire to cover their withdrawal. Williamson then devised a clever method for putting the basic infantry fire-and-maneuver tactic into operation. Numbering off the men by twos, he established a simple pair of whistle signals. On one whistle blast the "ones" would advance while the "twos" laid down covering fire. At two whistle blasts the "ones" hit the dirt and laid down covering fire while the "twos" advanced past the "ones."

Using his unorthodox method, Williamson's men drove the Japanese from the ambush area, pushing them down the trail about one hundred yards. But as the Japanese fell back, they moved into another prepared position. Reinforced, dug in, and heavily armed, the Japanese stopped the American advance in its tracks. Under heavy fire, the Americans retreated. But when they reached the clearing, they found that the Japanese had already retaken the area, and another well-sited machine gun blocked their way.

Under pressure from down the trail, men began to dash across the clearing, trying to reach the cover they had left earlier. Those who crawled made it, those who ran did not. But crawling was too slow, and the Japanese were pressing hard. Finally Williamson directed his men to move off the trail and climb up the ridge to a point where there was more cover to cross the clearing. In ones, twos, and whole bunches the men burst from the jungle and dashed across the clearing.

Williamson saw the man in front of him go down but there was nothing he could do. As he ran he could feel "cinders and rocks" striking his legs as the machine gun chewed up the ground.

It was nearly dark by the time the last man had crossed the clearing. For some reason the Japanese did not pursue Williamson's cut-up force beyond the clearing, which allowed the Americans to disengage and make it back to the ridge. Reoccupying their old position, the men dug in for the night, fully expecting a Japanese attack. Luckily, the night was quiet.

On 26 January the naval battalion rested. Hogaboom took a party down onto Lapiay to bury the American dead, but saw no signs of the Japanese. On the ridge the men were getting ready to attack again tomorrow. It was obvious to Bridget that the attack planned for 27 January was an all or nothing thing. He had asked for reinforcements, but there were none to be had. So far the naval battalion had held its own, but every time it ran into a strong Japanese position, casualties had been heavy. Holdridge's group alone had suffered nearly 50 percent casualties. Tomorrow Bridget was determined to commit his entire force to the assault on Longoskawayan Point. What he did not know was that the Japanese had about the same idea in mind.

At dawn a heavy barrage laid down by howitzers, mortars, and the USS *Quail*'s 3-inch guns pounded suspected Japanese positions. But as the naval battalion moved down the hill, the 75-mm fire was shifted—in the wrong direction. American artillery exploded among the advancing troops killing and wounding nearly a dozen men before it was stopped. The attack broken up by their own artillery fire, the Americans retreated to their foxholes.

A half hour later the battalion, again moving down the slope, ran into another wall of fire. This time it was Japanese machine-gun and rifle fire. The Americans hit the ground firing blindly into the thick jungle. Well-trained and organized, the Japanese slipped machine gunners through gaps in the American lines, catching them in a crossfire. The jungle was so dense that the sailors and marines could not see the enemy, but he seemed all around them.

Hogaboom moved forward, urging the men to move down the slope. He then tried to organize a special squad to deal with two machine guns that were causing real trouble. The guns quickly pinned Hogaboom down and cut off his flanking element.

The left and center of the American line continued to make slow progress. The fact that they made any movement at all is a tribute to their courage and tenacity. But courage and tenacity alone were not enough to sustain their advance. By mid-afternoon the Americans were stopped, and in serious trouble.

The Japanese had started their counterattack, supported by heavy covering fire. As more snipers and machine gunners slipped behind the Americans, threatening to cut them off, the order was given to fall back to the ridge and reform a defensive line. It was not an easy order to follow. The Japanese had cut the American line up into small sections, and many of those sections were trapped. But somehow those untrained sailors and few marines rose to the challenge. Unrestricted by set plans, or inhibited by convention, they banded together in small groups that savagely cut their way through the Japanese, to regain the ridge.

Once more the naval battalion formed a defensive line along the high ground. But this time the Japanese did not break off the pursuit. Attacking in force, they hammered at the American line, probing for an opening. The naval battalion hung on, but it looked like just a matter of time until the Japanese would break through. About midnight their luck changed. The 1st Battalion, 57th Infantry (PA) moved onto the ridge and relieved the naval battalion. The weary sailors gratefully gave up their places in the line and stumbled toward the rear.

Ensign Williamson was among the dog-tired men who streamed into the construction camp. As he walked past the switchboard center, RM2c James Gray hailed him and showed him a note. It was an order naming twelve pilots to be sent to Java aboard the submarine USS *Seawolf*. Williamson's name was not on the list.[37]

Williamson went to Bridget and asked why he had not been included. Bridget did not know, but looking at the list he noted Lieutenant Al Gray's name near the top. By that time, Gray was surely a prisoner of war, having been in the hospital in Manila when the Japanese entered the city. Bridget crossed off Gray's name and penciled in Williamson's.

The list included the name of another pilot who could not go, Ensign George Trudell. The young officer had been shot in the head and was paralyzed on one side of his body. He was at that moment lying helpless in a hospital on Corregidor.

When finally compiled, the list contained twenty-five names; eleven navy pilots, one yeoman, twelve army air force pilots, and a British major. They were lucky men. Few others would escape from Bataan and Corregidor.

On 28 January the USS *Seawolf* departed Corregidor with her passengers, en route to Java. The eleven PatWing-10 pilots felt uneasy about being taken out while so many others had to be left behind. Curiously, the men who were left were not too concerned about it. Things were certainly unpleasant on Bataan, but nearly all of them firmly believed the fleet was just over the horizon. In fact, for many the fleet was over three and a half years away. For more than half the PatWing-10 men on Bataan, the fleet would never come.

# 9
# Surabaja: Part I
# 17 January–2 February 1942

While the navy battalion was being organized on Bataan, the other half of PatWing-10 was setting up shop in Surabaja, on Java's northeast coast. The naval base at Surabaja was protected to the north by the large island, Madoera, which was separated from the mainland by a narrow strip of water. The naval base was at the meeting point of the natural channels that formed the east and west approaches. There was a commercial port to the west of the naval base, and the seaplane base, Morokrembangan, was west of that. The distance between the naval base and Morokrembangan was not too great, and the entire area was always referred to as Surabaja. But when the PBYs went to "Surabaja," they actually went to Morokrembangan.

Of the original twenty-eight planes in VPs-101 and 102, only eight PBY-4s remained. VP-22 was also down to eight planes, but a ninth, 22-P-7, was still in Ambon, damaged and unflyable. The five PBY-5s turned over by the Dutch were being serviced and would be ready to fly in a few days. At the moment, equipped with twenty-one flyable PBYs, and with plenty of extra aircrews, PatWing-10 looked pretty healthy.[1]

But the eight PBY-4s were in bad shape, long overdue for overhauls, and lacking some of the better design features found in the PBY-5s. The most notable difference between the two planes was the addition of blisters on the PBY-5 that replaced the sliding waist hatch found on the PBY-4. The blisters gave the waist gunners a much better field of fire. Bigger engines and an improved tail design were other features that made the PBY-5 a slightly better airplane than the PBY-4. The design improvements did not, however, make the PBY-5s any less vulnerable to fighter planes.

Morale in PatWing-10, especially among the Philippine veterans, was pretty shaky by 17 January 1942. There was a general feeling among those men that despite their efforts and the wing's losses, they had not accomplished anything. They were also bothered by the fact that about half the wing had been left in the Philippines. Added to those concerns were the widely held opinions that "Washington" had let the Asiatic Fleet down and that the high brass in Washington were sitting on their "duffs," while the Asiatic Fleet fought the war with inadequate equipment.[2] Tying all those unhappy feelings together was the fact that they had been forced to retreat "faster and farther than any army in history."[3]

VP-22, on the other hand, was in good spirits. In fact, the difference in morale between the men in VP-22 and the Philippine veterans was noted at that time, and later, by many VP-22 men. The newer arrivals owed their higher morale to a difference in circumstances.

In regard to its personnel, VP-22 had survived the Pearl Harbor attack pretty much intact. After the attack was over, they patched up their planes and flew patrols, but were not faced with additional attacks, or a visible threat of an enemy landing. When they moved west, they left a good share of their personnel behind, but those who were left behind were not cut off and surrounded by the Japanese. Probably the most important single factor was the fact that by moving west, VP-22 was not retreating, they were advancing to reinforce another unit.

Reinforced by VP-22, and enjoying the advantages of being based in Surabaja, the Philippine veterans' morale leveled off and started to rise. And the advantages in Surabaja certainly outweighed the disadvantages, which were irksome but not intolerable.

The advantages were many. The Dutch seaplane base, Morokrembangan, had excellent facilities that included two large hangars, three ramps, and a large work area. Cullen Bray was especially impressed with the Dutch boats used to service the seaplanes. He described them as "much like a tug boat with the towing bit nearly amidships, the cockpit forward." The design made the boat very maneuverable while towing a plane, and the plane "could be made to go just where it was supposed to go."[4]

The enlisted men were housed in an empty hangar, and some of the officers lived in quarters on the base. But most of the officers were given rooms in Surabaja at the Oranji Hotel. Generally, when not flying or working on the planes, everyone was given liberty. So it really did not make a lot of difference whether a man was living on the base or in Surabaja; everyone had access to the good things in town.[5]

For some, the good things included a steak dinner at the Europa and drinks at the Tambornie. And there were lots of girls in Surabaja whether at the Europa, Tambornie, the Planipitan, or any one of a dozen other night clubs. A few airmen spent time with Dutch families, enjoying the pleasant tropical evenings, sipping Bols Gin with their hosts.

Things were pretty good at Morokrembangan too. The Dutch served four meals a day that ranged from "good to excellent," and washed it down with plenty of Heineken beer.[6] One of the humorous sidelights to the early days in Surabaja had to do with the beer supply. Apparently the Dutch had complained to someone that the Americans were drinking up all the beer. So a Dutch officer told Captain Wagner that, as a result of the war, beer was rationed at six liters per man per day. He asked if the Americans could cooperate with that.[7]

Another benefit of duty in Surabaja was the rest camp in Tretes. Located high in the mountains, amidst lush foliage and with an almost unlimited view, the prewar resort was an ideal R and R center for the battle-weary airmen. The Commodore Hotel was luxurious, the food excellent, and the war seemed far away.

But few men stayed long in Surabaja, except those assigned to one of the staffs. After operating from Surabaja for a while, the aircrews would be sent to relieve other crews working off the tenders.

By rotating the planes and crews between tenders and Surabaja, time at sea and patrol time were fairly evenly distributed. Naturally, there were men who spent more time on a tender than in Surabaja, and some pilots who drew more missions than others, but the system was essentially equitable.

During the first week after the move from Ambon, the *Preston* and the *Heron* were at sea. The *Preston* was tending planes at Alor, and the *Heron* was operating around Boeton, on the southeast tip of the Celebes. The *Childs* had just completed an overhaul in Surabaja.

Because of losses, PatWing-10 had more aircrews than airplanes, so that usually there were two aircrews on each tender for each plane assigned. It was a good arrangement, one that made it possible for the tenders' captains to establish a day-on, day-off patrol schedule for each aircrew.

To avoid being caught on the water, the patrols took off at dawn and returned at dusk. While the planes were gone, the tenders got underway, maneuvering to avoid detection by the ever-present Japanese patrol planes. If a PBY could not take off, it was hidden along the shore, covered with foliage, until the tender returned. The tenders frequently changed location, rarely staying in one place more than two days, so that patrols often took off from one place and landed at another.[8]

Their mission was to locate the enemy at sea, though after 17 January it became increasingly a matter of simply going to where the Japanese were known to be. And the Japanese seemed to be everywhere. Sightings were made every day as the Central Force pushed down the Makassar Strait and the Eastern Force crossed the Molucca Sea. At the same time a carrier striking force had entered the Molucca Sea north of Ambon, providing the Japanese with fighter protection as far south as the Banda Sea.

Any spot north of a line drawn through Bandjarmasin-Kendari-Ambon was becoming increasingly unhealthy for the slow, lightly armed PBYs. Under the circumstances it is amazing that more PBYs were not shot down in less time than actually happened. The reason was that the pilots had become masters at concealment and defensive tactics.

Patrols were often made at very low altitude. The tactic ensured that the PBY's dark upper coloring blended with the sea and made the PBY harder for a fighter pilot to see. The low altitude, sometimes as low as fifty feet, also made it impossible for a fighter to attack from below. Pilots also flew along shorelines so that their planes blended with the dark jungle and shadows, making them hard to spot from ships farther out at sea.

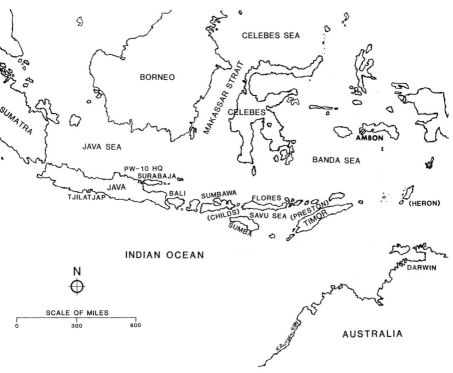

PatWing-10's area of operations 17 January–1 March 1942.

Low-level flights had, however, the disadvantage of providing shorter visual range for the pilots and crew, as demonstrated by what happened to VP-22 pilot Ensign Gene Geer and Ensign Douglas ("Doug") Davis.

> Gene Geer and I were coming around Kendari, low on the water, early one morning, and ran into a contingent of their fleet. We didn't have a torpedo or anything or we would have had them cold. We were only about thirty feet off the water, below the trees, and so close we damn near couldn't make a U-turn.[9]

The Japanese were as surprised as the pilots at the sudden confrontation. So surprised that not a round of antiaircraft was fired at the rapidly fleeing plane.

Low-level flight was often necessary just to survive, but every patrol involved a lot of time at higher altitudes. When that happened, the pilots noted the location of every cumulus cloud just as an infantryman looks for a rock or a tree to jump behind. If they saw a fighter, the PBYs headed for a cloud. Sometimes there were no clouds close enough to hide in, and when that happened the PBY was in serious trouble. A PBY caught in the open was almost a cinch to become "cold turkey" for the Japanese fighters. But not always.

On 17 January 1942, 22-P-1, flown by Ensign Jack F. Davis, was at 10,000 feet when it was attacked by a lone Zero. Davis had taken off that morning from Boeton to patrol north of the Gulf of Tomini. The flight came very close to the airfield at Menado, and that is probably where the Zero came from. It was a bright cloudless day when the port waist gunner AMM2c J. C. ("Jack") Behney spotted the Zero boring in on 22-P-1's port quarter.[10]

Davis responded to Behney's warning by turning into the attack and slipping to the left. The PBY was diving, placing the starboard waist gunner RM1c Bill Draper on the high side facing the fighter. As the PBY lost altitude, the Zero turned sharply, did a wingover, and dove to attack. The Japanese pilot fired a burst into the American, but Davis's maneuvers had spoiled his aim, and only a few rounds hit the PBY.

In the cockpit, Davis heard rounds hitting aft and above him. He was losing altitude in a left slip, at about 200 knots, when the fighter roared past below him, and started to climb for a new attack. Davis watched the Zero pull out of its dive, climb across his bow until it was well above the PBY, and start its wingover.

The Zero seemed to hang motionless for just a moment as it made the wingover transition from climb to dive. In that moment Davis rolled the PBY over into a right slip, exposing his port waist gun, and again upsetting the fighter's aim as he dove and fired, tracers streaking beneath the PBY. At 200 yards Jack Behney fired a single forty-round burst that nailed the Zero in the engine. Smoke poured from the fighter as it flashed past the PBY. Davis rolled the PBY over on the other wing, turned left, and watched the stricken fighter go down. On a steady, unaltered dive, the smoking fighter hit the sea.

Davis pushed his microphone button, "That was good gunnery, Behney."

"That was good maneuvering, sir."

They were, of course, both right. But it was also good luck. Despite all that had happened to them since the start of the war, Pat-Wing-10 aircrews had enjoyed quite a lot of good luck. Considering their losses in aircraft so far, the casualties had been low, and their luck in getting downed aircrews back was particularly notable. However, when it came to getting downed airplanes back, their luck was not good at all. One of the most frustrating examples occurred when they tried to recover Donaho's plane at Ambon.

After being shot up and partially burned on 15 January, the Dutch had hauled 22-P-7 into the hangar at Ambon. Donaho and several others, certain the plane could be repaired and flown out, wanted to go back and get it. They had good reasons for being optimistic. The wing on a PBY-5 was all metal except for the trailing edge and the aileron, which were covered with dope-treated fabric. On 22-P-7, the fabric had been burned away, but the rest of the wing was intact, and essentially undamaged. It seemed to be a straightforward matter of re-covering the trailing edge and fitting a new aileron. Early on 9 January, P-22 took off from Surabaja with some of the best talent aboard that could be found anywhere. John Hyland, Hawk Barrett, and George Webber were up front in P-22. The passengers included Ducky Donaho and Doug Davis, who would fly 22-P-7 back, and twelve enlisted volunteers. Among the enlisted men were Herb Casey and Ed Aeschliman. Material to make the repairs—dope, fabric, needles, and thread—were stowed aft. Beneath the port wing, strapped to a bomb rack, was a replacement aileron.[11]

The first leg of the trip took them to Alor to refuel, and to delay their arrival in Ambon until dusk. No one wanted to arrive in Ambon and be caught in a Japanese raid. It looked for a while, however, as if they were going to be caught in a raid at Alor.

As we taxied to the stern of the *Preston*, the air-raid alarm sounded. We cast off immediately and buoyed near shore while the *Preston* raised her hook and steamed in circles. Half an hour passed with no signs of enemy planes, and we finally gassed. . . .[12]

Since it was too late to reach Ambon before dark, the decision was made to lay over in Alor until the next afternoon. It was a good decision, because the layover provided the men with an unexpected opportunity for recreation. Barrett found a fresh-water swimming pool on the island complete with a ten-foot diving board, and the men spent the morning of 20 January lolling in the sun or paddling in "the delicious water." Refreshed, the men returned to their plane and took off for Ambon at 1430.

The seaplane base was reached at sundown as planned, but the Dutch, not expecting a plane, sounded the air-raid alert. As P-22 dropped toward the water, Dutch antiaircraft batteries trained on them, the gunners waiting for the order to fire. Fortunately, in the fast-fading light, a sharp-eyed spotter recognized the American star. It was a close call. Fifteen minutes later there might not have been enough light to make the identification, but there would have been plenty of light to shoot down the PBY.

As soon as they were ashore, the men went to work on 22-P-7's damaged wing. They were short on time and had none to waste on breaks, sleep, or even food. Everybody worked, officers and enlisted men, and even a few Dutch sailors pitched in. The main concern, as they hurried to finish the job, was that the freshly doped fabric might not dry enough by morning to hold.

Dope was painted on the metal frames to act as an adhesive, new fabric sections were laid across the frames, trimmed, and lashed to the frames with "baseball stitches." The newly surfaced area was doped layer upon layer, even before the first layers had time to dry. It was not being done according to the book, but there was no other choice. By the time the sun came up the re-covering job was done, and the new aileron was fitted in place. 22-P-7 was rolled out of the hangar and down the ramp.

Having completed their final checks, Donaho and Davis taxied out into the harbor, turning toward the harbor entrance. P-22 sat on the water near the shore while 22-P-7 started her takeoff run. If Donaho got airborne, and if the wing held together, Hyland would follow. If not, he would pick up Donaho's crew and return to Surabaja.

22-P-7 made a normal takeoff without incident and started a slow climb. Things seemed to be going well, and Ducky Donaho was about to believe that the airflow across the wing was actually drying the dope, ensuring that the fabric held. It was wishful thinking. Without warning the fabric lifted, ballooned, and tore off in one big, flapping chunk. Quickly Donaho landed, narrowly missing a mine near the harbor entrance, and taxied back to the ramp. The attempt to salvage 22-P-7 had failed.

The oil port of Balikpapan under attack. This was a common scene for PatWing-10 aircrews that patrolled up the Makassar Strait. (National Archives)

Disappointed, they left 22-P-7 to the Dutch, climbed aboard Hyland's plane, and returned to Surabaja. After they left, the Dutch hauled 22-P-7 back into the large hangar. Maybe the Dutch expected the Americans to come back and try again, or they may have given some thought to fixing it themselves. In fact, 22-P-7 had been written off.

If there was a single feature that could be called characteristic of PatWing-10 after 16 January 1942, it was that they were always on the move. There was no lack of assignments. They flew patrols, picked up downed Army bomber crews, evacuated allied military personnel and civilians, carried supplies to outposts, investigated suspicious reports at sea, and were shifted to assignments in Darwin, Surabaja, and aboard the tenders.

There were more assignments than available planes. Tony Antonides and his maintenance crew were working overtime to keep the PBYs flying, but a lack of essential spare parts made the task difficult. Spare engines were nonexistent, and the situation made it impossible to rebuild the old ones. A plane simply could not be kept out of service for the time required to complete an overhaul. The demand was too great. Under the circumstances, the loss of a PBY was a serious setback. Fortunately, for the moment, the PBYs were either avoiding the Japanese fighters or managing to scramble into cloud cover before they were shot down. Antonides knew that the good luck could not last long. He was right. On 21 January, a PBY-4 crashed and was written off. The crash was caused by a tired engine that finally gave out.

The plane was P-23, the oil-burning wreck that Hyland and Barrett had flown out of the Philippines. On 21 January both pilots and their plane were at Alor, assigned to the *Preston*. They had arrived that morning from Surabaja, after dropping off Donaho and his repair crew, and were not scheduled to fly that day.

At noon a report was received aboard the *Preston* that Don Chay and his J2F were down somewhere off Timor. His plane had run out of gas, and Dennis Szabo and Andy Reid were sent off in P-23 to deliver fuel in several five-gallon cans. It was a routine mission that involved little risk, but at that point in the war PatWing-10's pilots had come to expect the worst. What had happened to Don Chay, and what was about to happen to Reid and Szabo, were the sorts of things that made them feel that way.

Chay had left Darwin that morning en route to Surabaja via Alor. The Darwin-Alor leg would have used all his fuel even under favorable conditions, but what he ran into was far from favorable. From the start of the trip he encountered strong head winds and foul weather. It was only by a combination of luck and skill that he made it as far as Timor before being forced down. In fact, the conditions had been so bad that Chay figured he was "a gone gosling."[13]

Several hours after Chay had landed, Szabo and Reid arrived with enough gas to get the Duck to the *Preston*. The Duck was fueled, and Szabo taxied to take off. P-23 lifted off, the starboard engine lost power, and the PBY went into a "vicious slip." The plane hit the water, hull plates buckled, and "solid water poured in." P-23 sank to the wings almost immediately. No one was hurt.[14]

Aboard the *Preston*, Chay reported what had happened, and John Ogle went out in P-22 to pick up Szabo, Reid, and their crew. In the meantime, Chay entertained his old buddies aboard the *Preston* with an account of how P-23 had gone in and sunk.

"Goddamn it. My log book was in the drawer of that plane."[15] John Hyland was "graveled" over the loss of his old plane.

"It's an ignoble ending for such a close companion," was Hawk Barrett's written reaction to the news.[16]

In the days that followed, the very popular Dennis Szabo, took a lot of ribbing about his recent experience. Recalling that he had lost another PBY on Lake Lanao, his friends suggested that he be recommended for a Japanese medal. Someone else said that, insofar as PatWing-10 was concerned, Szabo was Japan's highest scoring "ace." To which was added, that with two confirmed "kills" he was Pat-Wing-10's highest scoring "ace."[17]

There was not much time to reflect on the loss of P-23, other than to note that the wing was down one more plane, and the war was heating up again. On the 22nd, Japanese transports and destroyers were spotted in the Mangkalihat Strait and Vice Admiral Chuichi Nagumo's carrier striking force was reported near Kema. Dick Roberts reported Japanese transports, cruisers, and destroyers headed toward Balikpapan, and Robbie Robinson discovered that the Japanese were already using the rivers near Balikpapan as advance bases for Mavis flying boats.

While those sightings were being made and reported, the *Childs* was steaming toward Kendari, loaded with 30,000 gallons of aviation fuel—5,000 gallons of it as deck load. Her mission was to deliver the fuel to a jungle airstrip at Kendari that was used as an emergency field by B-17s operating out of Java. It was a particularly dangerous assignment.

If the Japanese scored a hit on the fuel-laden *Childs*, there would be few pieces left to pick up. Even after she reached her goal, the tender would be stuck in what amounted to a small cul-de-sac, without room to maneuver. Doc Pratt later wrote, "No one on board was happy about this mission," and it is easy to see why.[18]

To improve their chances, Doc Pratt had ordered the entire ship painted jungle green, from waterline to top mast. Steaming close to shore during the early mornings and late afternoons, he took advantage of the deep shadows and lush rain forests with which his ship blended. When the sun was high, he holed up in small coves or inlets. Drawing on his experience in Manila Bay, he had also rigged a large canvas between the bridge structure and the number one stack to alter the ship's appearance. The fifty-five gallon drums stacked on deck added to the deception. The camouflage, disguise, and sailing tactics worked, the *Childs* arriving safely in Kendari on the evening of 22 January.

Kendari, a small town on a very small harbor on Staring Bay, was accessible through two channels across the coral-choked bay—one from the south and one from the north. The *Childs* had entered the south channel on course 312 degrees true. As the *Childs* glided up the channel, Pratt noticed that the ship's compasses "conformed exactly with the channel on the Dutch charts."[19] It was somewhat unusual and, as it turned out, a very lucky circumstance.

Throughout the night of 22–23 January, the ship's crew worked to unload the fuel into lighters and get it ashore before daylight. They nearly made it, but not quite. And on the morning of 23 January, the *Childs* was moved to a place of concealment near the harbor entrance where she was made fast to several large coconut trees.

The hiding place had been picked by the Dutch, and it was a good one. But they had forgotten to tell Pratt that when the tide fell, the *Childs* would be left sitting on the mud. Sure enough, the tide dropped, and the *Childs* settled onto the mud, heeling over more and more as the water ran out from under her. The mooring lines were soon bar-taut, and Pratt feared his ship might end up on her beam ends.

At the height of the crisis, a Japanese observation plane flew over Kendari. Apparently the *Childs*'s jungle-green paint, her altered appearance, or the fact that she looked like a derelict allowed her to go unnoticed by the Japanese pilot. All in all, it was a long morning for everyone on board. Finally the crew was able to give a collective sigh of relief when the tide started to flood.

As the ship came "back to the vertical," a man in a small boat hailed them. The man, who spoke English with an accent, had come from a schooner anchored in the harbor. The sailboat was the only other vessel in the harbor, and the men on the *Childs* had been aware of it since early in the morning. The main attraction was a good-looking girl who spent much of her time on deck, to the delight of the bridge crew who watched her through the big telescope.

The man, who called himself Argana, told Pratt that he had just brought a cargo of rice from Makassar. For some reason the *Childs*'s skipper was suspicious, and wanting to learn more invited the man to lunch. As the man came aboard, Pratt sent one of his men to the schooner to look around.

During lunch Argana urged Pratt and his officers to go ashore with him, where he would show them a "good time." He was very insistent, but when it finally became clear that his invitation was being flatly refused, he changed to a different subject. He wanted to know when the *Childs* would be leaving Kendari.

By the time lunch was over and Argana had left, Pratt's man was back with his report. The information hardened Pratt's suspicions about Argana. The sailor told his captain that there were no signs that rice had ever been carried in the schooner. Furthermore, the girl spoke English, and had said that they had come from Ambon— the opposite direction from Makassar. The most disturbing bit of news, however, was that the schooner was equipped with "a complete radio installation." With that information, Doc Pratt "decided to accelerate the operation and get the hell out of there. . . ."[20]

The unloading nearly completed, preparations were made to get underway. At 0525, as the sky began to pale, the *Childs* cleared Kendari harbor and turned toward the south channel. Eight miles away, Pratt and the bridge crew saw four ships headed their way. Soon

Rodney Nordfelt was a signalman on the bridge of the *Childs* when she went to Kendari. Nordfelt sent the recognition signal to the Japanese destroyers that caused them to hesitate long enough for the *Childs* to escape. (Courtesy R. Nordfelt)

there were a dozen ships, five transports, six destroyers, and a cruiser. The Japanese had arrived.

At 0532 a Japanese destroyer challenged the *Childs*, A8Y, A8Y, A8Y. The signalman, Rod Nordfelt, returned the same challenge, and everyone on the *Childs* waited to see what would happen next. Nordfelt's reply had momentarily stumped the Japanese, but three minutes later they challenged again. At that moment a heavy squall passed over the *Childs*, hiding her.[21]

Taking advantage of the passing squall, Pratt changed course to

132 degrees true and raced down the south channel. Enveloped in heavy rain, the tender charged down the narrow channel, "her propellers washing the coral heads dry on either side astern." What would otherwise have been a mad dash in near zero visibility, was made possible by Pratt having noticed on the trip in that the compasses conformed exactly to the channel on the Dutch charts. In the boiler room "engineers popped the safety valves as they built up steam."

Seeing the rain slacken as the *Childs* reached the end of the channel, Pratt turned right, slowed to 15 knots to reduce his wake, and headed for the beach. He wanted to hide against the dark jungle backdrop. As the rain cleared away, the *Childs* backed down and stopped.

While a contact report was being sent to Admiral Hart's headquarters, four landing boats were seen entering the north channel. The tender moved forward, coasting along close to the eastern shore of Staring Bay. As the *Childs* crept along the shore, the bridge crew watched the transports and two destroyers come abeam about ten miles away. At the same time four other destroyers "deployed into line and headed toward the *Childs*."

It looked like the situation had gone from bad to disastrous, especially when heavy black smoke unexpectedly poured from the *Childs*'s funnels.

"Knock off that smoke!" Pratt warned. "Flank speed. Give me all she's got."[22]

The *Childs* charged forward, every man on the bridge expecting to see puffs of smoke or the splash from launched torpedoes. None appeared. Apparently the Japanese were fooled by the *Childs* disguise, thinking she was just a tramp steamer. The sudden burst of smoke may have reinforced that opinion. Whatever the reason, the four destroyers abruptly "deployed into column on a westerly and opposite course."

As soon as the destroyers turned, the *Childs*, at full speed, hooked around the headland, and sped south down Winwoni Strait. Thirty-five minutes later three fighters took a look at the *Childs* and were driven off by heavy antiaircraft fire. The fighters, probably sent by the destroyers to investigate the odd ship, knew now that they had more than a tramp steamer on their hands.

When the fighters backed off, Pratt crossed to the east side of Boeton Strait and turned north. Five minutes later three more fighters came at the *Childs* and were also driven away, the lead plane trailing smoke. During the next six hours the tender passed north of Boeton Island and raced southeast to reach the Toekangbesi Islands. The ship was not bothered during that time.

Having reached the Toekangbesi Islands, the *Childs* cruised slowly down the west side of the chain, using the islands for cover whenever practical. At 1415 a single-engine float plane, probably from a cruiser, spotted the ship and sent the challenge A8Y. Again the *Childs* returned the same challenge, but this time the Japanese did not hesitate. At 1422 he dropped two bombs. Both missed, and he did not hang around to cause any more trouble. But Pratt, absolutely certain there was a cruiser in the area, headed the *Childs* to the southeast at "high speed." Two days later the tender was safely in Surabaja, having survived mainly as a result of her skipper's foresight and skill—not to mention some luck. Several days later Surabaja was bombed for the first time, causing Doc Pratt to wryly observe, "probably with our gas."[23]

While the *Childs* had been unloading the last of the fuel and making her narrow escape, the Japanese had taken a major step forward. PatWing-10 planes had been reporting large concentrations of Japanese transports and warships approaching Balikpapan, about half way down the Makassar Strait. In response to those reports, the army air force attacked the Central Force fleet on 23 January, sinking the transport *Nana Maru*, and that night a Dutch submarine torpedoed the *Tsurga Maru*. But the heavy blow was to be delivered by four American destroyers.

On 20 January, Admiral Glassford had sent two cruisers, the *Boise* and *Marblehead*, escorted by six destroyers, north to attack the Japanese at Balikpapan. It was a big order that soon got bigger. The force they were to attack consisted of a light cruiser, the *Naha*, fourteen destroyers, and eighteen transports. Those already formidable odds became greater when both American cruisers were partially disabled by an accident and a turbine failure. Escorted by two destroyers, the cruisers returned to Warorade Bay, Soembawa, leaving just four old "four pipers" to carry on.

During the late afternoon on 23 January, the four destroyers, the

*John D. Ford* (DD 228), *Pope* (DD 225), *Parrott* (DD 218), and *Paul Jones* (DD 230), were in Makassar Strait, approaching Balikpapan. At 1750 they were spotted by 22-P-6, flown by Dick Roberts and Ed Bergstrom.[24]

The PBY had left Surabaja four hours earlier on a special patrol up the Makassar Strait. Both Roberts and Bergstrom had just completed a ten-hour patrol when they were told to go out again:

> We were told to fly up to Balikpapan and report anything we saw. I asked if there was anything I ought to know about enemy activity in the area—any fighters, and how about anything friendly. I was told there was no information.[25]

Roberts and Bergstrom used cloud cover to work their way north along the Borneo coast, passing inland of Balikpapan. Popping in and out of the clouds, they sent continuous reports of the size and disposition of the Japanese fleet until they ran out of cloud cover north of Balikpapan. Doubling back, they flew south, and then east across Makassar Strait, to investigate Mandar Bay in the Celebes. Finding nothing, Roberts went down to 500 feet, below the cloud cover, and headed for home.

As 22-P-6 flew south, Bergstrom spotted four ships on the horizon, coming their way. At the same time Roberts heard a crewman report three aircraft ahead and above them, very near the four ships.

> The ships looked like Jap cruisers to us. Four stacks, plus three planes near them, and no report of friendly ships in the area, convinced us they were Jap cruisers.[26]

On the *John D. Ford*, lookouts spotted the PBY, but apparently missed the three Japanese planes.[27] Thinking the still unidentified plane was a Japanese patrol plane, Commander P. H. Talbot ordered the four destroyers to change course to 035 degrees true. He wanted the patrol plane pilot to think the destroyers were Japanese headed toward Mandar Bay. Commander Talbot's ploy worked. For the next thirty minutes, 22-P-6 shadowed the four ships, reporting their course and speed to ComPatWing-10. At 1800, low fuel and a darkening sky caused Roberts to break away, turning toward Surabaja.

That night the four American destroyers attacked the Japanese transports at Balikpapan with torpedoes and guns, sinking four transports, damaging another, and sinking a patrol boat. It was the first American naval engagement since the Spanish-American War, and the Allies' first, albeit small, naval victory against the Japanese since 7 December.

The following day, Roberts learned that the four ships he had identified as Japanese cruisers were really four American destroyers en route to attack Balikpapan. Concerned that he had steadily reported their course and speed for a half hour, Roberts later went aboard the *John D. Ford* to apologize to Commander Talbot.

"I understand," Talbot told him. "But you sent us enough information for us to get in and out, and that's what counts."[28] Roberts was greatly relieved.

On the other side of the Celebes the Eastern Force kept step with the Central Force with the landing at Kendari that had very nearly caught the *Childs*. That same day Japanese carrier-based bombers and fighters hit Ambon in the first of three successive raids that knocked out both the airfield and the seaplane base.

Duke Campbell and Ira Brown were sent up Makassar Strait on 24 January to report on the situation, and to send MOs to guide in a flight of eight B-17s. The two planes arrived over Balikpapan separately, and never saw each other during the three or four hours that they remained over the burning oil fields.[29]

It was a bright day with scattered clouds, and it was only because of the clouds that the two PBYs eventually made it home. As soon as the PBYs showed up at Balikpapan, the Zeros climbed to attack.

> "There's one below us, coming up at us."
> "Jap fighter coming in from starboard."
> "Watch out you got one on top."
> We would duck into a pretty good size cloud, and as soon as we poked our nose out, the fighters would attack. We would come out of a cloud, take a quick look at the fleet, and head for another cloud.[30]

The heavy pounding noise of the .50-caliber machine guns, and the chatter of the smaller .30-caliber gun in the bow, marked the plane's brief periods of exposure. Throughout the time they were over the fleet, Campbell's radioman sent continuous sighting reports.

Brown was having the same experience, but his job was to send the MOs to guide in the B-17s.

It burned hell out of us because its the simplest thing in the world
to find Balikpapan from Surabaja. There were fighters everywhere,
and it's hard for a pilot to see those damn things until they go by. A
PBY pilot's best friend was a cumulus cloud.[31]

Believing that nine lives for a cat are too few when outnumbered
ten to one, both pilots headed south toward Makassar where they
planned to spend the night. But there was no rest for the crew, who
were busy all night plugging holes and pumping out the water that
spurted fountain-like through the hulls. As with the *Childs*, the
planes had survived because of a combination of skill demonstrated
by their pilots and crews, adequate concealment, and luck.

In addition to patrols up the Makassar Strait, PatWing-10 planes
patrolled the Molucca Sea and the Gulf of Tomini. They also shifted
from Surabaja to the *Preston* at Timor, the *Heron* at Boeton, and reported on conditions in Ambon. With all that movement and exposure to the enemy, it is surprising that only one PBY was lost that
day. And it went down due to engine failure rather than enemy
action.

John Ogle had taken off from Timor in P-22, the same plane
Marcy had flown out of Manila and that Hyland had used to fly the
salvage crews in and out of Ambon. By 24 January 1942, P-22 was a
nearly worn-out PBY-4, badly in need of an overhaul. About an
hour after takeoff, an oil seal blew in the starboard engine, and
Ogle set the plane down in a cove at Alor.[32]

Ogle and his crew beached their plane and spent the rest of the
day covering the plane with foliage. After sending a report to the
*Preston*, at Sumlaki in the Taninbar Islands, the crew waited. It was
too late in the day to send a plane on the 24th, and there were none
available the next day. But on 26 January, the *Heron*, operating out
of Koepang on Timor, sent Ensign Jack Martin and his crew to Alor
to give Ogle a hand.[33]

Martin found the small bay on the west end of Alor without any
problem, but neither he nor any one in his crew could spot Ogle's
plane. After making two low passes over the bay without seeing any
sign of Ogle's plane or his crew, Martin landed. Taxiing along the
beach, they still could not see the plane and had gone right past it
when Ogle's crew ran out onto the beach, shouting and waving.

The rescue plane had extra tools and a few spare parts aboard in the hope that P-22 could be repaired. But an examination of the damaged engine showed it too far gone to repair, and there were no replacements. In every other respect P-22 was in good shape, but without a replacement engine the plane was a total loss.

Disappointed, the two crews stripped everything useful from the plane, including some engine parts. Before they boarded Martin's plane, P-22 was destroyed. The situation illustrates how hard-pressed PatWing-10 was. They could not afford to lose an airplane, but they often lacked the spare parts needed to keep them flying.

Again and again PatWing-10 planes were sent to the hot spots to report the situation or act as a radio beacon for army bombers. At-tacking in small numbers, and without fighter escort, the B-17s and B-24s were badly shot up. Distress calls and requests to pick up downed bomber crews flooded PatWing-10 headquarters. Typical of the rescue missions flown by the PBYs was the rescue of 1st Lieutenant J. E. Dougherty and his crew.

Dougherty had flown an LB-30 on a raid against Menado on 16 January. Only five planes—two B-17s and three LB-30s—had flown the mission, and two went down. Dougherty's plane limped as far as Masolembo Island, about halfway between Borneo and Java, be-fore it folded up and ditched. Dougherty and his crew, four of whom were wounded, spent the next nine days without shelter, medical treatment, or food, hoping to be found. But heavily over-cast skies and frequent storms had reduced visibility to nearly zero. Then on the 24th, a bomber returning at wave-top level from a raid on Balikpapan flew over the crash site and reported the position to Surabaja.[34]

Duke Campbell had just taken off, after his overnight stay in Makassar, when he was directed to pick up the downed bomber crew. Thirty minutes later his NAP spotted the dark form of a large plane beneath the water, on Masolembo's southeast coast. The sky was overcast, and the sea, whipped up by a strong wind, was very rough. A moment later Campbell spotted the bomber crew running from cover onto the beach, dragging their rubber life raft.[35]

To the men on the beach, the PBY looked like a miracle. For nine days they had survived on coconuts and hope. Now, weakened by hunger and exposure, hope was about gone. Throughout the nine days they had heard the sound of aircraft engines above the overcast as patrol planes and bombers flew along the Surabaja-Balikpapan route. When on the eighth day the lone B-17 roared low across their camp, they had been delirious with joy. But as day faded into night, they began to doubt that they had been seen. Now, at what amounted to the eleventh hour, a PBY was flying toward them at just 200 feet. They knew they were going to be rescued.

Campbell also knew they were going to be rescued, but he had to figure out how to do it without wrecking his plane. His first step was to pull up to the base of the overcast, head out to sea and dump the two 500-pound bombs he carried. When Dougherty and his crew saw Campbell turn away and climb, their hearts sank. But as soon as they saw the bombs fall and explode, they realized he was lightening his load in preparation for a landing on the rough sea.

The bomber crew was already struggling through the surf with their rubber boat as Campbell made his landing. Taxiing to a point about a half mile off the beach, the PBY turned into the wind. Campbell was taxiing forward slowly trying to hold his position until the men in the raft reached the plane. Heavy seas broke over the bow, inundating the cockpit windshield.

"We got them aboard." The waist gunner's report came as a relief. "Close the hatch." Campbell glanced at his copilot. "Let's go."

The copilot pushed the throttles forward. There was a pretty damn rough sea running. Green water was coming right over the cockpit, so we couldn't see a thing forward. We had full power, but it wasn't a normal takeoff. The plane just plowed through the waves hitting each one like a wall. We finally got up enough speed that we started bouncing, and finally bounced up into the air. We fell back, kissed a couple of waves, and then kept going.

The rough landing and takeoff had blown out all the plugs and patches in the hull. As the PBY climbed, water poured out through the reopened bullet holes.

Rescue and evacuation flights became routine as the rapid Japanese advance threatened to trap dozens of people, military and civilian, who were in isolated places. Few of those places were accessible to land-based planes, but all were located near a river, a lake, or a harbor. So the job of getting those people out fell to the PBYs.

Those missions were no pieces of cake. Because the Japanese had complete air superiority, the flights in to pick people up were made at night. Arrival was timed for dawn, followed by a rapid loading of passengers and an immediate takeoff. Landing in poor light, especially on rivers, was hazardous. Rivers twisted and turned, trees overhung the water, and there might be rocks and logs just beneath the water's surface. Lakes were a little less hazardous, but rocks, logs, and minimum room were often a problem.

Because of the danger of being caught on the water, the arrival time was critical. Generally, the Japanese land-based planes bombed their targets around noon every day, but the planes launched from Admiral Nagumo's carrier strike force usually came in around 0900.[36] It was, therefore, important to get away well before the bombers and their fighter escort showed up. That was particularly true when Ambon was evacuated.

Ambon had been considered by the Australians as vital to the defense of Java, and since December 1941 there had been 1,090 Australian troops garrisoned there. There were also 2,600 Netherlands East Indies Army troops, plus the RAAF Hudson squadron, and until 16 January a major share of PatWing-10's planes and crews.[37] Even after PatWing-10 had pulled out of Ambon on 16 January, the seaplane base continued to be used by an independent detachment of three or four PBYs commanded by Lieutenant Thomas Moorer. No tender was there, but the Dutch seaplane base provided fuel, beaching, and maintenance facilities.

But on 25 January the Japanese hit Ambon hard, concentrating on the seaplane base. While a squadron of Zeros worked over the RAAF base, eighteen Nells pasted the harbor area, laying waste the shore facilities. Living quarters, repair shops, and fuel dumps went up in smoke. The hangar in which Donaho's 22-P-7 was stored was smashed to rubble, eliminating any lingering hope that the plane might be salvaged. On the water 22-P-5 and 22-P-11 were shot up, set afire, and sunk by strafers. The only plane to survive was Tom Moorer's 22-P-4, out on patrol during the Japanese attack.

The Japanese had placed a high priority on the seizure of Ambon, and were clearly moving to accomplish that goal. Under intense enemy pressure, his small command nearly destroyed, Tom Moorer decided it was time to get out. Even as he prepared to leave, the Japanese again pasted the seaplane base.

We had fueled our aircraft and the Japs came over and bombed the fuel storage. All the fuel storage was on fire, with flames 400 to 500 feet high when a Dutch captain came down to see me. I was on the beach. He wanted me to sign a fuel chit for the gas I had used plus the gas the Japs had blown up. He figured that if we hadn't been there, the Japs wouldn't have bombed the base.

After the bombing raid, I saw we were going to get stranded up there. We knew a Jap cruiser wasn't very far away, so I loaded the crews into the plane and left.[38]

22-P-4 took off with thirty-six people aboard—its own crew, two stranded crews, and some Dutch naval personnel. After dropping them in Surabaja, Moorer returned to the *Preston* at Alor. In the meantime Captain Wagner sent two more PBYs to Ambon to bring out more Dutch naval personnel and a few civilians, including women and children.

John Hyland, flying one of the ex-Dutch PBYs, and Lieutenant Francis ("Fuzzy") Drake in P-13 left Surabaja at 2200 on 27 January. Arriving in Ambon after a seven-hour flight, the PBYs moored to buoys, and the pilots were taken to the dock in a boat. Stepping out of the boat, the Americans saw several people, their baggage stacked around them.

Hyland had expected the people, especially the civilians, to bring more baggage than they could take. His expectations were met, but the grand prize went to a Dutch officer instead of a civilian. Sitting on the dock among the mountain of baggage was the officer's piano.[39]

Clearly the piano was staying, and so was most of the other baggage. Despite protests that everything on the dock was "essential," the twenty-five passengers were hustled aboard the PBYs with nothing more than a bag or a suitcase each.

With the PBYs gone, the evacuation of Ambon was complete. The harbor was now empty, the abandoned luggage on the dock an international symbol of retreat. In the middle of the boxes, bags, and cases stood a lone piano, the representative of an era that had ended. Three days later, when the Japanese landed on Ambon, over 3,000 Allied soldiers went into the bag.

The Japanese facing PatWing-10 held a line that ran from Balikpapan, through Kendari, to Ambon. PatWing-10 was strung out along a 1,300-mile, east-west line extending from Surabaja to the Tanimbar Islands. The *Childs* held the left end around Soembawa, the *Preston* was in the middle at Soemba, Alor, and Timor, and the *Heron* covered the right end between Timor and the Tanimbar Islands. To the north, only Makassar was still open, but so close to the Japanese that it could only be used in extreme circumstances. With the airfields at Balikpapan, Kendari, and Ambon in Japanese hands, there was no place that PatWing-10's planes and ships were safe.

Operating from tenders, the PatWing-10 aircrews reported on Japanese movements, rescued downed airmen, and plucked outpost garrisons from the path of the Japanese advance. They were also called on to evacuate civilians, often whole families, from remote plantation sites. There was, however, one evacuation mission that the wing was asked to handle that should have been handled by the Dutch.

Before the war a nationalist movement led by Achmed Sukarno had caused the Dutch considerable trouble. As a result Sukarno and many of his lieutenants had been arrested and sent to political prisons that were scattered throughout the Netherlands East Indies. As the Japanese moved closer, the Dutch feared the jailed nationalists would fall into Japanese hands and work for the Japanese. They were, of course, right.

To prevent that, or at least delay it, the Dutch began to move the prisoners back to Java in late January 1942. As a part of that program, P-14 was sent to Banda Island, situated about 120 miles southeast of Ambon, on 1 February 1942. The pilots, Guy Howard and Harvey Hop, were to bring out five political prisoners and deliver them to the Dutch authorities in Surabaja.

It was a dangerous assignment for at least two reasons. With the invasion of Ambon in high gear, Japanese air activity around the island was very heavy. Secondly, the water on which they were to land was very narrow and restricted. Howard and Hop were briefed aboard the *Heron*, operating at the east end of Timor. They were to make a night, open-sea takeoff, land at Banda at dawn, and then fly to Surabaja. It sounded simple, but for Harvey Hop "it was the most terrifying experience I have ever had. . . ." The takeoff was the first part of the terrifying experience.

There were large swells running, and Guy elected to take off into the wind, that is into the swells. My instructions were, if we got airborne, to two-block the throttles to try to keep us airborne. A daytime open sea takeoff is tough enough, but at least when you bounce off a swell you can judge your height and nose position, and pray. At night you don't know if you bounced ten or fifty feet into the air. After ten or fifteen of the most crunching, frightening bounces and crashes, we were finally airborne.[40]

At least a dozen rivets had popped out during the rough takeoff, requiring that all the navigation pencils be broken into three pieces to plug the holes. An hour and a half later P-14 was over Banda Island and Howard flew low to check the landing area.

The place they were to land was on a narrow strip of water between Banda Island and a much smaller island north of it. The strip looked to be about 300 feet wide and curved to the north. Heavy jungle growth and trees lined both shores, overhanging the water. It was a tight spot, but at least the water was smooth.

Howard set the plane down and guided it around the bend, the starboard wing very nearly brushing the foliage along the shore. There was a small pier jutting out from the beach with a boat tied up to it and several people standing around. After the plane had been anchored, Howard went ashore to find out what his passengers were all about. It was something of a surprise. The five political prisoners were a Javanese family consisting of an adult male about thirty-five, two women, one of whom may have been his mother, and two children—a girl about fourteen and a boy about eight.

After the passengers were brought out to the plane and put aboard, Howard planned his takeoff strategy. He did not want to get out into the open sea again, which meant that he had to make full use of the calm water between the islands. Taxiing around the curve he came about and started his run. Hop was sure he felt the wing tip brushing through the trees as they sped back around the curve. Two-thirds through the turn Howard straightened out, "gunned the engines," and took off.

During the thirteen-hour flight to Surabaja, the passengers huddled together in the living quarters, accepting coffee and sandwiches from the crew. They were no problem to anyone, and the children were quite attractive. Some of the crew members experienced a twinge of regret when the family was turned over to the Dutch authorities in Surabaja.

Patrols continued up the Makassar Strait and along the Celebes east coast to the Molucca Sea. Sightings were frequent, large numbers of ships being reported daily. PBYs were regularly attacked by Zeros on these patrols, but none were shot down. But even though planes were not being lost, the strain was starting to show on the aircrews, as more and more men began to suffer extreme fatigue and frayed nerves.

Typical of the patrols flown during that period was the flight made on 30–31 January by Art Jacobson and Hawk Barrett. Flying one of the ex-Dutch PBY-5s, P-42, they left Surabaja at 0630 to scout Balikpapan. ABDACOM knew the Japanese were there, but they wanted to know if the Japanese had started their next move south. At that same time, Leroy Deede, in P-41, made a similar flight to Kendari to check on the movements of the Eastern Force.

When Jacobson and Barrett arrived over Balikpapan at mid morning, they found forty-two Japanese ships anchored off the port. There were no ships moving south, and none had been seen on the flight up the strait. Ducking in and out of some scattered cumulus clouds, they stayed over the fleet for twenty minutes, sending back their report. They were not fired on, and no fighters came up to attack. But with the ceiling unlimited, and visibility excellent, it was no place to hang around. At 1020 they headed north "with great relief."[41]

For the next three and a half hours they patrolled north up Makassar Strait, to Mangkalihat, crossed to the east side of the strait, and flew south. At 1314 they strafed a Japanese barge near the south end of Makassar Strait, and then turned toward Makassar. At that point they were told to return to Balikpapan "to track and give disposition of enemy forces."

No one aboard P-42 appreciated being sent back to Balikpapan to redo what they had just done less than four hours earlier. They had been lucky the first time, and no one expected to have the same luck again. Time was also against them. It would be dark in four and a

half or five hours, about the time it would take to fly back to Balikpapan, "take a peek," and then fly to Makassar.

Tired and discouraged, "but duty bound," they turned back. At
1520 they again made contact, and tried to get closer to determine
"what rumors" had caused the staff to ask for course and speed. Maneuvering among the scattered clouds at 7,000 feet the PBY flew
within four miles of the fleet center. The whole fleet "lay at rest,
just as it had that morning." The ships were not moving, but the
fighters were.

Suddenly a waist gun cut loose.

"What the hell is going on back there?" Barrett, startled by the
burst of fire, looked aft. A Zero flashed upward, past the bow, continued up and over, and attacked again. Two more fighters attacked
from astern, their tracers flicking past the cockpit window. Barrett
had his answer.

Dropping P-42's nose, Jacobson dove for a large cloud, both waist
guns chattering in short, sharp bursts. Before P-42 reached the
clouds, one of the fighters rolled over, and dove for the water. There
were no other signs that it had been hit, and Jacobson assumed the
pilot was diving to cut off their escape below the clouds.

The PBY plunged into the thick cloud hotly pursued by two
Zeros. Both fighters fired until their target was completely enveloped in the cloud before breaking off. Jacobson made a series of
low-speed, 90-degree turns, popped out of the cloud, and darted to
the next one. For thirty minutes he played hide-and-seek with the
fighters, always working his way south. At 1613 he broke out of the
clouds, dove for the surface, and scooted toward Makassar at wave-
top level.

As they ran south they took stock of their plane. The hull and
tail surfaces were pretty well shot up, but there were no fuel or oil
leaks. There was only one injury, RM2c Charles R. Phillips Jr. had
a slight shrapnel wound. All in all they had been lucky again.

Their luck continued to hold. Before reaching Makassar they ran
into a violent storm that nearly wrecked the plane. Hawk Barrett
thought a crash was inevitable, and that they would never break
through.

But we did, finally, due to Jake's skill, courage, and everlasting hope. At 1905 we made a night landing in a stormy sea with no lights but our own.

The landing gave them something else to worry about.

I didn't realize we had so many holes until we landed. I felt the plane getting hard to handle on the water; I couldn't turn it. The plane kept sinking, so the crew took up the floor boards, saw the holes, and plugged them. After we pumped her out we were OK.[42]

Two days later, without a rest, they changed planes in Surabaja and joined the *Childs* at Koepang, at the south end of Timor. When they arrived at the harbor at 1530, the tender was still out, so they buoyed and waited. When the *Childs* came in that evening they learned that theirs was the only plane with the tender. That meant they would have to fly the long patrols every day until another plane joined them, or until they were relieved.

What Jacobson and his crew were experiencing was fairly common for many of the flight crews, and the men were starting to complain about what they perceived to be inequity in assignments. That was especially true among the Philippine veterans, but rarely among the VP-22 people.[43] The difference was due in part to the unusual rapport between all ranks that existed in VP-22, and the fact that the men from VP-101 and 102 had been taking a continuous beating since 8 December.

There were certainly enough aircrews to handle the flight assignments, though airplanes were in short supply, and several new pilots had arrived from the United States on 29 January. In fact, reading the PatWing-10 Diary shows that the assignments were pretty well distributed. There were a few men who were rarely assigned, and a few who never flew any missions. But for the most part, the distribution of assignments was equitable.

The problem was mainly the way assignments were made. Some men were on one day and off the next, but most found themselves flying several missions in a short period of time, followed by a down period. Discouraged about the war situation, frustrated over the Allies' apparent inability to act on their sighting reports, and often dead tired, the men focused their complaints on the men assigned to the several staffs that had been created along with ABDACOM.

It is an old story that everyone complains about the brass and the staff officers. The staff people are viewed as being out of touch with what is happening at the front, and are accused of having it soft while the lower ranks fight the war. That was the view many Pat-Wing-10 pilots had about their staff officers. Though not really accurate, the fact that the viewpoint existed is understandable.

The planes they flew were unsuited for the role they had been given. But there was no way out of it in January 1942. Flying slow, virtually defenseless planes into airspace totally dominated by the enemy, subjected the aircrews to tremendous stress. In many cases their contacts with the Dutch added to the stress.

Dutch-American relations at the working level were complicated; no single word, good or bad, can describe them. At some levels the relations were excellent, while at others they were poor. Generally, however, the two nationalities worked well together and cooperated. But the Americans were sensitive to Dutch complaints about America's war effort. The Dutch were unhappy with America's performance, and they let the Americans know it.

At the end of January, Surabaja had not yet been bombed, and life went on there as though there were no war at all. To the Pat-Wing-10 airmen the Dutch bitterness over having been "let down" by the United States was unwarranted. After all, PatWing-10 had been fighting the Japanese since 8 December, whereas the Dutch in Surabaja had not even seen a Japanese plane yet.

There were numerous petty irritations that added to the ill will and increased the stress. One was the Dutch insistence on strict uniform regulations. The Americans were a pretty shabby looking bunch when they arrived in Java, with nothing more than the soiled, ragged clothes on their backs. After arriving they continued their gypsy-like movements from tender to tender, base to base, and plane to plane. Under those conditions it was nearly impossible to maintain any kind of a wardrobe. Yet the Dutch continued to insist on prewar uniform standards, and tempers flared. The worst instances were several brawls between American and Dutch enlisted men.[44]

Many of the flare-ups and the complaints were the result of battle fatigue. It is undoubtedly true that many of the aircrews, especially those from the Philippines, were in need of a long rest. But other than a few days in Tretes, that was not going to happen. In fact, the situation was about to become much worse.

# 10

# Surabaja: Part II
# 3–19 February 1942

On 3 February, 138 Kendari-based bombers and fighters struck the Surabaja area, destroying five Dutch flying boats, six B-17s, thirteen Dutch fighters, and one American P-40. The loss of the fighters left the Allies with just eleven P-40s and a handful of nearly worthless Curtiss Interceptors.[1]

During the violent raid, only one PatWing-10 PBY, P-7, was caught on the water. Of the other five, three were on patrol, one was en route to deliver Admiral Purnell to the RNNS *De Ruyter*, and the fifth was in a hangar being repaired. P-7 survived, but a crewman, AMM2c Roger W. Kampfer, was killed.

Kampfer, William Gough, and a radioman were aboard the plane when the air-raid alarm sounded. Unable to get the starboard engine started, Gough ordered everyone over the side as the strafers were coming in. The radioman and Gough went out the bow, but Kampfer stayed aboard to break out the life raft. When Gough was just fifteen yards from the plane he saw Kampfer jump from the waist hatch. No life raft was launched.

The pilot was about half way to the beach when he heard someone calling him. Gough stopped, turned around, and saw the radioman struggling toward him.

"Who's calling?" Gough treaded water about ten yards from the radioman.

"Kampfer. He's back there." The man was out of breath and having a hard time. "This life jacket is useless, and I'm getting tired fast."

"You'll be OK, just take your time. It's only about fifty yards to the beach. I'll go back and check on Kampfer."[2]

Gough swam back toward the plane, his head out of the water, looking for Kampfer. He saw no sign of him. The pilot reached the plane, climbed through the waist hatch, and hurried forward. Despite the fact that the Zeros were still strafing, he climbed atop the wing and scanned the water around the plane. He still saw no sign of the missing mechanic.

As he stood on the wing, a fighter made another run down the line of planes, of which P-7 was the last. The roar of the engine as it drew closer, the rattle of machine-gun fire, and the clearly defined bullet path told Gough it was time to go. Diving deep he "distinctly heard bullets striking the water or the plane." Surfacing, he saw gas pouring from the port fuel tank, but otherwise P-7 appeared intact, and not on fire.

Unable to locate Kampfer, and directly in the line of fire, Gough's immediate concern was getting to shore. While strafers continued to beat up the rows of planes, Gough alternately dove to avoid the bullets and swam toward the beach.

The radioman had reached the shore exhausted, but unhurt, and Gough joined him several minutes later. Kampfer's body was recovered the next day. He had been hit just after he left the plane and, unable to stay afloat, had drowned.[3]

The raid on Surabaja was a sign that the Allied defense of Java was doomed. That same day the Japanese completed their operations on Ambon and began to move planes onto the old RAAF field at Laha. At the same time, the Central Force seized the Samarinda oilfield.

The Central Force was now ready to roll through the south end of the Makassar Strait, turn right and seize Bandjermasin. With Ambon secured, the Eastern Force was free to hook around the end of the Celebes and take Makassar, thus securing the entire length of the Makassar Strait. They were also well positioned to launch attacks on Bali and Timor. Their objectives were the Den Passar airfield on Bali, just 190 miles away from Surabaja, and to cut the air corridor between Australia and Java. When those objectives were accomplished, Java would be isolated and trapped between the Japanese pincers. It was only a matter of time.

Though the Allies were having strong doubts, they were not fully convinced that Java was lost. As long as Singapore could be held, a combined striking force made up of Allied warships might be able to blunt the Japanese threat to the eastern flank. At the same time air strength in Java, particularly fighter strength, could be built up by bringing P-40s into Java along the Darwin-Timor-Bali-Surabaja air corridor.

There were, however, problems with that plan. Singapore was drawing off much of the Allied strength, especially warships. Most of the British warships, tied up escorting convoys to Singapore or across the Indian Ocean, were unavailable to join a combined striking force, and thus reduced whatever punch such a force might have had.

Additionally, because of age and long service without needed maintenance, the remaining Allied warships were qualitatively inferior to the Japanese. Most important, however, was the lack of air cover.

The Brewster Buffalo, the Curtiss Interceptor, and the P-40 were no match for the Japanese Zero. And the Allied pilots were not adequately trained or experienced to meet the Japanese veterans of China and the Philippines. In fact, the last attempt to fly P-40s into Java was a dismal failure in which 60 percent of the planes were lost in landing and takeoff accidents.[4]

But on 3 February, those shortcomings were not universally recognized by the ABDA commanders, especially the Dutch. On that day Admiral Purnell flew to Vice Admiral K. W. F. M. Doorman's flagship, RNNS *De Ruyter*, to discuss a proposed strike against the Japanese. Despite the fact that the Japanese had complete air superiority, the Dutch wanted to send a combined force of Allied surface ships into the Makassar Strait.

At 1030, Leroy Deede landed P-27 alongside the Dutch warship. As Admiral Purnell left the plane he told Deede to fly to a scatter base and await his call. Forty-five minutes later, the brief conference over, P-27 was recalled, and while heading back toward the *De Ruyter*, stumbled onto a lone Zero.

Deede was at 400 feet when he saw the Zero, down on the deck, shooting up a bunch of native boats. The range now very close, Deede warned his gunners of the threat, while looking for a cloud to hide in. But before he could find a place to hide, the Japanese pilot spotted him and climbed to attack.[5]

The Japanese pilot probably figured he had an easy kill, but he was mistaken. Deede's gunners opened fire on the Zero as soon as it started its climb. Climbing head-on into the stream of tracers, the Zero reached 200 feet before it suddenly "fell off on one wing and flew directly into the water." It is hard to say who was more surprised, Deede and his crew, or the Japanese pilot. One thing is certain: Deede and his crew were the only people cheering.

The fighter had gone down like a rock, leaving only an oil slick and some debris on the water. Curious, Deede decided to land and "pick up anything of interest which we might find." Deede's curiosity paid off. Floating on the surface was a large piece of the pilot's chart. The valuable piece of intelligence was fished out of the water, and Deede took off.[6]

Again headed toward the *De Ruyter*, P-27 ran into a formation of Japanese twin-engine bombers. Flashing a warning to Surabaja, Deede headed for the surface closely pursued by eight bombers. As the hare and the hounds leveled off at fifty feet, Deede's gunners blazed away, putting out such a volume of fire that six of the bombers immediately broke away. The remaining two tagged along, keeping a safe distance for another five minutes before turning back to rejoin their formation.

Deede was not the only one dodging Japanese bullets on 3 February. Ira Brown and Don Chay, in P-43, had the "unenviable job of investigating Balikpapan."[7] Flying a parallel route up the middle of the Makassar Strait were Dick Roberts and Jim Nolan in P-44. Roberts and Nolan made it up and back without a problem, but Brown and Chay ran into a hornet's nest over Balikpapan:

Ran into two bombers and five fighters, and what a merry chase that was. They chased us into the middle of Borneo. Thanks again for the clouds.[8]

Both planes that flew up the Makassar Strait reported Japanese naval activity south of Balikpapan. The Japanese were clearly moving south to take Banjermasin on the Borneo side of the strait. To the east, Barrett and Jacobson in P-41 were reporting many ships anchored at Ambon, while they dodged antiaircraft fire from a patrolling destroyer. They then flew north, at wave-top level, through Greyhound Strait and ran into three more destroyers, a cruiser, and five transports. Again dodging antiaircraft fire, P-41 climbed for the clouds and headed for home.

The next day three PBYs were sent out on patrol from Surabaja. P-43 and P-45 went up the Makassar Strait, and P-45, flown by Ed Bergstrom, very nearly did not come back. South of Balikpapan Bergstrom ran into a large bomber formation escorted by Zeros. A contact report was sent to ComPatWing-10 while P-45 scrambled for the clouds. Closely harried by three Zeros, the PBY ducked in and out of the clouds, working her way south.

The Zero pilots seemed to have Bergstrom's number, because every time he popped out of a cloud a fighter was there waiting. Bergstrom's violent maneuvers to avoid the fighters overtaxed his already tired engines, and near the end of the chase an oil line broke. One engine dead and the plane riddled with holes, it looked as though P-45 had lost the battle. But Bergstrom, remaining cool and determined, continued to dart from cloud to cloud until the Zeros gave up and rejoined the bomber formation.[9]

Surabaja, alerted by P-45's report, was prepared for the air raid. Even men who had nothing more than a .45 Colt pistol were waiting to blaze away at the enemy.[10] But as the morning dragged on, no bombers showed up. The planes reported by P-45 had, in fact, been headed toward Surabaja, but along the way they came upon a better target.

The ABDA Combined Striking Force, under Admiral Doorman, was steaming to attack the Japanese in the Makassar Strait. The fleet, made up of three cruisers, RNNS *De Ruyter*, USS *Houston* (CA 30), and USS *Marblehead* (CL 12), plus eight destroyers, was discovered by the Japanese bombers near the Kangean Islands. With only four Dutch flying boats for air cover, the fleet was virtually defenseless.[11]

Japanese fighters quickly accounted for the four flying boats, while the bombers went after the cruisers. The flagship, *De Ruyter*, took a hit that knocked out her antiaircraft control, and the *Houston*'s after 8-inch turret was destroyed by a hit that killed most of the turret crew. But the *Marblehead* was hardest hit. Near misses jammed her rudder to port and opened seams through which tons of water poured. Two more hits ripped open her after deck, as the heavy flooding caused the ship to list heavily to starboard.

It was clearly evident that without fighter protection the Combined Striking Force had no hope of reaching the Japanese in the Makassar Strait. With two cruisers already badly damaged, it would not have made any difference if they had been able to reach the Makassar Strait. The Combined Striking Force was no longer an effective fighting unit. The only move open to Admiral Doorman was a retreat to Tjilatjap, still out of range for Japanese aircraft.

While the Combined Striking Force was being clobbered, the other two patrol planes were having their own adventures. Bill Gough had taken P-7 on patrol over Ambon where he, too, dodged antiaircraft fire thrown up by a patrolling destroyer. He got away from the destroyer without any difficulty, reporting two destroyers and two transports in Ambon harbor. But the picket ship had apparently warned Ambon about the PBY, because Gough was quickly jumped by half a dozen Zeros. Again, the presence of cumulus clouds saved the PBY, and Gough brought P-7 back full of holes but in one piece. It was the second day in a row that P-7 had escaped nearly certain destruction.[12]

In the meantime, Duke Campbell was patrolling up the Makassar Strait in P-43. His copilot was Ensign E. J. Pendola, who had arrived in Surabaja on 29 January with two other new ensigns, including Jim Nolan. This was Pendola's first patrol.[13]

Off Balikpapan they reported a convoy of fourteen transports in three columns, escorted by six destroyers. They must not have been spotted, because there was no antiaircraft fire and no fighters bothered them. A short time later they reported another fourteen-transport convoy with eleven escorts. Again they were not attacked. At that point ComPatWing-10 told them to look for a downed B-17 on Arends Island, fifty-five nautical miles due south of Point Selatan on the southern tip of Borneo.

The B-17, flown by Lieutenant T. B. Swanson, had bombed Balikpapan on the 3rd. Out of eight B-17s sent from Java only Swanson's had gone down, making a wheels-down landing, with one engine afire, on the tiny island. They had radioed their position, put out the fire, and waited.[14]

Campbell found the island without any trouble, and saw the

bomber crew gathered near their B-17. Using an Aldis lamp, Campbell's radioman signaled the men on the beach to come out to the plane in their rubber raft. The signal was acknowledged and Campbell put P-43 down on the water.

Unlike his earlier rescue, the water around Arends Island was calm, but there were other problems.

> The island was surrounded by coral reefs that extended quite a way out. We landed as close to the outer coral as possible, but it was a long way from the beach. It was too deep to anchor so I had to keep taxiing while we waited for the B-17 crew to come out. Since we were coming back from patrol, I was really concerned about running out of gas from taxiing so long. I also wanted to get away so that we would get back before dark. I didn't want to make a night landing at Morokrembangan because of the shallows, and I was concerned about going up the channel to the seaplane base.[15]

While P-43 taxied back and forth, Campbell and Pendola watched the B-17 crew still milling around on the beach. Growing increasingly impatient, Campbell sent another message to the beach telling them to hurry up. An answer came back saying they were destroying the Nordon bombsight and classified documents.

> I was getting awfully impatient, and I wondered why the hell they didn't just bring the bombsight out in the raft and set the damn plane afire. Our plugs were starting to foul because of the idling, and every now and then we'd gun it to clear the plugs.

After what seemed like forever to Campbell, the army crew pushed off from the beach, paddled out to the PBY, and climbed aboard. In the cockpit, Campbell waited for the plane captain to report every one aboard. No report came.

"What the hell is going on back there?"

"We're trying to deflate the life raft."

The answer stumped Campbell for a split second, but he quickly recovered. "What the hell for?" he demanded. "Cast the damn thing off, and let's go!"

"Well, sir, the pilot of the B-17 insists we deflate it and take it with us."

"I don't give a damn what he insists. Cast the damn thing off, we're going."

"Aye aye, sir."

The yellow raft floated away, P-43 turned into the wind, and started her takeoff run. Campbell's worst fear, running out of gas, was not realized, but he did have to make a night landing at Moro-krembangan. Despite the shallow water, P-43 did not run aground, and the narrow channel to the seaplane base was negotiated without difficulty.

Two hundred miles to the east, P-42 was also making a late return from patrol. Art Jacobson and Hawk Barrett had taken off from the *Childs* at Soembawa and flown north to Peleng Strait. There they spotted a lone freighter, but could not bomb her because P-42 lacked a bombsight. Turning south through Greyhound Strait they ran into three destroyers and two transports, "reported same and got the hell out."[16]

On the way home, flying just fifty feet above the water, bone tired for want of enough sleep, Jacobson nodded off. In the right-hand seat Barrett was also having trouble staying awake. Something snapped Barrett out of his stupor in time to grab the controls before the plane flew into the water. Opening the top window, Barrett sat in a blast of air and concentrated on staying awake.

Several hours later, P-42 landed alongside the *Childs*, taxied up to the stern, and started refueling. To the crew's delight, they learned that Howard and Hop had come out in P-27 to relieve them. Because P-27 was too worn out for patrol work, the crews traded planes, causing Barrett to record in his diary, "The boys can have our plane, and gladly."[17]

On the morning of 5 February, PatWing-10 had seventeen PBYs in its inventory. Six were in Darwin, five were at Surabaja, two were en route from Darwin to Surabaja, two were with the *Heron* in the Tanimbar Islands, and two were with the *Childs* at Soembawa. Of those seventeen planes, six were either under repair or too worn out to send on patrol. That left eleven first-line planes.[18] By the end of the day there would be only six.

As dawn was breaking, 22-P-6 and 22-P-9, based on the *Heron* in the Tanimbar Islands, started their takeoff runs. 22-P-6, flown by Lieutenant (j.g.) Richard ("Dick") Bull and Ensign William ("Bill") Hargrave, made a normal takeoff. But 22-P-9 hit a reef and sank in shallow water. The plane was a write-off, and PatWing-10 was down to ten operational PBYs.[19]

At about the same time, P-45 took off from Surabaja to patrol up

Makassar Strait. P-7 and P-42 flew to a scatter base a few miles out-side of Morokrembangan, and P-14 was still in the hangar under repair. Why P-43 was left moored to a buoy is not explained, but there must have been some reason for not sending the plane to the scatter base.

Three hundred miles east, P-41 took off from the *Childs* and headed north toward the Celebes east coast. P-27, renumbered P-4, was too worn out for patrol use and remained moored to a buoy. By 0700 all planes available for patrol were in the air. So were the Japanese.

At about 1000 22-P-6 arrived at its assigned patrol sector off Ambon.

> At that time Lt(j.g.) Bull said we would fly over Ambon, drop bombs, and then go on with our patrol. Bull took over the bomb-sight and I was flying the plane. We climbed to 12,000 feet . . . and could see it [Ambon] was full of ships. I thought I saw two aircraft carriers and many smaller ships.[20]

RM1c Claude L. Nelson sent out the contact report as 22-P-6 started her bombing run. Visibility was excellent with scattered cumulus clouds at 12,000 feet. As 22-P-6 approached the anchorage, a wall of antiaircraft fire rose up from the ships below. Fighters roared down the runway at Laha, rising to intercept the lone American plane.

Looking through the bomb window at the flak and fighters, Bull told Hargrave, "There are too many ships here. Let's get into the clouds."

Hargrave banked right, diving for the clouds. But the fighters got to 22-P-6 first. Hargrave "attempted to slip the plane toward and down under" the fighters, but that did not work either. 22-P-6 was taking a beating. Machine gun and cannon fire tore holes in the wings, fuselage, and tail.

Gasoline from a ruptured wing tank poured into the hull. RM3c Ralph Cusak was bleeding profusely from wounds in the body, right arm, and left leg. Then disaster struck. Just as 22-P-6 entered the clouds, the port engine stopped, and the plane started to lose altitude. Struggling to stay in the clouds, Hargrave dropped the bombs. It did not do any good. The plane continued to lose altitude. By now the crew was being overcome by the fumes from the raw gasoline sloshing in the bilges, and the plane was in real danger of blowing up. Hargrave told Bull they had to land. Bull agreed, returning to the pilot's seat. In the meantime a waist gunner, AMM3c Cliff Sharp clipped on his parachute and jumped.

When 22-P-6 broke through the bottom of the cloud and landed off the north coast of Ambon, there was not a fighter in the sky. Unsure of where the Japanese were at the moment, they set about destroying the bombsight and codes. Bull attended to the wounded Cusak, but was unable to stop the bleeding. With help from Claude Nelson, Hargrave broke out one of the two life rafts, intending to get Cusak ashore and find a doctor for him as quickly as possible. Bull, AMM2c Lloyd Bean, ACMM Herbert Oliver, and AMM2c Robert Muller were breaking out the second raft.

Hargrave, Nelson, and Cusak were in their raft, under the wing, when a Japanese floatplane attacked the drifting PBY. Machine-gun and cannon fire beat the hull as the three men leaped into the water. Instantly the plane exploded in a fiery ball and sank. Patrol Wing ten now had nine serviceable PBYs left.

About an hour after 22-P-6 had blown up on the water off Ambon, the Japanese struck eastern Java again. The seaplane base, Morokrembangan, was especially hard hit. Virtually unopposed, the Japanese stayed over their target for an hour and two minutes, dropping thirty-eight 500-pound bombs with devastating accuracy. Repair shops were reduced to twisted, flaming wreckage. An entire hangar erupted in a ball of fire when a bomb plunged through the roof, struck 22-P-1, detonating four 500-pound bombs slung beneath its wings.[21] Quarters, fuel storage, and fire mains were smashed. Two Dutch PBYs were reduced to trash, while on the water, P-43 was strafed and burned. Surprisingly, there were no American casualties, but PatWing-10 was now down to seven serviceable PBYs. And the day was not over.

While men were still fighting fires in Morokrembangan, P-45 was being shot down in the Makassar Strait. The ex-Dutch PBY had taken off from Surabaja an hour before the air raid. Four and a half hours later ComPatWing-10 copied a single three letter message, FOJ—attacked by enemy fighters.[22]

The eight-man crew had come out of the Philippines. Ensign J. J.

Hogan and Ensign Carl Hendricks were from VP-101. The crew-men, AMM1c William Herren (NAP), AMM1c Dayton Treat, AMM1c Claude Jonon, Jr., RM1c Charles Pozanac, EM1c George Gardiner, and AMM3c Kenneth McCrary were all from VP-102.

Apparently the plane landed on the water rather than crashing, because the next day the Japanese reported finding an American PBY adrift. They also said they had found a radioman on board, but did not say if he was dead or alive, or if the man was Pozanac or Gardiner. A week later, Ed Bergstrom, patrolling up the Makassar Strait, spotted a partially inflated yellow, seven-man raft. There was no one in it.[23]

Though the clues are meager, we can reconstruct what probably happened. Like 22-P-6, the Makassar plane was jumped by fighters and forced down. The radioman was probably killed at his station, since had he been wounded, Hendricks and Hogan would not have left him aboard. The radioman the Japanese found was probably Pozanac. Since he was senior to Gardiner, he was probably man-ning the radio. The other seven men abandoned the plane in a rub-ber raft, were strafed, and forced to abandon it. They may have all been killed or wounded in the water, and were unable to regain their raft. That would account for the raft being partially deflated and empty. We will never know for sure what actually happened aboard P-45, but one thing is certain, PatWing-10 now had just six ser-viceable PBYs.

As darkness fell on 5 February, PatWing-10 knew that two of its planes were not coming back. They did not, however, know the fate of the crews, and all sixteen men were listed as missing. There was reason for some optimism and hope that all, or most, of the missing men would get back. That had been the case so far. But it was not the case this time. P-45's eight-man crew was never seen again, and only two men returned from the fiery destruction of 22-P-6. That they made it back was something of a miracle.

After the explosion, Hargrave and Nelson rescued Cusak and Muller, and got them to shore. Sharp, who had jumped, was never found, nor was Bull. Bean and Oliver both died in the explosion, and their bodies were found a few days later.

For nine days Hargrave did what he could for Cusak and Muller, who were badly burned. Because both men were suffering terribly, and Hargrave was unable to find medical help, he did the only thing he could. He turned them over to natives who agreed to take them to the Japanese hospital in Ambon. Muller died before he got there, and Cusak's fate is unknown, but he was not seen again.

Hargrave and Nelson escaped from Ambon in a small, native boat. After 17 days, during which they dodged the Japanese, fought storms, and suffered from exposure and malnutrition, they returned to Australia.[24] Long before they returned, however, PatWing-10 ceased to exist as an effective fighting unit. But on 6 February there was still some time left.

PatWing-10's losses were indicative of the Allies' critical shortage of aircraft. There were so many Japanese planes, and so few Allied planes, that the PBY crews felt very lonely on patrol. Their attitude was, "If you see something flying, it's either a bird or a Jap. And if the wings don't flap it's a Jap."[25] On 6 February, Jack Martin found out how true the axiom was.

He had been sent north to count the ships at Ambon. Thirty minutes south of his goal, a waist gunner's warning got his full attention.

"Do you think that's our airplane behind us?"

"What does it look like?" Martin asked.

"It's a single-engine floatplane."

We knew it wasn't our plane. We were above a lot of sea haze, an atmospheric condition that offered us some sort of cover. You could see through the stuff, clearly, straight down, but obliquely or hori-zontally it was really dense and hazy. It was caused by the sun reflecting on particles in the air. Close to the surface our upper surface paint blended perfectly with the water—sort of blue-grey.[26]

Martin dove to within fifty feet of the surface, flattened out, and scooted toward a small island several miles away. Fishtailing to give his waist gunners a view aft, he hugged the wave tops, and ducked behind the island. Staying close to the shore, Martin made a 360-degree turn around the island, watching to see if he had been followed. Either the Japanese pilot had not seen him at all, or had lost track of the PBY after it disappeared into the sea haze.

While Martin took advantage of every bit of concealment to avoid an immediate threat, the Americans and the British were growing increasingly pessimistic about the prospect of holding Java. And they had every reason to be pessimistic. On 6 February six transports filled with Imperial Japanese Marines left Kendari en route to take Makassar. Admiral Doorman made a feeble attempt to intercept the convoy, but broke off the attempt in the face of overwhelming Japanese air superiority.

Two days later the Japanese crossed the Johore Strait, starting their final drive on Singapore. The British naval base was now surrounded on land and sea by the enemy, and smothered by Japanese air power. Singapore was so obviously finished that the Japanese went ahead with their preparations to assault Java from the west.

Events moved very quickly now. On 9 February, Makassar fell, Bandjamasin on the tenth. The Japanese Central and Eastern Forces, now linked up, were prepared to seize Timor, Bali, and knock out the Allies' main staging area at Darwin. While four carriers steamed south to attack Darwin, air raids on Surabaja and Timor were stepped up. Four days later Japanese paratroopers jumped into Sumatra, seizing Palembang, the only oilfield still in allied hands. Banka Island was also taken, giving the Japanese Muntok airfield.

While those moves were being made, PatWing-10 was forced to start its move toward Australia. The *Heron* and the *Preston* were pulled back to Darwin, and the *Childs* was sent to Tjilatjap to bring out several pilots and enlisted men.

On 11 February, there were twelve PBYs left, but only five were in commission. Six of the planes were in Darwin with the *Preston*, but four were down for repairs. The other six were at Morokrembangan, three flyable and three not.[27] The planes based in Java patrolled up Makassar Strait to Balikpapan, and east across the Flores Sea to Flores Island. Because of heavy fighter opposition, the Makassar patrols were made "by moonlight and very early twilight."[28] The planes based in Darwin patrolled north to Ambon.

On the same day that the Allies were pushed out of Sumatra, Admiral Thomas C. Hart was relieved as ABDAFLOAT by Admiral Helfrich, and as ComSoWesPac by Admiral Glassford. The changes in command did not materially affect PatWing-10 operations, but they did affect the fate of the wing's flagship, the USS *Langley*.

By 14 February American and British planners had accepted the fact that Java could not be held. Any lingering doubts were eliminated the following day when Singapore surrendered. The western pincer was now in place on Java's western tip. The only thing to be done before the eastern pincer would be in place was for the Japanese to take Timor and Bali and smash Darwin. Actually, the Japanese could have accomplished their primary goal without making those last moves, but they were being cautious.

The ABDA supreme commander, Sir Archibald P. Wavell, British general, had already been told that no reinforcements would be sent to Java, but material resupply would be attempted if possible. The number one priority for resupply was fighter aircraft. As a result, a plan was hatched by the army to send ready-to-fly P-40s to Java aboard the *Langley*. Marked by confusion, mismanagement, and a lack of communication between the several commands involved, the plan went into motion on 11 February. On that day the *Langley* left Darwin en route to Perth/Fremantle where she was to take aboard thirty-two P-40s. Aboard the ship on her trip to West Australia were several pilots and enlisted men who represented Pat-Wing-10's growing surplus of aircrews.

With one flank anchored in Darwin and the other in Java, and surplus aircrews moving out of the operations area, it was evident to everyone in the wing that Java was a lost cause. The question they asked themselves was how long could Java be held? The answer was, not much longer; the invasion was just thirteen days away.

If any further evidence of the Allies' inability to stop the Japanese was needed, that evidence was provided on the same day Singapore fell. On the evening of 14 February Admiral Doorman's Combined Striking Force steamed out to attack the Japanese west of Java.

The damaged *Houston* and *Marblehead* had been replaced in the lineup by HMS *Exeter* and HMS *Hobart*. Together with three Dutch cruisers, four Dutch and six American destroyers, they steamed through the night of 14/15 February. At 0920 on 15 February, the Striking Force was spotted by Japanese carrier planes and attacked at noon. At 1320 Admiral Doorman turned back, pursued by attacking aircraft for another four and a half hours. Surprisingly, none of the ships were damaged by the bombing, but it was the same old story all over again—without air cover Allied surface ships could not operate at sea during daylight.[29]

Those events had an impact on PatWing-10's planes and aircrews. The PBYs already had "critically high engine hours," and at least three were too worn out to use for patrols. That meant that a few planes were used to fly most of the patrols. For example, at Morokrembangan three planes, P-7, P-42, and P-44, flew all the patrols up the Makassar Strait from 3 to 18 February. On the 18th, an old VP-102 plane, P-25, was put back in service and picked up part of the load.[30] Without relief, and without spare parts, those few planes were literally being run to death.

A shortage of spare parts had been a serious problem since the start of the war. VP-22 had brought all the spare parts the planes could carry when they left Pearl Harbor. The *Childs* had done the same when she left Sangley Point, and the *Heron* had brought in a small supply to Tjilatjap on 17 February. That meager supply, plus what could be salvaged from wrecks, was all that was available, and that was quickly used up.

Like their planes, the pilots and crewmen were also worn out. They all displayed signs of being under extreme stress—jumpiness, a nervous habit or twitch, fatigue, or a combination of those characteristics, plus others. Several men were in such bad shape that they had to be taken off flying status.[31]

There were good reasons for the conditions they were in. The huge loss of PBYs was demoralizing, and greatly increased the wear and tear on the remaining planes. Ambon had been touted as the place the Allies would make a stand. Twenty-three days later they had been forced to retreat to Surabaja and establish a line of tender bases along the Lesser Sunda Islands. Then the line had been pushed back to Darwin and the initial move toward Australia started. Clearly, the war was not going well for PatWing-10.

Repeated flights into Japanese-controlled areas, and futile attempts to mount bombing attacks, had revealed the PBY's glaring vulnerability. How the men felt about the plane they flew and their chances of survival is recorded in several of their diaries. None of the comments speak well of the PBY. In a letter dated 8 February 1942, Frank O'Beirne wrote to his brother Emmet, "I'd like to see you all out here, but not unless you can bring really good planes out—and that doesn't include any PBY models."[32]

The long letter had described in detail the operating conditions in the ABDA area. Frank had told his brother, the executive officer of VP-21, what spare parts and equipment VP-21 would need if and when it was sent to Australia. It was an accurate appraisal of the situation and offered excellent advice.

Despite the grim operating conditions, and the PBY's terrible vulnerability, morale was generally good. But there were some men whose morale had fallen pretty low. They were the men who made most of their flights up the Makassar Strait. Because the strait was literally infested with Zeros, the Americans called it "Cold Turkey Alley." The name derived from the common belief that any PBY jumped by Zeros was "cold turkey."

It was true that nearly every plane that flew up the strait came back looking like a colander. But surprisingly few were shot down in comparison to the number of flights that were made. In fact, of the fifteen planes shot down, only three were shot down in the Makassar Strait.[33]

Nevertheless, the possibility was good of being shot down if attacked by a Zero. Thus, the combination of all factors—the regular presence of Zeros in the Makassar Strait, the constant presence of shot-up planes at Morokrembangan, around the tenders, and the staggering losses due to all causes—produced the "cold turkey" attitude.

There was another situation that added to the stress the men were under. To report Japanese naval movements, they flew long patrols and faced incredible danger. They did a superb job, often reporting Japanese movements hourly. But little action was taken on their reports. It made little difference to the men in PatWing-10 that the Allies were, essentially, unable to respond to the reports. The fact was, they made the reports and nothing happened. It was terribly frustrating.

Another depressing situation was the daily appearance of large Japanese bomber and fighter formations over eastern Java. According to Admiral Glassford, the daily air raids created a "critical situation" in which "it was becoming increasingly evident that Surabaja would soon be untenable as a base for surface ships."[34] On 18 February, Glassford shifted his headquarters to Tjilatjap. The harbor was only marginally adequate, but was, for the moment, relatively remote from Japanese air bases in Borneo and the Celebes.

Captain Wagner, his headquarters already relocated in Bandoeng, was preparing to make another move to Tjilatjap. At the same time twenty-two officers and men, mostly pilots, were sent to Tjilatjap to go aboard the *Childs*.[35] Lieutenant Commander Peterson stayed in Surabaja to control PatWing-10's reconnaissance activity "until the end." The end was very close. In fact the final act opened on 18 February.

The Allies, expecting the Japanese to seize Timor, had sent reinforcements from Darwin to beef up the island's defenses. But the convoy, without air cover, was attacked and turned back. Two days later, on 18 February, the Japanese were ashore on Bali, and the Timor invasion fleet was just one day away from its goal. To safeguard the Timor-Bali operation, and to isolate Java from Australia, the Japanese launched a massive air raid on Darwin. The raid's first victim was 22-P-9, formerly designated 22-P-4.

22-P-9, piloted by Lieutenant Thomas Moorer and Ensign W. Mosley, took off from Darwin at 0800 on 19 February 1942. Moorer was to patrol north to Ambon, 675 nautical miles north of Darwin. A second PBY, 22-P-2 flown by Buzz LeFever and AMM1c Maynard Humphreys (NAP), was to cover the Tanimbar Islands and Timor. The other three PBYs, P-4 (ex 102-P-12), P-8, and P-41 were being serviced on the water.

At 0920, while investigating an unidentified freighter fifty miles off Melville Island, 22-P-4 was surprised by nine Zeros. Diving out of the sun, the fighters nailed the PBY on the first pass. 22-P-9 burst into flame, the fire fed by a stream of gasoline pouring from huge holes in the fuel tank. The radios were destroyed, the port engine quit, and flames crept back along the fuselage causing the port blister to melt. The wing floats were knocked out.[36]

Inside the plane, Mosley was hit by shrapnel in the head, Moorer was hit in the hip, RM1c Ralph C. Thomas suffered a head wound and a broken ankle, and RM3c F. E. Folmer took a chunk of shrapnel in the knee.

PBY 22-P-9 was down to 600 feet and losing altitude fast. Moorer tried to turn into the wind, but all the fabric had burned off the port wing, making it impossible to turn. His plane was headed toward the water at about 125 knots when Moorer:

> . . . glanced back and observed large streams of fuel pouring from both tanks, and fire extending along the port side almost to the tail.

Ralph C. Thomas was a radioman aboard
Tom Moorer's plane when it was shot down
on 19 February 1942. (Courtesy R. Thomas)

Small balls of fire were bouncing around inside the mechanic's compartment, and the noise caused by bullets striking the plane was
terriffic.[37]

The flaming PBY hit the water, bouncing three times before
slewing to a halt. AOM2c T. R. LeBaron switched to the starboard
gun and continued to fire at the fighters. Folmer, discovering that
the big life raft had been shot full of holes, dragged a smaller four-
man raft forward to the navigator's compartment. Aided by AMM2c

J. C. Shuler, ACM J. J. Ruzak (NAP), and AMM2c A. P. Fairchild, the radiomen launched the raft through the navigator's hatch.

The fire was now so hot that everything aft of the wings was melting. The situation outside was not much better—huge patches of burning gasoline surrounded the plane. Fearing strafers, the men went into the water without inflating the raft. Only after they saw the nine fighters rejoin the bomber group did they pull the $CO_2$ valves. While they were in the water, they had time to count the planes. There were seventy-two, all headed toward Darwin.

Despite a last-minute warning flashed from Timor, Darwin was virtually unprepared for the incoming raiders. Several ships, transports, freighters, ammunition ships, corvettes, and the *Peary* and the *Preston* were at anchor or alongside the only dock.

The sound of approaching engines caused Ed Aeschliman and Tom Anderson to look up. They were standing on a scaffold slung beneath the port engine on P-41. Two other PBYs, P-4 and P-8, were anchored next to them. Across the channel the *Preston* lay at anchor.

"Oh boy. Look at those reinforcements."[38] Anderson had mistaken the planes, that were now in clear view, for Americans.

Hearing the engine sounds and shouts, Herb Casey poked his head through the hatch over the pilots' seats. Anderson was counting the planes.

"We're finally getting a carrier out here." Anderson spoke as he counted. Suddenly he stopped counting. "Those aren't reinforcements, those are Japs." Anderson's observation was underscored by three Zeros diving to strafe the three helpless PBYs.

The fighters were already firing when Aeschliman and Anderson dove into the water. Casey ducked back into the plane, dragged out the life raft, and launched it through the port waist hatch. As he worked, bullets and cannon fire peppered the plane. There were now heavy explosions along the shore. Shrapnel and falling debris rained around the swimmers.

Aeschliman and Anderson shed their life jackets and ducked beneath the surface as the fighters made another pass. When they surfaced Casey was in the raft. Quickly they climbed in. Urged on by the nearness of the now burning PBYs, the three men paddled hard to get away. Flaming gasoline, spreading across the water, was being swept aft of the planes by the swift ebb tide. Paddling against the current the three men slowly drew ahead of the planes.

The strafers came in again, the three men leaped out of the raft, and the raft flipped over. Caught in the fast running current, the men were swept past the planes, toward the sea.

By now the three men were widely separated. Swimming hard, Aeschliman made it to a clump of mangrove trees where he watched a P-40 pilot bail out and parachute into the grove some distance away. In the meantime Casey was tiring fast and calling for help. Hearing Casey's calls, Anderson swam back and rescued his friend. A few moments later a motor whaleboat from the *Preston* came along and picked up both men. A few minutes later Aeschliman was picked up, and the boat headed toward the beach.

Unlike Pearl Harbor, where the Japanese concentrated on the ships, at Darwin the main targets were harbor facilities, docks, warehouses, and fuel storage. The purpose was to destroy Darwin as a useful port. The Japanese, however, did not ignore the several ships anchored in the harbor.

When the first wave of attackers came over, the *Preston* was anchored alongside the three PBYs. Within five minutes she was underway, her antiaircraft guns hammering at the enemy. On the bridge, Lieutenant Lester O. Wood, the executive officer, was in command.[39] The *Preston*'s skipper, Lieutenant Commander Etheridge Grant, had gone ashore at 0800 to complete arrangements for delivering aviation fuel. When the first wave came over at 0955 he was in a launch returning to the ship. Halfway to his goal, the alarm was sounded, and the *Preston* got underway. Grant had two things to worry about—the safety of his ship and his own survival. Grant was in good physical shape, a condition that saved his life.

Wood headed for the open sea, quickly working the tender up to twenty knots. Moments after getting underway, Frank O'Beirne reported a group of bombers directly overhead. Wood conned the ship hard right to dodge the salvo, but was almost at once forced to go over hard left to stay in the channel. Charging down the channel, Wood saw the USS *Peary* on his starboard bow, 300 yards away. The destroyer had just gotten underway, moving slowly ahead, turning

Left to right, Ted Shuler, Jack Haines, and Charles Fraser. Shuler and his brother, Joseph, were both in VP-22. Ted survived, but his brother was killed after Moorer's plane was shot down. Fraser was one of the heroes during the Darwin attack on 19 February 1942. (Courtesy T. Shuler)

to starboard. Wood slowed to two-thirds, recognized that " . . . we had sufficient differential in speed to . . . cross outside and ahead of the *Peary*," and rang down full speed.

As the *Preston* gathered speed, curving right past the *Peary*'s bow, a Val dive bomber nosed over high above the tender. Dive brakes extended, its bomb swung clear of the fuselage, the Val closed on its target.

Heavy antiaircraft fire rose up to meet the Val. Machine-gun bullets splattered the hull and wings. A chunk of the canopy flew off, but the Val bore in. The bomb dropped clear and plunged toward the *Preston*.

At 1010 the bomb struck the *Preston* a few inches aft of "frame 137, main deck, port." The bomb exploded just forward of the after deckhouse, ripping a seven-foot hole in the steel deck. Flame and shrapnel fanned out, exploding fourteen 4-inch rounds in a ready service rack. The compounded explosion virtually demolished the after deckhouse, took out the ship's steering, smashed the after 4-inch gun, and started a raging fire. Ten seamen were instantly killed.

Gorden Ebbe was running forward along the port side when the bomb hit. The blast knocked him down, but the shrapnel that would have killed him killed the man behind him.[40] Don Burham was equally lucky. He too was running forward when the bomb struck, but was abaft the deckhouse. The deck seemed to rise up in front of him before he was knocked off his feet. Lying on the deck Burham checked himself for wounds, expecting to find one. There were none. The man lying next to him looked OK too. There were no visible wounds. But when Burham tried to revive him, he saw the man was dead.[41]

Jack Martin was forward, near the forecastle, when the *Preston* was hit. He remained on his feet, but a man near him was blown over the side. Running to the rail, Martin grabbed the man, who was still clutching the edge of the deck. Heaving the man back on deck, Martin found he had hold of a bloody mess, but one that was still alive.

The pilot cleaned the man up as best he could with some rags, and then told him, "Stay right here and don't go wandering around." Running to the aid station, Martin obtained morphine and quick instructions on how to administer it. He then returned, stabbed the needle into the man's arm, and organized a party to carry the wounded sailor below.[42]

On the bridge, Wood had his hands full. The fire aft was so strong that no one could reach the steering engine room, and his ship was without steering. Dead ahead, just 500 yards away, was an Australian hospital ship. At that moment the *Peary*, still only a short distance away, was hit. There was one huge explosion. The ship was instantly enveloped in flame, another explosion burst from the center of the inferno, and the destroyer simply disappeared. There was only one survivor.

Under intense pressure, Lieutenant Wood remained cool, steering the *Preston* with her engines. Backing down, he narrowly avoided the hospital ship and swung the *Preston*'s stern into the wind.

With no steering control it was found necessary to back the ship into the wind in order to have much semblance of control, it being much easier to turn the stern across the wind than the bow.[43]

1. F. T. Bond, 2. Ralph Thomas, 3. Ed Aeschliman. Bond was one of the few gunners to shoot down a Japanese Zero. Aeschliman was with Fraser during the Darwin attack and took part in the rescue of a downed American airman. (Courtesy R. Thomas)

Tied up at Darwin's only dock were two British ammunition ships, the SS *Neptuna* and SS *Zealandia*. Both were hit and exploded. The monstrous blast vaporized the dock, swept away warehouses, and sent a powerful shock wave rolling across the harbor. Lieutenant Commander Grant's boat was bowled over by the shock wave, Grant tumbling into the water. Grant surfaced, saw he was being swept out of the bay by the strong ebb tide, and swam to a buoy. Hanging on against the strong current, his arms and upper body lacerated by barnacles, he watched his ship fight her way out of Darwin harbor.[44]

The *Preston* was definitely putting up a fight. Wherever there was room, the crew had mounted .50-caliber and .30-caliber machine guns, salvaged from wrecked PBYs. In all, there were seventeen machine guns firing at the dive bombers. Before the battle ended they would fire a total of 18,000 rounds at the enemy.[45]

The harbor was now a mass of smoke and fire, littered with

burning ships and sunken hulks. Overhead the sky was filled with planes. Horizontal bombers flew in precision groups high above the others. Dive bombers dropped like hawks, and fighters looped and turned, attacking the few P-40s that were airborne. Others swept in low to strafe.

Amidst the carnage and destruction, Wood maneuvered the *Preston* stern-first toward the harbor entrance. Damage reports continued to come in, none of them good. All water, steam lines, and electrical cables abaft frame 137 were destroyed for a distance of about ten feet. Fuel-oil tank D203 was ruptured in several places, and the fire was now burning in the "immediate vicinity of 30,000 gallons of fuel oil, and fifty 500-pound bombs." The pyrotechnic locker was already burning. A scratch crew led by Lieutenant E. C. Rider was doing everything possible to bring the fire under control.

High overhead, shrapnel had cut the flag halyard, dropping the *Preston*'s colors to the deck. Looking up, WT1c W. E. Roache saw the flag fall. Snatching up the flag, he scrambled aloft, and lashed it to the mainmast. The apparently minor episode seemed to mark the turning point in the ship's fight to survive.

At 1030 Lieutenant Rider reported the fire under control. That was good news, but the fire was still hot and the *Preston* was still without steering. Until the fire was out, Lieutenant Wood would have to steer the ship with the engines. Dodging burning ships, sunken hulks, and dive bombers required all his skill. Luckily for the *Preston*, Lieutenant Wood had plenty of that.

Hand steering was accomplished at 1115, by which time the fire was essentially out. When first notified that he had rudimentary emergency steering, Wood intended to return to the plane anchorage. But two things caused him to change his mind. One was a report received from Buzz LeFever's 22-P-2 that a carrier, four cruisers, and three destroyers had been spotted 180 miles off Darwin.[46] The second was that the emergency steering was marginal at best.

Under normal conditions, the rudder was moved by a one-cylinder steam engine called the steering engine. Cables running aft from the bridge controlled a yoke that determined in which direction the engine ran, and thus which direction the rudder turned in response to the turning of the wheel on bridge. Those cables had been cut by the explosion. They could be replaced, but the same explosion had taken out the steam line that provided power for the steering engine. All communications lines aft and the power lines to the after two gyrocompasses were also gone.

In order to turn the rudder, a long steel bar, a sort of tiller, had been attached to the rudder post at right angles to the keel line. Several men were stationed on each arm of the "T" formed by the steel bar and the rudder post, and on command heaved and pushed the rudder from left to right. It was hard work, most of the muscle being provided by PatWing-10 aircrews.

Having resolved the steering problem, Lieutenant Wood next established a communications system between the bridge and sweating rudder crew, and sent a compass aft.

> A spare aviation compass was taken aft, and a system of hand signals improvised from the bridge whereby right rudder, left rudder, rudder amidships, and steady could be signaled.[47]

While maneuvering that way, the *Preston* was able to pick up a survivor from the USAT *Meigs*. The rescue completed, Woods brought the *Preston* back to twenty knots, passed through the submarine net, and made for the open sea. The time was 1145.

In the meantime Casey, Anderson, and Aeschliman had been returned to the beach by the *Preston*'s boat. Aeschliman had told the others about the P-40 pilot he had watched parachute into the mangrove swamp. He recounted how the pilot had been strafed in his chute as he descended, and it looked as though he had been hit. Anderson, who had also seen the pilot come down, suggested that he and Aeschliman find the injured American.

Joined by AOMM Joseph "Chopper" Smith, they found a rubber raft and paddled across the open water toward the area where the pilot had come down. By that time the second wave was over Darwin. Struggling against the powerful ebb tide they paddled through a rain of falling debris, shrapnel, and spent shell cases. Fortunately, the raiders were concentrating on the main harbor and not a bright yellow raft splashing across the water. Had that happened, the three men would have been caught like fish in a barrel.

They found 1st Lieutenant Robert F. McMahon, still in his parachute, hanging from a mango tree. McMahon had been shot in the leg, and though conscious, was unable to free himself from the chute. The three sailors cut the wounded officer down, loaded him into the raft, and paddled back across the open water. McMahon was taken to a hospital, and later he fully recovered.[48]

When the last Japanese plane was gone, Darwin was a gigantic flaming, twisted wreck. Few ships in the harbor had survived, nearly all the army and Australian aircraft had been destroyed, harbor facilities were smashed, and the only rail line had been cut. Pat-Wing-10 had lost four PBYs—three on the water, and one shot down. The *Preston* had escaped, but was badly crippled.

By the next afternoon Bali and Timor were in Japanese hands, and the final two-prong assault on Java was ready to go. As the battered survivors from Darwin made their way west toward Exmouth Gulf, and ultimately Perth, the evacuation of Java was moving into high gear.

## 11

# The Retreat to Australia
# 20 February – 5 March 1942

On 20 February 1942, the ABDA house of cards was about to collapse. It was common knowledge among the Allies that the British were about to pull out, and so was the air force. The navy's position was less certain, but noncombatant units and headquarters staffs were already in Australia, or headed there. PatWing-10 was still operating from Surabaja, with most of its remaining eight PBYs there. But the wing was, nonetheless, scattered and slowly moving toward a gathering point in Perth on Australia's west coast.

Both the *Preston* and the *Heron* were headed toward Western Australia, followed by the *Childs*, which left Tjilatjap on 21 February with twenty officers and one hundred enlisted passengers. At the same time PBYs started ferrying excess personnel between Surabaja, Derby, and Broome. Among the first to be shuttled west were the Darwin survivors, including Lieutenant Commander Grant, who were to join the *Preston* in Derby.

Grant rejoined his ship at 1140 on 21 February only to learn that she had been damaged when she hit a shoal entering Derby. The ship was watertight, but both screws were damaged and the port propeller shaft badly bent. Even with her steering repaired, the *Preston* was still a cripple, and the *Heron* was ordered to meet her in Broome to provide escort to Perth. At the same time the *Childs* was also ordered to Broome to assist the *Preston* and "land excess personnel."[1]

On the 22nd the British formally announced they were getting out, and General Brereton moved his headquarters to India. In Surabaja only two planes, P-42 and P-44, were available for patrol. Two others, P-3 and P-7, were at a scatter base eighty-five miles south of Surabaja. In Surabaja, a fifth plane was being built with salvaged parts.[2]

But 22 February contained an apparent contradiction. While Peterson maintained his headquarters in Surabaja and at the same time was shifting the wing to Australia, the wing's flagship, the USS *Langley*, left Fremantle en route to Tjilatjap. Tied down on her flight deck, and packed into the hangar deck, were thirty-two P-40s intended to bolster Java's air strength. As she headed toward Java, the hopelessness of her mission became increasingly evident. But bureaucratic bumbling, a total breakdown in communications between the various headquarters, and Dutch self-interest ensured that she would not be recalled. At the same time that Wagner and Peterson were trying to save what they could of PatWing-10, the *Langley* was steaming into a trap.

On the 23rd, Bill Deam and Ira Brown packed thirty-nine people and the wing's records into P-7, and taxied out into the channel. They knew now why P-7 had not been used for patrol, and they must have wondered about their chances of reaching Broome. The wings and tail were full of holes, the hull leaked like a sieve, and the starboard engine was loose in its frame. The plane's condition was typical of what the others were like. After two takeoff attempts, P-7 staggered into the air and headed for Broome.[3]

That same morning the Royal Navy announced it was pulling out, and General Wavell was ordered by the British government to get out too. But Admiral Glassford was ordered by the Commander in Chief, U.S. Fleet to report for duty to Vice Admiral Helfrich. The United States Navy was going to stand by the Dutch. Events in what was left of ABDACOM headquarters illustrate the confused, disorganized situation that accompanied the final collapse.

General Wavell had told Admiral Helfrich at 1300 on the 23rd that the British were leaving. That same day Rear Admiral Palliser told Glassford that the Royal Navy was leaving with the general, and that the defense of Java was being turned over to the Dutch. Admiral Glassford then suggested that his own chief of staff, Admiral Purnell, act as chief of staff to Helfrich, replacing Palliser. The offer was accepted, and Purnell was sent from Tjilatjap to Bandoeng, with instructions to be "prepared to remain indefinitely."[4]

But the next day Admiral Palliser received orders from London to "assume direction of H.M. naval forces in the ABDA area as the senior officer present." The reason for the apparent turnabout in British policy was evident in section C and D of Palliser's orders.

> (C) Withdraw the British Naval forces from Java when further resistance, in his judgement, served no useful purpose, and (D) make every effort to persuade the Dutch to preserve their naval forces by a timely and corresponding withdrawal.[5]

The change of mind directly affected PatWing-10. Obviously the British were not intending to make a last-ditch stand in Java. They just wanted to persuade the Dutch to give up a lost cause and save their ships. It was undoubtedly a good idea, but the Dutch were not going to go along with it. Regardless of the fact that the cause was hopeless, however, if the British stayed, the Americans also had to stay. That meant that the few planes left in PatWing-10 would have to fly patrols for a fleet that existed, largely, on paper. That was unfortunate, because the paper fleet was going to cost the lives of two PatWing-10 aircrews.

The first loss occurred the same day that Palliser announced that he was staying. With the Japanese operating from air bases along the Makassar Strait, and on Bali and Timor, daylight patrols were impossible. From 24 February until the final collapse of Java, all PBY patrols were flown at night. But even under cover of darkness the patrols were no picnic. On this particular day Lieutenant (j.g.) John Robertson, Duke Campbell, and Al Barthes were the three PPCs assigned to fly patrols. Robertson and Campbell flipped a coin to see who would fly up to Makassar; the other would cover Bali. Of the two assignments the flight to Makassar was considered the more dangerous. Campbell won the toss and the Bali flight. Robertson lost. Barthes, already assigned to a flight to Flores, did not take part in the coin toss.

Robertson flew P-42 north, arriving over Makassar harbor before dawn. In the dim light, the crewmen made out three transports at anchor and a submarine lying on the surface. Having accomplished his mission, Robertson sent a sighting report, and headed for home. Forty-five minutes later, ComPatWing-10 ordered P-42 to bomb the freighters.[6] It was a questionable order.

Ever since the massacre at Jolo, the debacle at Menado, and Dick Bull's futile, lone attack at Ambon, it was recognized throughout the wing that the PBY was unsuited as a day bomber. Experience showed that ordering P-42 to bomb would accomplish nothing, but would certainly put the crew in extreme jeopardy.

The order was not questioned, but Robertson must have given it a lot of thought. He apparently decided to make the best possible effort by waiting until there was enough light to see his target clearly. But that meant he would also be easier to see. Two hours later, before P-42 was even over the harbor, the PBY was attacked by fighters.[7]

Dodging from cloud to cloud, making maximum use of the available cover, Robertson flew relentlessly toward his target. Twenty-five minutes later, harried by fighters, he started his bombing run. The PBY was at 10,000 feet, rock steady, fighters swarming all over her, as the two 500-pound bombs fell away. Robertson noted one hit and a near miss before ducking back into a cloud.

For nearly two hours the PBY warded off her attackers, but it was just a matter of time. At 0716 P-42 sent a plain language message. "AM BEING ATTACKED BY AIRCRAFT. NORTH MANY PLANES AND FLEET." Nothing was ever again heard of P-42 or her crew.[8]

When the other two planes returned, Campbell reported lots of fighter activity on and around Bali. Barthes told about running into a cruiser, seven destroyers, and four submarines headed toward Bali, and had flak holes in his plane to prove it. Having made their reports, the pilots flew their planes to a scatter base. Shortly after they had taken off, fifty-four Nells and Bettys pasted the Navy Yard.

The loss of Robertson and his crew was a sad loss for PatWing-10, but there was hope that they might get them back. That had happened often enough before, and on 24 February it had happened again. Lieutenant Tom Moorer and his crew had been rescued by an Australian patrol boat. After being shot down, on the

19th, Moorer and his crew were picked up by the SS *Florence D.*, the freighter they had been investigating. Almost at once that ship was attacked and went down, putting the airmen back into the water.

Their experience in the water, still close to the *Florence D.*, was terrifying and painful.

> The attack continued and three bombs missed the ship and fell in my immediate vicinity, throwing great columns of water over all the men . . . It is impossible to describe the sensation experienced when in the water adjacent to the explosion of a 500-pound bomb. The pain is terrific in the testicles, stomach, back, and chest, and results in coughing and spitting blood.[9]

One of Moorer's crewmen, AM2c Joseph Shuler, died when a bomb exploded almost on top of him.

After an hour the Japanese went away, and two of the ship's boats picked up the swimmers. Commenting later, Moorer wrote, "Faced with the prospect of a sixty-mile swim, I was happy to observe that the crew . . . succeeded in lowering two life boats."

But conditions in the boats were grim. The native crewmen were in a state of panic, and many were badly burned. Because the ship's captain was badly burned, Tom Moorer took command of one boat, and assigned Mosley to the other. Things were far from organized, however. Terrified and unable to understand English, the native boatmen could not be made to row the boats properly. Finally ACMM Joe Ruzak manned the stroke oar while offering Tom Moorer many good suggestions on how to organize the natives. Progress was just being made when the Japanese roared low across the life boats to strafe the hulk of the *Florence D.* Instantly, every native strong enough to hurl himself over the side went into the water. The rescue process had to be repeated.

After an exhausting search for survivors, Moorer set course for an island he knew was close. Just before dark they sighted land, and were, in turn, spotted.

> At this time a plane came up from the south and circled the sunken ship. It then headed toward the life boats at which time I recognized it as a Lockheed Hudson. The Filipinos again attempted to go overboard, but were restrained with great effort.

The Hudson sent a signal that no one in the boat could read, but at least they had been spotted and that was reassuring. By 2400 they were ashore on Bathurst Island, and in bad shape.

> Ten men were suffering from major burns and about five were burned slightly. Thomas had further injured his ankle when he jumped overboard and was running a high fever . . . There was no medicine, no blankets, only a small amount of water which was instantly consumed by the injured, and a large quantity of condensed milk and crackers.

At 0800 the following morning, 20 February, Moorer led an attempt to walk around the west coast of Bathurst to the mission on the southeast coast of the island. The attempt ended in failure fifteen hard miles from its starting point. The return trip took the rest of the day, being completed the next morning, 21 February, after an overnight stop.

On the afternoon of 21 February, they were again spotted by an RAAF Hudson. Frantically clawing at the sand, the airmen spelled out a message that identified them and told their urgent need for food and water. Later in the day a plane dropped supplies and a note telling them that a boat would get them in the morning.

At 0700 the next morning a subchaser, HMAS *Warranambool*, appeared offshore and sent a small sailboat in to the beach. Seven airmen and five injured Filipino seamen were in the sailboat when a Japanese flying boat, appearing unexpectedly, dropped two 200-pound bombs. The bombs missed, the *Warranambool* made smoke, and the patrol plane flew away. From that point forward everything went according to plan, the rescued airmen arriving in Darwin at 0100 on 23 February.

The second loss occurred on 25 February after two planes left Surabaja on patrol. P-5, flown by Lieutenant (j.g.) Hoffman ran into a bunch of twin-engine bombers that chased him for two hours. A little later he was jumped by Zeros operating out of Makassar.[10] Hoffman made it back. The other plane, flown by Lieutenant (j.g.) Robinson, simply disappeared somewhere around Bali.[11]

That same day General Wavell left Java for India, and ABDACOM ceased to exist. Wavell's departure also signaled the start of the exodus. Though Admiral Glassford was obliged to stand by Admiral Helfrich until released, he ordered as many navy ships and personnel to Australia as he could. Among those sent to Australia on 25 February was Admiral Purnell, a move that coincidentally saved the *Childs* and her crew from nearly certain destruction six days later. But it almost eliminated a future Commander, U.S. Pacific Fleet.

P-26 was assigned to carry the admiral, his staff, and fifty pieces of baggage to Broome. Because the takeoff was being made late at night, and no one wanted Purnell's plane to go on the mud as a result of a taxiing accident, a boat was used to guide the plane out. It was a Dutch boat with a Dutch coxswain. But for some reason John Hyland was also put in the boat.

The boat led the way down the narrow channel, the PBY following closely. What nobody realized was that the boat had a top speed that was a little slower than the PBY's taxiing speed. It was a fact that John Hyland started to notice very quickly.

Glancing back frequently, Hyland saw the big PBY getting closer and closer. The Dutch coxswain stared ahead unaware that his boat was about to be run down. The PBY was nearly on top of the boat, and Hyland had just exclaimed, "God Almighty, they're going to chop us to pieces," when the Dutch seaman saw the danger. Putting the helm hard over he veered out of the channel as the PBY taxied through the spot the boat had just vacated.[12]

That same night Charles Hoffman flew more evacuees to Broome, and on the morning of 26 February John Hyland flew P-3 out of Surabaja with another seventeen on board. There was now only one plane left in Surabaja, 22-P-12, and it was still being repaired with parts from a wrecked Dutch PBY. The other five planes were in Broome along with the *Heron* and the *Preston*. The *Childs* was due to arrive about noon.[13]

Broome had become a major collecting point for military evacuees and a growing number of civilian refugees from Java. Its choice as a collection point was one of necessity rather than one based on the port's merits. Located on Roebuck Bay, Broome was a pearling center on Australia's northwest coast. Before the war the town had a population of 1,700 that included 600 Japanese pearl fishermen. Now the Japanese were interned in Perth, and most of the civilians had moved away.[14]

The harbor was equipped with a single pier that at high water extended about a half mile into the bay. But because of a twenty-nine-foot tidal range, at low water the pier ended about a half mile from the bay. Anchoring ships and flying boats off Broome required that their captains pay attention. Otherwise, at low water they ended up high and dry on acres of mud.[15]

Since the war started, the Australians had built an airfield at Broome, capable of handling B-24s and B-17s. In the harbor there were three mooring buoys for seaplanes, a limited ferry service operated by Qantas to take people from the flying boats to shore, and a single refueling lighter. The harbor had never been intended to handle a large volume of traffic.

But since the loss of Darwin, Broome had become the most important staging and refueling point on the evacuation route from Java. As many as fifty-seven planes per day were arriving in Broome, and in one day nearly 8,000 people.[16] People flown out of Java were taken to Broome where they were sorted out and sent on to Perth. Because of the sudden influx, the town was jammed with people, and even overnight housing was virtually impossible to find. For that reason nearly everyone who arrived in flying boats remained on board until the planes were refueled. That often took as long as twelve hours.

Both the *Preston* and the *Heron* were scheduled to depart for Perth on the 26th. The *Childs's* mission was unclear, but it looked as if she might stay in Broome and tend the flying boats that were using the port. That was certainly a good idea, since servicing facilities for flying boats were extremely limited and the tender would have greatly eased the problem.

But from the moment he arrived, Lieutenant Commander Pratt did not like the setup in Broome. In his opinion, Broome, with its concentration of people, planes, and ships, was an inviting target. He was sure that the Japanese would hit the port any day, and if the *Childs* were there she would be sunk. He was absolutely right on the first two points, and probably right on the third.

Pratt's idea was to leave one of the ship's boats, equipped to service planes, in Broome. The *Childs* would move to a place that was farther away and less likely to be attacked. There the *Childs* could tend seaplanes in relative safety, either sending them on patrol, or acting as a way station on the route to Perth.

It was a good plan, but without authorization Pratt could not put it into effect. So, shortly after his ship was safely anchored in deep water, he went ashore to see what he could do about getting his idea approved. After a long, hot, dusty walk through what looked like an "Arizona cow town," he came to a nondescript shack. Over the door was an improvised sign, "U.S. NAVY HEADQUARTERS." Entering, he found Admiral Purnell seated in a wooden chair, his suitcase beside him. The admiral was alone.

"Admiral, what are you doing here?"

"Doc, I can ask you the same question."

Before Pratt could answer, Admiral Purnell said that he was "more or less stuck" in Broome and needed to get to Perth. Pratt then explained his situation, pointing out that if the Japanese hit Broome the *Childs* was almost certainly going to be lost. He then went on to explain his alternate solution.

"Well, what are you waiting for?" Purnell said, getting out of the chair and picking up his suitcase.

Doc Pratt's foresight in leaving behind a boat when the *Childs* left Broome resulted in many lives being saved on 3 March 1942. (Courtesy T. Pollock)

Returning to the *Childs* with the admiral, Pratt had a boat, manned and supplied to service planes, put in the water, and he prepared to get underway. At 1745 the *Childs*, "with the authority of the senior Asiatic Fleet officer present," steamed out of Roebuck Bay and turned southwest toward Exmouth Gulf. Doc Pratt's coincidental meeting with Admiral Purnell accomplished two things. It saved his ship, and the boat he left behind saved dozens of lives five days later.[17]

The confusion that attended the evacuation of Java had worked out to be a stroke of luck for Doc Pratt. But for Commander Robert P. McConnell and the *Langley*, the resulting confusion was a fatal trap. While the *Childs* was steaming toward Exmouth Gulf, the *Langley* was starting her night run into Tjilatjap. It was imperative that she make the last 120 miles under cover of darkness to avoid being caught by Japanese planes. But during the night McConnell received orders, later rescinded, that forced him to double back for several hours. Going first one way and then another, the *Langley* found herself still 120 miles out at sea when the sun rose.

As the sun rose higher in the clear sky, the *Langley* met the destroyers that had been sent to escort her into Tjilatjap, the USS *Edsall* and the USS *Whipple*. At noon the inevitable happened— seventeen twin-engine bombers, escorted by Zeros, appeared overhead. The *Langley*'s crew went to general quarters, while the *Edsall* and the *Whipple* moved away from what was clearly the primary target.[18]

Machine-gun tracers arched above the three ships, and occasional black flak bursts splotched the blue, tropical sky. But the anti-aircraft fire was much too low to bother the Japanese, who took great care in setting up their attack. The *Langley* was making 13 knots, moving ahead in a straight line, when the Japanese dropped the first salvo. As the bombs fell away, Commander McConnell ordered the helm hard over, right. Columns of water rose up near the tender's bow as she swung away from the target zone. The bombers lined up for another run.

On the third pass, five 500-pound bombs struck the *Langley* from bow to stern. The hangar deck became an inferno, the flight deck was smashed, fire mains ruptured, and a huge fire burned fiercely on the stern. With her rudder jammed to port, trailing dense black

The USS *Langley*, shown here in the background as a recreation party goes ashore, was unsuited for operations in the combat zone. Nevertheless, she was sent on a pointless, one-way mission to Java as the Japanese closed in. She was sunk on 27 February 1942. (Courtesy Gordon Ebbe)

smoke, the *Langley* steamed in a circle, losing way. She was soon dead in the water, burning, and listing to port.

An hour later she was abandoned. Between 1340 and 1400 on 27 February 1942, the *Whipple* fired five 4-inch rounds and two torpedoes into the hulk. As the two destroyers, packed with *Langley* survivors, cleared the area, the *Langley* was down by the bow and burning. Ironically, the tender that had been kept in Australia because she was too vulnerable was the only PatWing-10 tender to be sunk by the Japanese.

At about the same time that the *Langley* was being attacked, the *Childs* was dodging bombs dropped by a Japanese flying boat. After shadowing the tender for a while, the plane made a run, attacking from the port beam. Pratt turned into the attack, the bombs missed, and the flying boat flew away toward Broome.[19]

On the afternoon of 27 February, PatWing-10 was still scattered from Java to Australia, and along the Australian coast from Broome to Perth. Two planes, P-7 and P-26, plus their crews were still in

Broome. The *Heron*, the *Preston*, and the *Childs* were either approaching Exmouth Gulf or just arriving. And a small group of early arrivals were setting up a base on the Swan River in Perth. The *Langley* survivors were aboard two destroyers in the Indian Ocean, and three planes, P-5, P-10, and P-46, were in Surabaja.[20]

The Japanese were also on the move. While the Allies were pulling out of Java, the Japanese invasion fleets moved toward assault positions on the west and east ends of Java. At 1427 a Dutch patrol plane reported a large Japanese convoy near Bawean Island. At 1500 Admiral Doorman's Combined Striking Force cleared the Surabaja minefield and steamed to meet the enemy.

Admiral Doorman had, on 26 February, asked that a B-24 be sent out, with naval observers aboard, to scout for the Japanese. But none was sent, the order to evacuate having been given instead. Thus, when the Combined Striking Force headed into the Java Sea, the ships had no air cover and no reconnaissance planes out ahead.[21]

At 1612 Doorman's force engaged the Japanese. For nearly an hour the two sides maneuvered and fired, the HMS *Exeter* and USS *Houston* suffering some damage. At 1708 the *Exeter* was badly hit and forced to withdraw. Four minutes later the Dutch destroyer *Kortenaer* was torpedoed; she broke in two and sank.

By now the battle area was "in a state of great confusion." Smoke from burning ships and from a screen put down by HMAS *Perth* blotched the area. Japanese planes circled overhead providing Rear Admiral T. Takagi, commander of the Fifth Cruiser Division, with blow-by-blow reports. It was an advantage Doorman did not have. In fact, without air reconnaissance, Doorman had been unable to locate his main objective, the invasion convoy. What he had run into was the tip of the Japanese lance.

At 1830, when the antagonists separated, Doorman had lost two destroyers, one cruiser was limping toward Surabaja, and the American destroyers were out of torpedoes.[22] On the Japanese side, the destroyer *Asagumo* had been badly damaged and forced to fall back to the transport fleet.

ENEMY RETREATING TO THE WEST. CONTACT BROKEN WHERE IS THE CONVOY?"[23] The message sent by Doorman at 1857 was the cry of a groping, blind man. Without air reconnaissance he had no hope of locating the transports.

Captain Wagner, acting on his own initiative, ordered a PatWing-10 PBY into the air at 1900. Flown by Duke Campbell, P-5 located the Combined Striking Force at 1955, and then flew north to search for the enemy. At 2222 P-5 located the invasion fleet, northwest of Bawaen Island, and sent a contact report.[24]

Until that time contact reports sent by Dutch patrol planes had been delayed for up to three hours before being received by Admiral Doorman. PatWing-10's reports, on the other hand, were routinely passed on with little or no delay.[25] The difference was in command structure and the communications organizations used by the Americans and the Dutch. Because of superior communications, ABDACOM had relied heavily on the American PBYs. In fact, PatWing-10's performance was so superior that its planes were regularly assigned to the most critical sectors.[26]

But on 27 February, at 2222, something went wrong. P-5's 2222 contact report was delayed an hour and a half before it reached Doorman. By then it was too late. His striking force, already reduced by one cruiser and three destroyers, was further reduced by the loss of two more Dutch cruisers at 2332.[27]

In the meantime Campbell stayed over the Japanese convoy making a careful count of the ships. In the pale moonlight his crew counted eighteen, then twenty-four, thirty-six, and finally fifty-nine ships. The invasion convoy was so large that the "running time from the head of the convoy to the tail . . . took exactly eight minutes."[28]

Heading back toward Surabaja Campbell came upon the night action that was the second phase of the Java Sea battle. Below he saw dark silhouettes and flashes of gunfire. He saw ships explode and burn, but he could not tell who they were. What he watched was a half-hour duel involving two Japanese heavy cruisers, *Haguro* and *Nachi*, and two Dutch light cruisers, the *Java* and *De Ruyter*. The explosions and fires Campbell saw were the Dutch ships being torpedoed at 2332 and 2334. The *Java* sank in twenty-three minutes. The *De Ruyter* hung on until 0104.[29]

Continuing his patrol, Campbell saw two dark shapes headed away from the battle area toward Tandjong Priok. They were the already damaged *Houston* and the Australian light cruiser *Perth*. The battle of the Java Sea was over, but the two cruisers had one more round to fight—and lose.

Campbell continued his patrol until dawn on 28 February. By that time the Japanese invasion fleet was nearly in position off the Java coast, and Surabaja was expecting an air raid at any moment. Because the naval base and the nearby seaplane base were now untenable, Campbell was told to take P-5 to the scatter base at Toloengoe.

After landing, Campbell walked to a small restaurant where he telephoned PatWing-10 headquarters in Surabaja to make his report. He was already dead tired and expected to be tied up for a short time making the report. Instead, he was on the phone for nearly two hours.[30]

The holdup was caused by Surabaja's concern that the phone lines were no longer secure. Campbell was told to encode his report and spell it out over the phone in the same manner that it would have been spelled out by radio. Because the report was detailed, and ComPatWing-10 needed specific details, the telephone call went on a lot longer than the very tired pilot had expected.

Campbell was not the only bone-tired man. In Surabaja, mechanics were working doggedly to bolt 22-P-12's wings to a Dutch PBY's fuselage, and perform what maintenance they could on the two remaining operational PBYs, P-5 and P-10. That afternoon, the salvaged PBY, P-46, rolled out of the hangar, and PatWing-10 had three PBYs in Surabaja.[31]

In Australia the three tenders had gathered in Exmouth Gulf, where the *Childs* tended Hyland's P-3. Two other PBYs, P-7 and P-26, were still in Broome, standing by to fly personnel to Exmouth Gulf.

Throughout the day the Japanese invasion fleet moved closer to Java's north coast. The attack by the Combined Striking Force had at least slowed the Japanese, delaying the invasion by twenty-four hours.[32] Delayed or not, the outcome would be the same, but the extra day made it possible to get more people out before the blow fell.

And people were getting out. In Bandoeng, Admiral Glassford's staff was burning records, code books, and other classified documents. The Dutch were destroying oil supplies at Surabaja and Tjilatjap. RAAF and Qantas flying boats were shuttling steadily between Tjilatjap and Broome with literally hundreds of civilians and military refugees. Adding to the growing crowd in Broome were Dutch Dornier flying boats loaded to over capacity with women and children. At the U.S. fighter base at Blimbing, the Americans burned their few remaining P-40s, and grabbed the last B-17 out.

That evening the *Houston* and the *Perth*, having refueled in Tandjong Priok, were at sea en route to Tjilatjap via the Sunda Strait. At about the same time the damaged *Exeter*, the HMS *Encounter*, and the USS *Pope* were steaming away from Surabaja. They were also going to Tjilatjap. Four American destroyers, the *John D. Edwards* (DD 216), *Alden* (DD 211), *John D. Ford* (DD 228), and *Paul Jones* (DD 230) were escaping via the eastern route through the Bali Strait.

While the scattered Combined Striking Force was trying to reach safety, Lieutenant Charles C. Hoffman and his crew were assigned to fly P-5 westward along Java's north coast. At about midnight, P-5 reported the Japanese Eastern Force eight miles off the beaches at Kragan.[33] Acting on Hoffman's report, Captain Wagner ordered Peterson to evacuate his people from Surabaja to Exmouth Gulf. By that time both the *Houston* and the *Perth* were sunk, and the first Japanese troops were coming ashore at Kragan.

When the word to get out reached the airmen, most of them were in their quarters in Surabaja. Hoffman and his crew, still out on patrol, were ordered to return. Surprisingly, many of the men, though very tired, were not asleep. Tom McCabe, Nick Keller, and four others were in the *Chez Willie* drinking gin when Lieutenant Commander Neale came in and told them the wing was pulling out.[34] Next, Neale went over to the Oranji Hotel to tell the others.

In the meantime Duke Campbell had gone to the Polo Club to eat dinner. He had already downed "a few drinks" and was waiting for his dinner when Jack Dawley located him and said they were pulling out. Campbell protested that he had not had dinner yet and had not eaten for over twenty-four hours.

"You'll have to eat later," Dawley said, tugging him toward the door.[35]

Arriving an hour later at the seaplane base, Campbell found that preparations were being made to load about sixty or seventy people into two PBYs for the flight to Australia. Walking up to Campbell, Neale reminded him that he was to fly one of the planes.

"Look. I haven't eaten anything since yesterday, and I'm not fly-

ing anywhere unless I get something to eat." Campbell stood looking down at the Lieutenant Commander. Exasperated, Neale told
the stubborn pilot to get something to eat in the Dutch messhall.
Campbell hurried off to eat while the evacuation went on.

At 0340 on 1 March, P-10, piloted by Buzz LeFever, taxied
down the long channel, turned into the wind, and took off. There
were thirty-two people jammed into his plane. Two hours later,
Campbell followed in P-46, equally overloaded. Shortly after P-46
had left, Hoffman returned from his patrol and landed. He stayed
in Surabaja just long enough to take aboard Lieutenant Commander
Peterson, Charlie Eisenbach, and a few others. P-5 then flew to the
scatter base to await further orders.[36]

By mid-morning the Allied Naval Command in the Netherlands
East Indies had been dissolved. Two hours later Admiral Glassford,
Captain Wagner, and their staffs were driving toward Tjilatjap to be
flown to Australia. One hundred miles northwest of Bawean Island
the *Exeter, Encounter,* and *Pope* were being sunk by Japanese ships
and planes. Japanese troops were ashore at both ends of Java.

In the meantime LeFever and Campbell had arrived with their
passengers at Exmouth Gulf, and Hoffman was still standing by at
the scatter base south of Surabaja. At 1700 the *Childs* received orders to send all available PBYs to Tjilatjap to evacuate U.S. naval
personnel. Three hours later LeFever, Hyland, and Campbell were
on their way.[37]

As the three planes were taking off from Exmouth Gulf, P-5 was
taking off from Tjilatjap. Hoffman and his copilot, Ensign B. C.
Nolan, had gone there from the scatter base to pick up Admiral
Glassford and his staff. Still with Hoffman and Nolan were Lieutenant Commander Peterson, Charlie Eisenbach, and Peterson's
staff. Though the two staff officers knew what the situation in Java
was, they were not prepared for what they saw in Tjilatjap.

The harbor was jammed with ships of all sizes and types. On the
dock hundreds of civilians and soldiers were clamoring to be taken
aboard. The entire waterfront was afire, and heavy explosions rolled
from the area behind it as the Dutch systematically destroyed the
port and its oil storage. Amidst the smoke, noise, and confusion,
P-5 taxied to a service ramp to refuel. When the job was done, a
Dutch officer insisted that Peterson sign for the fuel.[38]

It was dark by the time Admiral Glassford and his staff were aboard. Despite warnings from Dutch officers that a night takeoff in Tjilatjap was "suicidal," Hoffman and Nolan taxied out into the crowded anchorage.[39] The Dutch officers had good reason to feel as they did. Tjilatjap harbor was little more than a wide place on the narrow, twisting, Shildpadden River. With only the light from the burning waterfront to show the way, P-5 shot across the crowded anchorage and lifted off.

Coming the other way P-3, P-10, and P-46 had become separated, and were heading independently toward Tjilatjap. In P-46, Duke Campbell had only a Navy box compass with which to navigate. John Hyland in P-3 was no better off. His only chart was a page torn from a World Atlas. But Hyland had even bigger problems. At the time he should have been over Tjilatjap, Hyland looked down and saw the Sunda Strait. He was 150 miles west of his goal.[40]

Other than time lost, Hyland was not too concerned. All he had to do was fly east along Java's south coast until he came to Tjilatjap. What did worry him was that his starboard engine had started backfiring and missing. He was caught between two problems. He had to land to repair the engine, but he "would never try to land in Tjilatjap at night." For the last hour he circled outside the port, nursing the sick engine and hoping the sun would come up before he went down.

At first light Hyland landed safely in the crowded harbor. As he taxied to the fuel dock, he saw people "swarming all over the dock, wanting to get out." While the plane was being refueled a man offered to give Hyland a new Cadillac in exchange for a place in his plane. Others pleaded to be let aboard, but Hyland had no choice but to turn them down.

After refueling, the crew worked about an hour on the engine, changing plugs. When the plane captain had buttoned up the engine cowl, Hyland started the engines and taxied out to make a test hop. Everything went fine at first, but then the engine started cutting out again. Worried and irritated, Hyland landed. It was now mid-morning and because an air raid was expected at any time the American PBYs were sent up river with orders to "nose into a bank" and remain hidden until evening.

That night the three planes moved back down to the dock and

anchored out. Almost at once several boats left the dock, moving toward them. Duke Campbell stood on the bow of his plane watching the boats approach. As the first boat came alongside, Campbell saw it was heavily loaded with baggage and passengers.

> There were twenty-six people in that boat—four admirals, a bunch of captains, and one commander. They were a mix of American, British, and Dutch. They came up to the bow and I saw they all had their damned luggage. I was worried about gas, and that luggage was heavy.[41]

"We can't take any luggage, only people. We'll never make it back if we take all that luggage."

The senior officers looked up at the tall, unshaven ensign in the tattered uniform. Quickly a captain stood up, a sword in one hand and a suitcase in the other.

"You heard what the man said." The captain threw his sword in the bay and dropped the suitcase. As the captain came aboard, Campbell heard more splashes and watched with relief as the empty-handed officers clambered over their abandoned luggage toward the plane.

His plane loaded, Campbell cast off the buoy, and taxied away. Moments later he was airborne. Hyland and Buzz LeFever were taking their last passengers aboard when P-46 cleared the harbor. Captain Wagner and his staff were aboard P-3 with their baggage, but Hyland could not get the starboard engine to start. After several fruitless tries, Hyland told Wagner that P-3 was unable to take-off.

"Leave it here. We'll take the other one." Wagner indicated LeFever's P-10 as he turned toward the waist hatch.[42]

Some time later Hyland, his crew, Captain Wagner, and his staff were aboard P-3. As senior pilot aboard, Hyland replaced LeFever in the left-hand seat. While the plane taxied out to take off, Captain Wagner sadly recalled his departure from Bandoeng.

> Prior to our departure, Commander Linder, RN, said that Admiral Helfrich had left Java for Ceylon. In saying goodbye to our Dutch friends in Bandoeng I noted no bitterness about the United States leaving, but keen disappointment and hurt over the lack of help from the United States. They depended on us, not the British.[43]

Had Wagner, or any other American officer been able to do something, he would have. But the fact was that the United States had done all it could—there just was not any more.

After a long takeoff run, P-10 climbed to just 300 feet, and headed toward Australia. Fully aware that the Japanese were out in force and that a carrier group was somewhere in the Indian Ocean, Hyland and LeFever figured their chances were better on the deck.

Two hours later, however, the Japanese menace took second place to an on-board fire. The two pilots became aware of the electrical fire in the panel behind them when the cockpit filled with acrid smoke.

> When the fire broke out I had a triple heart failure. All my engine problems and now this. The wind was blowing hard, making the sea very rough. There was no way you could land in that ocean because it was just too damn rough.[44]

The situation looked grim for several minutes while Spitzer and another crewman fought the fire. Then, as suddenly as it had started, the fire burned itself out. Everything seemed to be working, and everyone aboard gave a half-sigh of relief.

Many miles ahead of them, Campbell in P-46 was having his scary problems too. Fuel consumption was way too high, and one tank was nearly empty. Campbell told his plane captain to transfer fuel from one tank to the other until the levels were about even. When the mechanic opened the valves, raw gas spurted out, cascading into the bilge. When he tried to shut the valve, it would not close all the way, allowing gasoline to continue spraying into the bilge. After several moments the valve was closed, but raw gasoline sloshed in the bilge.

Campbell immediately put out a no-smoking order, knowing that P-46 was nothing less than a flying bomb. A short time later Campbell went aft to see what was being done about getting rid of the raw gasoline. As he stepped into the crew compartment he saw one of the "foreign admirals," an unlighted cigarette dangling from his mouth, patting his pockets in search of a match.

"What the hell are you doing?" Campbell shouted as he jerked the cigarette away from the admiral's lip. "This is survival. That's raw gas there. You light a match, and we'll all be blown to hell."

Before the startled officer could answer, Campbell threw the cigarette down and walked forward. There was no smoking for the rest of the trip.[45]

P-46 was the first down, and was already astern of the *Childs*, being refueled, when P-10 landed at 0615. For the rest of the day Admiral Glassford conferred with his staff, Captain Wagner, and Lieutenant Commander Peterson about the next move. It was their decision that Exmouth Gulf was too exposed to the elements and the Japanese to be a suitable advance base for ships, submarines, and flying boats.

It was decided to move everything to Perth. The *Preston* and the *Heron* were already en route there for repairs. The *Childs* was ordered to follow on 4 March, after she had tended the last PBY and sent it on its way toward southwest Australia. Along the way the *Childs* was to stop at Shark Bay to tend PBYs before they started the last leg of their journey. Admiral Glassford, his staff, and Captain Wagner would fly out that night, aboard P-10 and P-46, for Perth. Lieutenant Commander Peterson would stay aboard the *Childs*.

At 2300 Tom Pollock and a fresh crew boarded P-5, while Nick Keller and a new crew took over P-46 for a trip to Perth/Fremantle. As the two planes took off, the *Childs* sent a message to Bill Deam and his two crews in Broome telling them to come down to Exmouth Gulf. Unfortunately, the message was garbled. Deam knew he should do something, but he did not know what, and for some reason failed to ask for more information.[46]

With the invasion of Java, Broome became, for the moment, the most heavily used port in Australia. Its airfield and harbor began to receive aircraft in numbers that would set records in many large commercial airports. Flying boats of the Royal Netherlands Air Force, the RAAF, and Qantas were making, literally, non-stop round trips between Tjilatjap and Broome. One pilot recorded eighty-four hours without sleep during the massive air lift.[47]

People were being sent west as fast as possible, but the sudden influx vastly overtaxed the resources available. Priority was given to wounded, women, and children for the flights to Port Hedland or Perth. Those who had to wait had little shelter, little to eat, and a good chance of coming down with dengue fever, which had reached epidemic proportions among the refugees.

By 2 March the Qantas operations officer in Broome and most military men were certain that the Japanese would hit the port at any time. Their fears were reinforced by reports of evacuation planes having been shot down, or ships having been bombed close to Australia's coast. At 1500 on 2 March, a Japanese reconnaissance plane flew over the crowded harbor, and they knew their worst fears were about to come true.

On the morning of 3 March there were sixteen flying boats moored or anchored in an area about one mile square. Two of them, P-7 and P-26, belonged to PatWing-10, three were Dutch Dorniers filled with women and children, one belonged to Qantas, and the rest were either Australian or British.

At 0920 six Zeros came in low and fast over the tightly packed anchorage. There was no warning and no opposition as the six fighters blasted flying boats with machine guns and cannons. Immediately the flying boats started to explode and burn. Terrified passengers, mostly Dutch women and children, leaped into the water. Others died in the planes, shot or burned to death. The chatter of machine gun fire mingled with the screams of helpless women and children. Ammunition in the planes crackled and exploded in the heat and flames.

The long wharf was packed with people, civilian refugees, and service men. When the fighters swept in, many fled toward the town in panic, others hit the deck. Among the crowd was Al Armbruster, who had come into Broome with thirty others in P-7. Lying on the dock, Armbruster watched the flying boats go up in flames as fighters flew so low and so close that he could see the pilots in the cockpits.[48] Near Armbruster was Qantas pilot, Captain L. R. Armbrose.

> All of us on the jetty expected to get it any minute. We were powerless to help the poor devils in the aircrafts or those in the water. We just had to wait.[49]

The wait seemed to last forever, but in fact the raid was quickly over. Within five minutes the Zeros had destroyed all sixteen flying boats, including P-7 and P-26, and then roared over the town to attack the airfield. In moments, seven land-based planes were burning, including a B-24 that was shot down and crashed at sea.[50]

Even as the attack was going on, several small boats were moving among the struggling women and children. Most of the boats were rafts and dinghys from the military aircraft, a few came from the beach. The moment the last Zero cleared the harbor, more boats pushed off from shore. Al Armbruster was in one of the boats.

> After they were gone we started the rescue mission. We tried to get anyone who was alive first, then we collected the dead bodies that were floating. There was a little flat car on the jetty, and we stacked the bodies on it like cord wood. The wounded were horribly smashed, arms, and legs, the bones shattered. It seemed there was a bullet hole every inch up their arms.[51]

The sailors and airmen in Broome had all seen war and its result. But to many, the butchery of helpless women and children, the sights of drowned infants, and dead mothers clutching dead babies, was too much. Al Armbruster said that for him 3 March 1942 was the most horrible day of the war. Many others felt the same way.

Cullen Bray put the whole thing in perspective when he wrote:

> As a result of sinking of my plane at Davao Gulf, and sinking my plane again in Broome, I had only one thing left, a whole skin. That was the best of the lot I think.[52]

The attack on Broome effectively ended PatWing-10's war for many of the men. The survivors from Broome, and the ships and planes at Exmouth Gulf, were ordered to Perth. On 5 March half of the men who had reached Australia, plus the men who had survived the *Langley*, were sent home aboard the USS *Mt. Vernon*.[53] The rest, according to Captain Wagner, had "earned the right to stay."[54]

What selection process was used to decide who stayed and who went home is a mystery. Some of the enlisted men insist they were lined up, told to count off by twos, and the even numbers went home. Several officers who wanted to stay were sent home, several who had come out of the Philippines stayed. A high number of missions flown was no sure ticket home, though it worked for some. Hawk Barrett and Duke Campbell came home, while Tom McCabe and John Hyland stayed. Most of the Bataan evacuees went home, but Tom Pollock stayed.

Those who had "earned the right to stay" established a small seaplane base on the Swan River near Perth. But they had little to work with. Out of four tenders only the *Childs* was still in service. Only three PBYs had survived, a Philippine veteran, P-5, and two of VP-22's planes, P-10 and P-46. Actually, P-46 was only half of a VP-22 plane—its wings and engines being Dutch.[55] None of those planes were suitable for regular operations because they were simply worn out. The only useful planes available were two SOCs and an OS2U, left behind by the *Langley*, that were used for antisubmarine patrols. Tired and without adequate facilities or equipment, the survivors started to rebuild the wing. They called themselves "The Swan River Flying Club."

# 12

# The Swan River Flying Club
# 7 March–27 April 1942

During the next fifty-two days the remnants of PatWing-10 established a new base at Pelican Point, rested, recovered, and flew patrols. Formerly the Swan River Yacht Club in the district of Crawley, the new base was the ideal place for the battered wing to rebuild. Lovely surroundings, friendly people, and an informal daily routine caused the aviators to dub their new quarters the Swan River Flying Club.

> We have taken over the Yacht Club basin as our mooring field, and the club house as our headquarters. The club offers a beautiful beach for gassing and working on our planes, and also for swimming. Working in shorts, we all have a fine tan.[1]

Quarters were obtained in nearby houses and the Nedlands Hotel. According to John Hyland, the quarters were as pleasant as the Yacht Club headquarters.

> A senior group of us, Tom Moorer, Ducky Donaho, Harmon Utter, Jack Lamede, Nick Keller, and I, were put in a house that had been owned by a very wealthy Australian lady. The house had a name, The Bend in the Road. It was a lovely house, with a grass tennis court in the front yard. I have always been a tennis buff, and I had a lot of fun playing tennis there.[2]

The officers housed in the Nedlands Hotel were also happy with their accommodations. Within a few days they had recovered sufficiently from the rigors of war and diseases to "notice that Perth had pretty girls." One officer recorded, ". . . we have good water, lights and girls at hand. So it is heaven."[3]

They also had transportation. Somewhere, somehow, four jeeps had been acquired. But keeping them running was as much work as keeping the three surviving PBYs flying. And for much the same reason. The jeeps were subjected to hard service, as evidenced by one status report, "4 jeeps: 2 rolled by joyriders, 1 wrecked, 1 being used for dates."[4]

In addition to good quarters and an improved social life, the duty was easy. Because of the limited number of aircraft and their generally rundown condition, patrols were limited to one each day. Each morning a PBY patrolled to the northwest, while two utility planes made a forenoon antisubmarine sweep.[5] Under the circumstances—few planes and an excess of aircrews—the men had a lot of free time. Administrative duties and some special assignments took little

In Perth, PatWing-10 set up a base at the Swan River Yacht Club. The facilities were very pleasant and gave the battle-weary airmen a much needed rest. They called themselves the Swan River Flying Club. (Courtesy J. Antonides)

The airmen enjoyed a relaxed duty schedule, but the maintenance and repair crew headed by Joseph Antonides worked from morning until night.
They had to build from scratch a complete set of workshops and repair
facilities. This shop is set up in an old stable. (Courtesy J. Antonides)

of their time. In fact, the atmosphere was so relaxed that they made
up and posted a dummy duty roster.

> We had a roster that somebody dreamed up. One guy was assigned
> as the officer in charge of bicycles, and we only had one bicycle.
> Another officer was in charge of flashlights, and he had two as-
> sistants—one for batteries and one for bulbs. The list went on and
> on so that every officer had some silly responsibility assigned to
> him.[6]

Though the aircrews had a relaxed work schedule, that was not
the case for Joseph Antonides and his busy maintenance crew. Their
job was to create seaplane service facilities, scrounge spare parts,
and get the three PBYs back into shape. It was a big job, accomplished with a lot of ingenuity.

Antonides' people built a nose hangar, set up a complete machine shop, and a sheet metal shop. There was, however, one vitally important item missing. The rivets used to grip the seams in PBY hulls and wings had to be softened before they were driven, but Antonides had no way to do that.

A stop-gap solution was found when they located a man in Perth who made and repaired artificial limbs. He heated his rivets in a ceramic bowl, with a blow torch. An arrangement was made whereby he would heat the rivets for PatWing-10 as they were needed, but the process was limited in capacity, and slow. It was also necessary to pack the softened rivets in ice for transportation back to Pelican Point.

Always on the lookout for a good thing, Antonides' scroungers found what they needed in a shop aboard the USS *Wright*. The old ship was scheduled to be scrapped, and everything in her was there for the taking. It was a gold mine of aircraft parts, shop equipment, and hardware.

> One of the things we got was a salt bath that you need to soften and heat-treat rivets before you drive them. We were told the salt bath was a piece of junk that hadn't worked in fourteen years. But we took it anyway. When we got back I asked one of our electrical engineers if he could find out what the hell was wrong with it. He worked on it for days, took it all apart. And he got it so that we could not only heat-treat rivets, but we could even temper steel on the damn thing.[7]

The maintenance crew scrounged more than just shop equipment. They regularly haunted the distressed-cargo warehouse looking for anything that they could use, or adapt for use. Though they were mainly on the lookout for aviation items, they were quick to grab such things as an outboard engine and an ice-cream maker. Among their more valuable finds were a BSA motorcycle and sidecar and several 7X50 binoculars. Unfortunately, there were no usable aircraft parts among the distressed cargo.

In the meantime, the maintenance people got the three battered PBYs into shape, which increased the number of serviceable utility planes to five. Between 7 March and 7 April, PatWing-10 carried out its mission with those few, tired planes. Fortunately, the Japanese offensive had stopped at Java, and other than raids on Darwin, Broome, and Derby, there was little activity around Australia.

PatWing-10's area of operations 1 March–9 May 1942.

In anticipation of reinforcements and increased operations, Pat-Wing-10 started to establish advance bases at Geraldton and Shark Bay. The *Childs* spent much of her time at those places. At the same time that PatWing-10 was preparing for reinforcements, there were several personnel changes among the old crowd.

Frank O'Beirne relieved Doc Pratt on the *Childs*, and Pratt returned to the United States. Captain Wagner went home, Peterson taking over the duties of the Commander Aircraft, Asiatic Fleet, but not the title. He remained ComPatWing-10. VPs-101, -102, and -22 were merged into one squadron, VP-101, with Ducky Donaho the squadron's skipper. Lieutenant Commander Neale moved to a slightly different staff position, but remained involved in the wing's activities.

On 7 April 1942, the first three-plane section of reinforcements arrived at Pelican Point. VP-21, commanded by Lieutenant Commander George Mundorf, had come out from Pearl Harbor along the same route used by VP-22 two months earlier. The twelve PBY-5s were a welcome sight, but they meant that Antonides had a big job cut out for him.

VP-21 had brought as many spare parts as they could carry. But there was still a serious parts shortage. Antonides cabled for the urgently needed parts, generators, starters, and instruments, and those were sent out aboard ships and aircraft. But most of the parts never reached Australia. Because every time a ship put into a port, or a plane landed, where there was a PBY squadron, the parts were "requisitioned."[8]

VP-21 did not maintain its identity once it reached Perth. George Mundorf was put on the PatWing-10 staff almost at once, and VP-21 was merged into VP-101. The merger was not well received by the VP-21 people because their aircrews were "thoroughly mixed up with VP-101, and changed around."[9]

Despite being broken up and shuffled around, the newcomers did fit in with the oldtimers, mostly because so many of the men knew each other. At one time or another, nearly all of them had been at Pearl Harbor, and VPs-21 and -22 had been sister squadrons in PatWing-2. The situation was illustrated by the case of Frank and Emmet O'Beirne. Frank had been VP-22's skipper when it came west, and his brother Emmet was VP-21's executive officer.

Three days after VP-21 arrived, John Hyland was put in command of a three-plane detachment at Geraldton. Hyland figured he had been given the assignment because he was the "most junior of the seniors." Despite the fact that Geraldton was "an excellent base, with good facilities for gassing from shore, and excellent quarters," the assignment was not a popular one. In part, that was because Geraldton was 400 miles from the "action in Perth." "Action," of course, meant the social life. But for John Hyland there was more to Geraldton's remoteness than the absence of social life and pleasant living. He did not know it at the time, but by being sent to Geraldton he missed out on the Gridiron Flight.

# 13

# Operation Flight Gridiron
# 27 April–3 May 1942

On 9 March 1942 Java capitulated. The Japanese now occupied the southwest Pacific inside an arc that ran from northern New Guinea through Sumatra. The Malay Peninsula, Burma, Thailand, and Indochina were under Japanese control. American and Filipino troops still held Bataan and Mindanao, but their battle was already lost. When Bataan surrendered on 9 April, only Corregidor and part of Mindanao were in American hands.[1]

A few escapees from the Philippines, Borneo, the Celebes, and Java made their way south in small, open boats. Hiding ashore by day and sailing at night, a few—very few—reached Australia.

PatWing-10 picked up some of those escapees. The most notable instance occurred on 21 April 1942 when a VP-21 plane spotted an open boat with eleven men in it, about 100 miles north of Exmouth Gulf. The PBY landed to pick up the five RAAF officers and six enlisted men who had escaped from Java, but only three enlisted men agreed to go aboard the PBY. The others told the Americans that they had been at sea forty-six days, were in good health, and preferred to sail on to Port Roeburne, about 200 miles away.[2] The incident was a reminder that PatWing-10 still had people in the Philippines.

By the middle of April it was obvious that it was only a matter of time before Corregidor fell, and plans to get selected people to Australia were started. But since the Japanese controlled nearly everything between Australia and Corregidor, that was not going to be easy.

The Japanese had still not taken Mindanao, though they were pushing north from Davao and through Zamboanga. That meant that the army still controlled the big airfield at Del Monte. But that was as close as a B-17 or a B-24 could get, because the field on Corregidor was too small to handle a bomber. So, the problem was how to get the evacuees from Corregidor to the airfield at Del Monte. That could only be accomplished with a seaplane. Using two types of planes was, however, a waste of resources, and the logical solution was to use a seaplane for the entire mission.

Selecting the people to be flown out was another tough job. Deciding who would stay and "who would go free," was done by several people, including General Douglas MacArthur, General Jonathan M. Wainwright, Admiral Glassford, and Captain Wagner.[3] MacArthur and Glassford selected men who had specific skills needed to continue the war against Japan. For example, an intelligence officer, Colonel Stuart Wood, was selected because he had spent several years in Japan, spoke Japanese, and understood Japanese military thinking. Navy Lieutenant Thomas K. Bowers, and Commanders E. W. Hastings and C. H. Williams were selected for their specific skills.

Captain Wagner wanted the two PatWing-10 pilots brought out, but Ensign George Trudell's head wound kept him off the list. Commander Bridget, still in good shape, was included. General Wainwright's major concern was the 150 army nurses on Corregidor. Obviously, they all could not go, and choosing the few who could was a particularly difficult task. In the end, about fifty-four people were selected, among them nineteen nurses. The job would require two planes.[4]

The planning for the flight, and the selection of pilots, was done by Lieutenant Commander Neale.[5] Since a PBY could not reach Lake Lanao or Corregidor by direct flight from Perth, it was necessary to stage through Darwin. The Perth-Darwin leg alone was an 1,800-mile flight along the coast, and the Darwin-Corregidor leg was another 1,800 miles. Clearly, the planes would have to refuel before reaching Corregidor, and again on the flight back. Fortunately, Lake Lanao was still in American hands, and fuel stores were still available there.

Another major concern was the presence of Japanese fighter bases along the Darwin-Corregidor route. Even the initial staging point, Darwin, was under frequent air attack, and both Broome and Exmouth Gulf were within range of Japanese fighters. Therefore, the threat of being shot down was present for most of the flight.

The danger could be reduced considerably by making the hops at night, and that was how it was done. But that meant that the planes would have to hole up somewhere during the day. PatWing-10 had lost twenty-five of its forty-six planes on the ground, and the shoot-ups at Olongapo and Laguna de Bay were still fresh in Neale's mind. So, a decrease in danger in one area increased the danger in another.

Lieutenant Commander Neale's last problem was pilot selection. Understandably, he wanted men who had flown in the Philippines, and his choice was limited to the the VP-101 and VP-102 veterans. That was still a large group to choose from, with many pilots qualified for the assignment. Three lieutenants (j.g.) were selected, Tom Pollock, Leroy Deede, and William Gough, plus one enlisted pilot, David Bounds. Neale assigned himself to Pollock's plane as the mission commander. The pilots selected their own crews.[6]

The army arranged to have men ready at Lake Lanao to refuel the planes, provide weather information, and establish special operation codes. When completed, the plan called for each PBY to load a half ton of artillery nose fuses, medical supplies, and radio parts in Darwin. They would then fly all night to Lake Lanao, refuel, and hide there during the day. The next night they would fly to Corregidor, land between the "Rock" and Caballo Island, unload the supplies, embark the passengers, and return to Lake Lanao where they would again refuel, and hide for the day. That night they would make the return flight to Darwin, arriving at about dawn on the third day.

The plan went into effect on 27 April at 1000. Neale, Pollock, and Bounds led the way in 21-P-1, Deede and Gough flying wing in

21-P-7. After a short stop in Shark Bay to refuel and eat, the two planes went on to Darwin, encountering heavy weather that made navigation difficult, causing the planes to become separated for part of the flight. But both arrived together at Darwin at dawn on 28 April, their low-level approach causing an air-raid alarm when they came in from the wrong direction.

The crews spent the 28th in Darwin trying unsuccessfully to rest in the 110-degree heat. That afternoon the planes were refueled while a ton and a half of artillery fuses, radio equipment, and medical supplies were loaded into each plane. The three-times increase in cargo was a surprise that necessitated the recalculation of fuel consumption schedules. In fact, the planes were so full that to move fore and aft, the crewmen had to crawl on their hands and knees across the stacked fuses.[7]

Tom Pollock added two other items to his load, a couple of yards of muslin cloth, a pint of marine glue, and an extra medical kit to supplement the one carried in the plane. Pollock was not expecting to patch a hole or treat a wound, he was just being prepared. It was a good thing.

At 1600 on 28 April the PBYs, each loaded with 3,000 pounds of cargo, 5,000 pounds of fuel, seven crewmen, and fully armed, rose slowly off the water, on the first leg of the trip to Lake Lanao, 1,350 miles north. Their initial course, 327 degrees true, took them east of Timor, then across the Banda Sea to Peleng Island. The route perfectly split the distance between the Japanese fighter bases on Timor and Ambon. At Peleng, the planes turned to 358 degrees true, crossed the Molucca Sea, the northern arm of the Celebes, and entered the Celebes Sea. To their right they saw Menado "lit up like a Christmas tree," a reassuring sign that the Japanese were unaware of their presence.

One hundred and twenty miles south of Lake Lanao they jinked left for about thirty-two miles and then came right to line up on Lake Lanao. The purpose for the course change was to bring them in across the middle of the Moro Gulf and Illana Bay. They wanted to stay as far away from the shoreline as possible until the last moment, so not to alert the Japanese.

At 0430 on 29 April they landed on Lake Lanao in "pitch black." It was not easy since the pilots could not see the lake's surface. That meant that a normal full-stall landing was impossible, since they might drop the plane onto the water with a destructive "thud." Instead, they had to make "standard power landings," essentially flying their planes onto the water, or landing by feel. The darkness also kept them from knowing the wind direction, so that they had to guess. Both guessed wrong.

At 300 feet they brought the noses of their planes up, maintaining lift, but slowing their rate of descent. Nose up, descending steadily, the planes neared the invisible lake surface. Pollock was the first one to touch, making a down-wind landing. As soon as the hull touched, Dave Bounds jerked the throttles back and the big flying boat settled onto the water. Moments later Deede made a successful cross-wind landing.

A signal flashed from the shore, followed shortly by two native boats that guided the planes to their hiding places. Soldiers and sailors came out of the dark to help the airmen cover their planes with foliage. By the time the job was done, the two aircrews had been without sleep for nearly forty-eight hours. They hoped to get at least a few hours' sleep while they laid over on Lake Lanao, but a crowd of curious, noisy Moros shot down that plan.

At 1300, with "no sleep, but some rest," the planes were refueled and stripped of all "non-essential gear." Left on the beach were their guns, ammunition, oxygen, blankets, food, and tools. Only navigation equipment, code books, and emergency rations were kept aboard. Much of the removed weight was replaced with additional cargo.

Refueled, loaded with cargo to the overheads, the PBYs took off from Lake Lanao and turned west. Over the Sulu Sea the planes turned to 335 degrees true. Their flight was again over water to avoid detection by the Japanese.

> We were told where to rendezvous with the escape party boats near Corregidor. The place selected was off Caballo Island. We had expected to land in the protected harbor area on the east side of the main island, hence we had many misgivings to find we would have to land at night with a heavy load, and in the open sea where ground swells can bounce a seaplane like a rock skipping over a lake.

Five hundred miles north the people upon whom fortune had smiled were making their final preparations. Some had known for several hours that they were going out. Others had heard the good news only moments earlier. Army Nurse Evelyn Whitlow was one of the first to be told.

> I had malaria and was no good to anyone. Sometime in the afternoon Chief Nurse Maude Davidson called a group of us into a cubicle, and told us we were going to be flown out about midnight. We were sent down to the headquarters finance department to draw 200 dollars, and told to take only a tooth brush and what small things we could carry on our laps.[8]

Another army nurse, Sally Blaine, heard the welcome news much later.

> After the evening meal, some of us were called into the dining room. I had malaria and wondered why I had been ordered out of bed. We were told it was top secret, we were going home. But word got around anyway. I guess we were selected because we were old, sick, or married. Being married was a no no. We could only take a musette bag so I put in a matching silk skirt, turban, and sweater. We all wore coveralls, white sox, and white nurses shoes.[9]

Sally Blaine had a long-standing date with a young army officer when she got to Australia. It was a date she never kept.

Helen Gardnier was among the last to learn that she was to be flown out.

> I never did find out how I was picked to go. We were working in the Malinta Tunnel Hospital. None of us had malaria, but we were working long hours. The Chief Nurse called some of us together and said we were going to be flown out that night. There was very little time between the notification and the departure. Two of the people who went with us were General Seals and his wife. He was a very old man, and she was terribly crippled with arthritis.[10]

While the passengers waited, the PBYs were slugging their way north through thick weather. Unable to see any landmarks through the soup, with all navigation aids extinguished, and Manila's radio station off the air, navigation was done by dead reckoning. Finally, Pollock tried to fix their position by dropping low enough to spot landmarks through the gloom. He was starting to worry when he spotted an oil tank burning on Corregidor.

By aid of this "flare," we could tell the wind direction. . . . As soon as I cut my engines to glide down, Deede lost me in the haze because there was no exhaust to show my position. We landed independently and started for the rendezvous.[11]

Throughout the day, Japanese had pounded Corregidor with the heaviest bombardment to date, in celebration of the Emperor's birthday. But the bombardment ceased at sundown, as the celebration took a more conventional form. Therefore, when the PBYs landed there was little or no enemy fire.

Despite the relative quiet, it seemed to Pollock that hours passed before the first boat appeared. Actually it was about five minutes. Empty boats quickly came alongside the drifting planes and took aboard the precious cargo. Pollock later wrote, "I have never witnessed such a speedy job of unloading cargo." Exchanging cargo for passengers, the boats hurried back to the planes. General Wainwright wished each man and woman Godspeed.

Pollock had been impressed at the speed with which the cargo had been taken out of his plane, but the loading of passengers was another matter. His impatience was prompted by the nearness of his plane to "some rocky pinnacles." As the plane drifted closer to the rocks, he and Bounds used the engines to slow their drift.

"After station from pilot. Get those old women aboard, and let's get out of here. There is Jap artillery on both sides that can make us very unhappy."

Dave Bounds stepped into the pilot's compartment.

"Well, you were right about the women. There are fourteen aboard."

"All women?" He expected a number of male VIPs. "Where's Commander Bridget?"

"Don't worry," Bounds reassured him. "He's aboard."

"How many people are aboard the plane?" It was beginning to dawn on Pollock that he had more passengers than he had expected.

"I can't be sure." Bounds was buckling himself into his seat. "But there must be thirty. You can't walk from one end to the other."

Bounds may have over-estimated by a few heads. Using Pollock's reconstructed passenger list, postwar newspaper and survivor interviews, it appears there were twenty-five passengers aboard 21-P-1. There were eleven nurses, Brigadier General O. Seals and his wife, four navy officers, four army officers, two civilian women, and two Filipino army officers.

There were twenty-nine people in Deede's plane, nine of whom were nurses. But Deede added two more people to his load. As the last passengers were being helped aboard, Bill Gough recognized a sailor standing in the nearly empty boat. The man, recorded only as Donnell, had been Gough's radioman before the war. Grabbing Donnell by the hand, Gough pulled him through the waist hatch.[12]

At the same time, Deede's NAP, W. D. Eddy, recognized one of Deede's old crewmen, Alvin "Abe" Kall. He pointed him out to Deede, who shouted back, "Bring him aboard." The lucky sailor lost no time getting out of the boat.[13]

Coincidentally, the bow hook in the last boat to come alongside 21-P-1 was Burt Fuller, who had been with Pollock on the trips to Manila to get supplies. He was the gun-wielding chief that had convinced the captain to cooperate in bringing out the ammunition barge. Sadly, Pollock did not see his old friend, and Fuller was again left behind. Tom Pollock felt very badly when he learned that he had missed Fuller.

> In the Philippines one of the saddest things I experienced was leaving my shipmates in Bataan. I knew they had little chance of escape. It was particularly hard to shake the hands of the crew who flew with Harmon Utter and me. They were all happy that we had a chance to evacuate and wished us the best. All we could offer was that we hoped we could be coming back. This was in my mind when I "volunteered" for the Corregidor flight in the hopes that I could bring out some of our people—and what happened? I did not recognize in the dark that Burt Fuller, CRM, who had been with me on my convoy trips, was the bow hook on the boat with the passengers. I was too busy keeping the plane from drifting on the rocks.[14]

The passengers aboard, the two planes took off in the order they had landed—21-P-1 and then 21-P-7. On the uneventful trip back to Lake Lanao, Sally Blaine contemplated a bundle of letters given to her by an army chaplain. He had asked her to mail them when she got to Australia, and had given her $200 for postage. Next to her a nurse was crying. Sally thought the girl was afraid, but it turned out that the woman was upset because her best friend had gone in the other plane. As it worked out, the nurse had good reason to cry.[15]

By the time they reached Mindanao, Lake Lanao was covered with heavy haze and mist, so thick that the planes became separated. Pollock, finding a hole, spiraled down to the lake, but Deede landed at sea, and waited for dawn. About an hour after sunrise, 21-P-7 "came sailing into land."

While the passengers were taken to a hotel in Dansalan to rest and eat, the aircrews, with less than seven hours rest since leaving Perth, stayed behind to camouflage the planes. Their work was hurried along by the appearance of a Japanese reconnassiance plane, apparently looking for army planes at Del Monte.

Deede's plane was tailed into a slot in the trees, but Pollock's plane had to be nosed into the bank. Pollock would have preferred to be tailed in but the nature of the hiding place made that impossible. Anyway, it did not seem to make any difference. There were two small tug boats, a huge outrigger and a small launch, both equipped with one-cylinder engines. They had pulled 21-P-1 away from the bank last night, and there was no reason to doubt they could do it again.

At 1500 the passengers returned to the planes, were given a few instructions, and told to take a break until time to board. Takeoff was set for 1830. In the meantime, the planes were refueled, and the guns were put back aboard.

At 1830 Deede taxied out onto the lake. But Pollock was already having trouble. The launch had broken down, leaving only the large, under-powered outrigger to pull 21-P-1 off the beach. The outrigger's skipper was inexperienced, and it took "about twenty passes" before he finally picked up the tow.[16]

The outrigger tugged feebly on the line, 22-P-1 moved slowly back, and the bow line was slacked. The plane continued its slow rearward movement until the bow lines reached the bitter end, and were cast off. Suddenly a gust of wind hit 22-P-1 on the starboard quarter. All rearward motion stopped.

Unable to overcome the wind, the tug stalled. As the plane drifted to port, the tow line was cut, the PBY's tail swinging away from the wind as the plane tried to weather-cock. Crewman ran onto the wings to fend off overhanging limbs. In the cockpit, Pollock and

Bounds prayed the plane would drift past the island so they could start the engines and taxi out. The plane hit a rock.

The plane struck hard, tearing a huge hole "in the mechanic's compartment, . . . outboard from the keel on the port side."[17] Water rushed in through the big hole and a half dozen smaller ones. The moment the plane touched, Pollock started his engines, swung into the wind, and started his takeoff run.

Water was pouring in. Sally Blaine had taken a sleeping pill and was asleep while the plane was being warped out. The shuddering blow and the abrupt roar of two Pratt Whitney engines at full power woke her with a start. As the plane plowed across the lake, water quickly rose to three feet in Blaine's compartment. Around her, some of the nurses made a futile attempt to avoid the rising water by climbing onto anything they could find.

"I don't think we're going to make it. Do you?" Neale handed Sally Blaine a code book.

"Why ask me?" Sally was still groggy from the pill.

"Throw that over the side." Neale was already pushing his way aft to check on the situation there.[18]

Rosemary Hogan jerked a petticoat from her musette bag, plunged into the water, stuffing the garment into the ragged hole. Looking down from his tower perch, ACMM Mario Ferrara saw Rosemary grab her musette bag and plunge back into the water in a second vain attempt to plug the hole. He later described her as "especially courageous."[19]

By now the water was waist deep and 21-P-1 was sinking fast. From the after station, Commander Bridget told Pollock to abort the takeoff and head for the beach.[20]

As soon as Pollock put the bow on the beach, the passengers surged forward to get out.

"Come on, Sally, let's get out." Rita Palmer tugged her friend's sleeve as she started forward.[21] Ahead of them General and Mrs. Seals were first out through the bow hatch. Age and arthritis slowed their exit while the water rose swiftly in the after compartment. Someone opened a waist hatch, a crewman shouted an order to close it, and the hatch slammed shut.[22] Baggage and soggy letters swirled in the bilges as the last passenger sloshed his way forward and out.

With the last passenger out, the plane crew slammed shut the watertight hatches between the compartments. Water now covered the bunks. Wasting no time, they started stripping the plane of its radio gear, guns, and ammunition, in an attempt to save what they could. Pollock was sure at that point that the plane was finished.

Deede's plane was airborne by the time Pollock had beached 21-P-1 and his passengers were out. While Deede circled overhead, Pollock tried to raise him on the voice radio. But apparently Deede's receiver was out; he did not answer. Grabbing a signal lamp, Pollock pointed it skyward. GO ON. GO ON. Deede acknowledged the message, gained altitude, and turned south. The men on the beach were still stripping the plane when the sound of Deede's engines faded to silence.

It took two hours to strip the plane. 21-P-1 was now lying with her bow and port wing tip float on the beach, but the tail and starboard wing were afloat in deep water. Water lapped at the bottom of the blisters as the tail sank deeper into the lake. To add buoyancy, three empty gas drums were lashed on each side of the fuselage near the tail. A drum raft, padded with army blankets, was pushed under the starboard engine to support the wing.

Pollock and his crew were exhausted. But still they worked to save the plane, now helped by four soldier volunteers and several PT boat sailors. Pollock later said, "Four soldiers did the finest piece of ordinary labor I have ever witnessed."[23] Divers plunged beneath the plane, running their hands along the hull looking for holes. Inside, men ducked beneath the surface, groping in the black water along the stringers and cross frames.

They found a large L-shaped hole, about 18 inches along each arm, in the mechanic's compartment. Farther aft, in the crew quarters, a large section of the chine had been stove in. Several smaller holes were discovered in the hull from the navigator's compartment to a point beneath the waist hatch. All were on the port side.[24]

Unable to use the plane's bilge pump, the men started bailing. At the same time, Pollock supervised the application of marine glue and muslin patches over the smaller holes. It was a discouraging job. Water was four feet deep in some places and clear over the navigator's table. Despite their hard work, they were not gaining.

At 2230 a small gasoline-driven pump arrived. By a combination of bailing and pumping, they began to make progress in the waist compartment, but simultaneous attempts to patch the big hole failed. It was also discovered that the watertight door between the mechanic's and navigator's compartment leaked, allowing water to pass from the mechanic's compartment into the navigator's compartment. There was no way to stop it.

To stop the flow of water through the big hole, a collision mat was rigged over the hull using an army blanket. The blanket did not keep the water out, but it slowed the flow enough that some of the water could be bailed out of the mechanic's compartment. As the water pressure on the inside decreased, the outside pressure pressed the blanket more securely against the hull.

By 0330 all leaks had been stopped aft and the waist compartment was relatively dry. With one compartment watertight, plus the added buoyancy from the six gas drums, Pollock was sure the tail would stay afloat. That major gain came at the right time because at that point the pump engine threw a rod.

Dead tired, disappointed, but still hopeful, Pollock set a watch and told his crew to get some rest. Reassured that the plane was no longer sinking, Pollock "wearily stumbled ashore to collapse in . . . wet clothes on the ground."

Just after dawn on 1 May, Commander Bridget woke Pollock. With Bridget was Captain J. L. McGuigan, a naval constructor. Captain McGuigan had brought carpenter's tools, native laborers, and a two-man hand pump.

Bridget told Pollock that arrangements were being made to have an army B-17 come to pick up everybody. He asked Pollock what he thought the chances were to repair the plane.

"As long as she still floats, we have a chance."

"Very well, go to it. And if the plane isn't OK by the time the B-17 comes, we'll send for you. You can sink the plane and ride with the army."[25]

When Bridget left, Pollock conferred with McGuigan.

> By the time Captain McGuigan arrived the flooding was under control, but I was shot. From there on McGuigan did most of the physical work while I supervised the structural aspects of the plane.[26]

Using a bucket brigade and the hand pump, McGuigan soon

lowered the water level in the mechanic's and navigator's compartments. In the meantime Dave Bounds repaired the broken pump,
and with the second pump on line, the water was lowered to the
point that McGuigan could make an accurate survey of the damage.

> The holes in the mechanic's compartment were between the sec-
> ond, third, and fourth stringers, outboard of the keel on the port
> side. One stringer was broken.

The smaller hole, nearest the keel, was repaired first.

> The inboard hole was plugged by laying a double thickness of can-
> vas covered with marine glue between the stringers and extending
> well beyond the two main cross members. A thin piece of wood
> was fitted over the canvas. A thick piece of wood was placed over
> this and was braced to the keel with a two-inch brace every three
> inches.

The large hole, the L-shaped tear, was more difficult to patch.

> Finally, the large tear was covered with sponge rubber, taken from
> the back of a parachute harness. This was forced between the
> stringers and was covered with a thin board forced under the cross
> members. Bracing was accomplished with a two-inch board. The
> leak in the third section was badly battered and the surrounding
> area was very weak. No four-by-four was available so a small tree
> was hewn to fit between the stringers. Another length was cut to fit
> over the first two patches to prevent the bracing from springing out
> on takeoff. The collision mat was removed, but the leak was still
> too fast, so it was replaced. The pump had again broken down, but
> bailing easily kept the water down when the blanket was in place.[27]

Six hours after he had started, McGuigan declared the job finished.
    It was now 1630 on 1 May. Bridget and the other passengers had
already left for the Del Monte airfield and could not be recalled.
But there were other people who could be taken out. In addition to
Captain McGuigan and another officer, five sailors who had worked
on the plane were told they could go too.
    As the radio gear and guns were being put back aboard, Pollock
noticed the spare medical kit he had picked up in Perth. Opening
the box, he found a pint of "medicinal brandy." Holding the bottle
up for the crew to see he asked, "Do you guys think this is an emergency?" They did.[28]

The passengers were climbing aboard when three soldiers who had worked on the plane walked up to Pollock. They wanted to go too. One of the soldiers said that he had malaria three times and was sure he could not survive in a POW camp. Pollock was sympathetic, but he had no authority to authorize their evacuation. He told them to see a particular officer for permission to go aboard. The officer gave them an "emphatic no." [29]

There was no wind as the patched-up PBY was again towed tail-first from the beach. The tow was cast off, the engines started, and 21-P-1 turned away from the shore. As the plane moved forward, the blanket lashed beneath the hull pulled away, and water poured in around the interior patch. Immediately the crew formed a bailing party.

> Word was passed to me that we were taking water fast. With cold engines, I used full throttle on one of the longest runs of my life. We were forced to take off heading into a mountain. Slowly, I could feel the plane get on the step. I could not wait to fly the plane off as the shore was approaching fast. I pulled it off the water and staggered through the air gradually picking up speed. We were airborne but we faced two dangers. The aircraft was very unstable due to the several thousand pounds of water in the hull and continued to stagger through the air until we could let it drain out. [30]

The sky was not yet dark. To avoid being spotted by patrolling Japanese fighters, Pollock and Bounds turned the shuddering PBY toward some storm clouds on the east side of the lake. Streaming water from the hole in her side, 21-P-1 entered the clouds and slowly spiraled up. When there was enough altitude to clear the island, the pilots turned south. Somewhere over the Sulu Sea Pollock found out that he had three stowaways aboard. They were the three soldiers that had been refused permission to go aboard.

> After we were airborne, I spotted one soldier sitting up in the bow compartment. He was between the two ammunition racks and was covered with rags. I found out later that one had lain across the two aluminum supports under one of the bunks in the mechanic's compartment, and the third in the tail section behind a metal plate designed to give the tunnel gunner some protection. This last man, along with the heavy load of water, helped cause the plane to be

dangerously unstable for takeoff. I never asked if the plane crew helped, but I had my suspicions.[31]

A few hours after finding the stowaways, Pollock was sleeping on a berth when Mario Ferrara woke him. Still half asleep he heard the plane captain say that they were low on fuel. That woke Pollock up completely. Looking at the fuel gauges, a cork float in a glass tube, Pollock and Ferrara calculated that they could not reach Darwin. But they might be able to glide to an island north of Australia.

> After our experience at Lanao, this was the clincher and I was pretty low, but did not tell the passengers. The crew were well aware of the situation. We were positive we had filled the tanks at Lanao. We finally concluded that the gauges were stuck, although it had never happened before. As it worked out we landed at Darwin with plenty of gas to spare.[32]

Darwin was reached on the morning of 2 May. During the flight from Lake Lanao, the crew removed the patch from the big hole, replacing it with a stronger installation. Overtired, Pollock misjudged the altitude, cutting the power too soon. The plane dropped like a rock, hitting the water so hard that it bounced three times. Rivets popped out and the big patch squirted water, but it held. Nevertheless, water poured in, requiring steady bailing to keep the plane afloat.

After breakfast and refueling, 21-P-1 took off for Perth. Ignoring the coast route, Pollock made a beeline across Australia to Perth, arriving at 0130 on 3 May 1942. This time he made a more sedate landing, but because of the mangled, leaking bottom, the plane was beached immediately. Elated at being safely in Australia, the crew and passengers leaped ashore. Their elation was somewhat dampened, however, when they heard that no plane had been sent to pick up the people left behind.

For Tom Pollock, the failure to get Bridget, the nurses, and the others out, was particularly distressing.

> When I returned to Perth and was checking out the plane the next day, I found nearly all of the nurses' musette bags stowed under the bunks and in some of the bilges. They were all water-soaked and soggy but I dug them out and emptied the contents to find all kinds

of clothing, personal items, keepsakes, watches and some pistols ranging from .32s to Army .45s. I picked out all the personal items and guns and turned them over to Military Intelligence in Perth, but I am not sure about their intelligence because they did not seem to know what to do with them.

The clothing I turned over to a lady in Perth, who helped in some of the houses used to billet our personnel, to wash and distribute to local ladies who were in short supply of these kinds of things, due to the war.[33]

# 14

# Surrender

When the wing had pulled out of the Philippines in December 1941, 178 enlisted men were left behind. When the remnants of that group were sent to Corregidor late in March, twenty-two were missing. On Corregidor they were split up, 122 to Caballo Island to man the guns and searchlights at Fort Hughes, and thirty-four were assigned duties on the "Rock." Commander Bridget, who had not been evacuated with the other pilots on 11 January, went to Fort Hughes. The only other officer not evacuated on 11 January, Ensign Trudell, was in the Malinta Tunnel Hospital.[1]

Among those left on Corregidor were Arthur Burkholder and his friend AM2c T. W. Young, better known as "Duck Butt." Most of the thirty-four PatWing-10 people were sent to Company L, 3rd Battalion, 4th Marines. The marines' positions, out in the open, were shelled every day, and as the shelling grew heavier, the fox-holes got deeper and deeper.

> We went over there without any cover or anything, so we started digging. And we had to dig fast, because if the Japs saw anything moving, they put in a salvo. So we dug a hole that went down, then back, and then to the right. We dug all day and night making a place for the six of us. We dug down about six feet and then back

four feet before we started right. We put in a piece of water pipe so that if it caved in on us we could get a little air.

Like all soldiers who are subjected regularly to heavy shelling and air raids, the sailors soon learned to reach their foxholes with spectacular speed. None, however, were faster than Duck Butt, whose disappearing act became legendary.

> We called Young the fastest man alive. We could be sitting around the foxhole taking a break, and when the first shell hit, old Duck Butt was always the first man in. You couldn't beat him; no way. So I told myself that one of these days I'll get there first. So I happen to be sitting right at the edge of the hole when a round came in. I just fell over backwards, but you know what? He still beat me in.

The men on Corregidor lived under the most miserable conditions, and things were only slightly better for those at Fort Hughes, on Caballo Island, 1,000 yards southeast of the "Rock."

The island was armed with two 14-inch rifles, designated Battery Woodruff and Battery Gillespie. There were also Battery Craighill, armed with four 12-inch mortars, a 3-inch antiaircraft battery called Idaho, and two World War I, 3-inch guns similar to the "French 75s." Including 400 navy and civilian personnel sent to the island in late March, there were about 1,000 men on the island.[2]

When the PatWing-10 people arrived on Caballo Island, they were "pretty well discouraged." Conditions on Bataan had been bad—little food, little water, and inadequate shelter. Conditions at Fort Hughes were little better. The island had no water. Instead, water was brought over in barges and pumped into two holding tanks, one made of cement, the other of wood. Initially, the PatWing-10 people were housed in a single wooden building that served as barracks, galley, messhall, and for whatever other purpose came up.

When they first arrived, Fort Hughes had not yet been heavily shelled or bombed. In fact, most of the rounds that hit the island were "overs" intended for Corregidor. But by the middle of April, Fort Hughes was increasingly subjected to artillery fire and bombing attacks. During an early bombardment PatWing-10's quarters were destroyed, and both water tanks were smashed.

George Gaboury, the carpenter's mate who had built the dummy

PBYs at Olongapo, was given the job of repairing the wooden water tank and constructing a new building. The water tank was beyond repair, but Gaboury found a solution that worked pretty well.

He gathered all the 12-inch and 14-inch powder cans he could get, rinsed them out with sea water, and buried them in the ground "right to the very top." Like the water tanks, the cans were kept filled with water brought over from Corregidor. But their capacity was limited, making it necessary to dole out water each day, at two canteens per man.

The new building was constructed with timber salvaged from the old building. Double walls were built with a two-foot space in between that was filled with dirt. A direct hit would certainly take it out, but anyone inside was, at least, safe from shell splinters.

As the end drew near, Gaboury and others were put to work preparing beach defenses. Caballo Island is seventy-five acres atop steep cliffs rising one hundred feet above the sea, and the narrow beaches at the base of the cliffs provided poor landing spots. Along the tops of the cliffs Gaboury and his helpers built wooden chutes, "well greased," down which they intended to slide 30-pound fragmentation bombs. They also built wooden mines, using small bombs and artillery rounds as the explosive, that they buried in the small beaches.

After the middle of April, food became a critical problem on the island.

> By this time we had almost all the crews from the inshore patrol ships that had been sunk. We also had some Filipino civilians who worked for the army. They had to be fed, which made things more critical with food and water.

The island's entire food supply was stored in a magazine for 12-inch and 14-inch ammunition. During one of the bombardments, a large caliber round landed squarely on the magazine's roof. The huge projectile plowed through fifteen inches of dirt cover, smashed through a concrete wall, bounced off a pillar, and punched through the half-inch steel doors to the powder room, where it exploded. When the smoke cleared and the dust settled, bits and pieces of food were all that remained. The men were ordered not to eat the food because it was contaminated—an order that the now-starving men ignored.

George Gaboury and many other PatWing-10 men had watched the planes of the Gridiron Flight arrive, load up, and leave. Before he left to board the PBY, Commander Bridget went to every PatWing-10 man at Fort Hughes to say goodbye. The men viewed his departure with mixed feelings. On one hand they were glad for him because he was very popular, and they sincerely wished him the best of luck. But they also hated to see him go. Bridget was the only PatWing-10 officer left, other than the wounded George Trudell, and Bridget had performed magnificently among them.

Many recalled that during a particularly heavy bombardment, Bridget had broken from cover and raced into the open to drag wounded men to safety. He had done it alone, and it took several trips to bring all of them in. He had constantly looked after their interests in many other ways, and did his best to keep their sagging morale from hitting bottom. They would miss him.

One week after Commander Bridget left, the defenders at Fort Hughes were prisoners of war. Corregidor had surrendered on 6 May, but the Japanese did not come ashore on Caballo Island until 0230 on 7 May 1942. From that point forward, George Gaboury and his mates were subjected to an ordeal so horrible that less than half survived.

With the surrender of Fort Hughes, there remained only one more act before the original PatWing-10's war ended. On Mindanao, Commander Bridget, Colonel Stuart Wood, and eleven army nurses were still hoping that an army bomber would come get them.[3]

After returning to the Dansalan Hotel, they had been taken by bus to Del Monte airfield to wait for a plane. The Japanese were just thirty-seven miles away, pushing slowly closer. At Del Monte they were told to go to Valencia Field, seventy kilometers south, where they might find a plane to fly them out. At the time they were unaware that Pollock and his crew had salvaged the plane and had taken off. It is probably just as well that they did not know.

Another thing they did not know was that a few days after they walked south, away from Del Monte, a B-24 landed there to pick them up. By that time the group was waiting at Valencia, but no one told the pilot. Again, it probably would not have made much difference in the outcome, because the B-24 crashed at sea on its return flight to Australia.[4]

Forced out of Valencia by the Japanese approach, they were "hustled from place to place" trying to avoid capture, finally ending up at a place called Ford Ranch. Despite all that had happened, they still believed they would be picked up. But after midnight on 11 May, Sally Blaine heard the truth.

The nurses were all asleep on the ranch house floor except Sally Blaine, who was sick and sleeping fitfully. Lying awake she heard two men talking, but could not understand what they were saying, partly because their voices were drowned out by the noise of an approaching airplane's engine.

Thinking it was the plane coming to get them, she got up and walked outside where the two men were still talking. Colonel Wood and Commander Bridget told the nurse that the engine she heard was a Grumman Duck, and that possibly one nurse at a time could be flown out. Where they would be taken was not mentioned, but it sounded good to Blaine. But when the plane landed to refuel, they found it was flown by a Filipino pilot who was "flying the last plane out, to home." He had no intention of taking any passengers. And certainly was not going to make twenty-five round trips. After the plane had taken off and its engine noise had faded away, Colonel Wood and Commander Bridget turned to Sally Blaine.

"Sally, we'll tell you something if you promise not to cry." The tall colonel's voice showed his discouragement and fatigue.

"I won't."

"But you mustn't tell anyone."

"I won't."

Colonel Wood looked at the ground, and Bridget looked at Sally, while Wood spoke the words that the nurse now fully expected.

"We're going to surrender this morning."[5]

Sally did not cry.

An hour later the two officers assembled the nurses to give them the news. Colonel Wood told them to burn the letters they had agreed to carry out, but to keep their money. Later that morning Japanese troops arrived at the ranch and took them prisoners. It was 11 May 1942, when Commander Frank Bridget surrendered, the last PatWing-10 man to go into captivity. He never came back.

# Epilogue

"We didn't accomplish a thing."

That somewhat bitter statement is made by many of the men who were in PatWing-10, but it is not entirely correct. Statistically the wing suffered badly, but the figures can be misleading. The wing lost forty-one out of forty-five planes, fourteen being shot down, twenty-four destroyed on the ground, and three lost in accidents. Three made it to Perth, and one was abandoned in Tjilatjap, but was flown out by the Dutch. Considering that they were operating in air space totally controlled by the Japanese, it is remarkable that only fourteen PBYs were shot down. Even more remarkable is the fact that most of those aircrews returned safely. Unfortunately, the wing's casualty figures soared, because about half its personnel were captured in the Philippines when Corregidor fell. Of those, over 60 percent died in captivity.

Certainly, the wing did not win any major victories, its attempts to bomb the Japanese Fleet proved futile, and its excellent reporting seldom resulted in an Allied countermove. But their rescue and evacuation flights saved many lives, and their almost hourly reports on Japanese movements caused delays in the Japanese advance—delays that made it possible for several hundred more Allied troops to escape. Those are substantial accomplishments.

Because they were the only U.S. Navy aviation unit fighting the Japanese during the war's early weeks, they were the first to learn that prewar plans for using the PBYs were all wrong. The solutions to the problems they faced became the basis for American wartime use of the PBY. They certainly laid the groundwork for the highly successful rescue missions for which the PBY is most famous, and they definitely set the stage for the equally successful Black Cat operations. Those were substantial accomplishments.

Many of the aircrews, particularly those from VP-22, took their experience to the Aleutians. Others became instructors in the United States, and many more were salted into unseasoned units to provide leadership and direction. In every instance PatWing-10's experience was a valuable contribution to the navy's war effort.

PatWing-10 produced an unusually high percentage of very suc-

Hawk Barrett and Lanson Ditto in San Francisco in April 1942. They were among the men who returned on the USS *Mt. Vernon*. Barrett had a hard time with the Military Police because of the unusual flier's wings on his jacket. The wings were made in Australia by a tailor who had never seen U.S. naval aviators' wings. Ditto was on the *Langley* when she went down and was one of the few survivors to be rescued after the *Pecos* was sunk two days later. (Courtesy R. Barrett)

This picture was taken at a postwar reunion. 1. Joseph Antonides, 2. J. V. Peterson, 3. Frank O'Bierne, 4. Tom Pollock, 5. John Hyland, 6. Frank Wagner, 7. J. C. Renard, 8. Etheridge Grant, 9. Don Chay, 10. Amos Wooten, 11. Arthur Jacobson, 12. Bishop, 13. Duke Campbell, 14. Charles Holt, 15. W. G. Winslow, 16. Edgar Neale, 17. Al Burgess, 18. T. E. L. McCabe, 19. Ed Bergstrom, 20. Guy Howard, 21. William Kabler, 22. Richard Roberts. (Courtesy Tom Pollock)

cessful navy careers. Many of the enlisted men, and all the NAPs, were commissioned before the war ended. Nearly all the pilots who remained in the navy rose to the rank of captain, and several achieved flag rank. Two, John Hyland and Tom Moorer, became full admirals. Hyland commanded the Pacific Fleet before he retired, and Moorer held the navy's top job as chief of naval operations. Three tender skippers, Grant, Kabler, and Pratt, all became rear admirals, and R. P. McConnell of the *Langley* retired a vice admiral. Tom Warfield, who brought several PatWing-10 pilots out of Manila in the MS *Maréchal Joffre*, also became a rear admiral. The collective success of the men of PatWing-10 reflects on the high quality of the organization.

There were, sadly, several who died during and after the war in various accidents. Leroy Deede was killed in Australia when the Douglas SBD "Dauntless" he was flying crashed on takeoff. Earl McConnell also died in a flying accident, as did Doug Norris,

Charles Van Dusen, Burt Nolan, and Charles Holt. E. L. Christman was killed on the ground on Iwo Jima. Harmon Utter, who with Tom Pollock hit the barge on Christmas Eve, survived the war only to be killed in a postwar auto accident. A similar accident claimed Bob Foster, who had manned all the guns on P-2 on Laguna de Bay on 25 December. There were others.

Jim Baldwin, who had survived a cartwheeling crash in an OS2U at Ambon, was lost when the *Langley* went down. Both Frank Bridget and Al Gray died while prisoners of war. The exact events surrounding their deaths are unknown, but both apparently died aboard Japanese ships in 1944.

Natural causes have taken many of the others. Most of the leaders are gone—Frank Wagner, Edgar Neale, John Peterson, and D. G. Donaho. But Frank O'Beirne is still active. Most of the men still living are retired, but many are working at a second career. A. L. Armbruster is a successful physician, Harvey Hop operates his own airline in Florida. Duke Campbell is an investment broker, and Hawk Barrett runs a maple sugar business in Vermont.

George Gaboury and Art Burkholder survived terrible ordeals while prisoners of war. Burt Fuller, Pollock's right-hand man on the trips back into Manila, escaped from the Japanese and became a guerrilla fighter. Those three men are representative of the men who made up PatWing-10. All exhibited, to one degree or another, tenacity, resourcefulness, and courage.

Those qualities are also represented in the many awards and commendations that were given PatWing-10. Nine destroyers were named for PatWing-10 pilots, and four were named for PatWing-10 enlisted men. The officers were Frank Bridget, Richard Bull, Russell Chambers, Leroy Deede, Burden Hastings, W. H. Mosley, A. L. Seaman, and Russell Snyder. The enlisted men were Joseph Bangust, Otis Lee Dennis, Earl Hall, and Andrew Waterman. Eight Navy Crosses, ten Distinguished Flying Crosses, and fourteen Army Silver Stars were awarded to the officers and men of PatWing-10. Thirty-six enlisted men received commendations and promotions for meritorious conduct, and Presidential Unit Citations were awarded to VP-101, 102, and 22.

In view of the record, PatWing-10 accomplished a lot in the face of enormous odds.

# Source Notes

A shortened source note form has been used to save space. The complete source descriptions are given in the Bibliography. All bibliographical material is in the author's collection.

*Chapter 1*

1. Campbell and Ebbe interviews. The account that follows is taken from those sources.

2. Bray and Burgess, letters to the author; and Campbell and Reid interviews.

3. Reid, letter to the author.

4. Hyland interview.

5. Nordfelt interview.

6. Ibid.; and "Operations of Patrol Wing Ten, 7 December–5 March 1942," undated. (Hereafter cited as "Ops. PW-10").

7. Barrett Diary.

8. Bray, letter to the author.

9. Barrett Diary; and Campbell, McCabe, Pollock, and Williamson interviews. The following account is based on those sources.

10. Hyland and Swenson interviews; and "PatWing-10 War Diary."

11. Swenson interview. All the conversations came from that source.

12. Ebbe interview.

13. Barrett Diary; "PatWing-10 War Diary"; and "Ops. PW-10."
14. Ebbe interview.
15. Peterson Narrative.
16. Campbell interview.
17. Barrett, Hyland, and McCabe interviews.
18. Kelly interview.
19. Peterson Narrative.
20. Johnson interview.
21. Gaboury, letter to the author.
22. Wagner Narrative.
23. Burgess interview.
24. McCabe interview.
25. Burgess interview.
26. Swenson interview.
27. Campbell interview.

*Chapter 2*

1. Hyland interview.
2. Johnson interview.
3. Ralston interview.
4. "PatWing-10 War Diary"; Action Report, USS *William B. Preston*, 8 December 1941, and USS *William B. Preston*, Log.
5. Swenson interview.
6. Williamson interview.
7. Grant, "The Saga of the USS *Preston*."
8. Bray interview.
9. Ebbe interview.
10. Brown interview.
11. "PatWing-10 War Diary."
12. Ibid.
13. Shimada, "Japanese Naval Air Operations in the Philippine Invasion," *Proceedings*, January 1955, p. 9.
14. Antonides interview.
15. Edmonds, *They Fought with What They Had*, p. 81.
16. Campbell interview.
17. Wagner Narrative.
18. Edmonds, *They Fought with What They Had*, p. 99.
19. Chay Diary.
20. Wagner Narrative.
21. "PatWing-10 War Diary."

22. Ibid.; and Swenson interview.

23. Swenson interview.

24. "PatWing-10 War Diary."

25. Gaboury interview.

26. Reid interview.

27. Keller, "Contact With Enemy Forces on December 10, 1941; Report of."

28. Palm and Swenson interviews.

29. Peterson, "Bombing Attack on Japanese Battleships on 10 December 1941; Report on." (Hereafter cited as Peterson Report.)

30. *Chicago Daily News.*

31. Peterson Report.

32. Palm interview.

33. Jacobson interview.

34. Peterson Report.

35. "PatWing-10 War Diary."

36. Ibid.

37. Wagner Narrative; and "Ops. PW-10."

38. Roberts interview.

39. Ibid.

40. Burgess and Webber interviews.

41. Pollock Papers.

42. Pollock, letter to the author.

43. Antonides interview.

44. Pollock Papers.

45. Wagner Narrative.

46. Edmonds, *They Fought with What They Had*, p. 108.

47. Armbruster, Campbell, and Johnson interviews. The following account is taken from those sources.

48. Wagner Narrative.

49. Hart, "Narrative of Events, Asiatic Fleet, leading up to War and from 8 December 1941 to 15 February 1942." (Hereafter cited as Hart Narrative).

50. Grayson, Jacobson, McCabe, Reid, and Williamson interviews. The following account is taken from those sources.

51. Chay Diary.

52. Keller Narrative.

53. "PatWing-10 War Diary."

54. Hyland interview.

55. Hart Narrative.

*Chapter 3*

1. Keller Narrative.
2. Antonides interview.
3. Burkholder interview.
4. Ibid.
5. Barrett Diary.
6. Hart Narrative.
7. "MS *Maréchal Joffre* War History."
8. Wagner Narrative.
9. Chay Diary.
10. Hart Narrative.
11. Ibid.
12. VP-101 and VP-102 Muster Rolls; and "Status of Certain Personnel (Patrol Wing Ten)," 21 September 1942.
13. Ebbe interview.
14. Ibid.
15. "War Activities, Utility Squadron, Asiatic Fleet."
16. Barrett Diary.
17. Chay Diary.
18. Hart Narrative.
19. Grayson interview.
20. Barrett Diary; "PatWing-10 War Diary"; and Peterson Report.
21. Barrett Diary.
22. USS *Childs*, Log.
23. Pratt, letter to the author.
24. Kuhn interview.
25. Burgess interview.
26. Nordfelt interview; and Wagner Narrative.
27. Kuhn interview.
28. Chay Diary.
29. Barrett Diary.
30. Ibid.
31. Ralston interview.
32. Grayson interview.
33. Warfield interview.
34. Grayson and Ralston interviews; "PatWing-10 War Diary"; "*Maréchal Joffre* War History"; and Warfield, "*Maréchal Joffre* Report and Recommendations."
35. Barrett Diary; and Hyland interview.

36. *Pilot's Handbook, U.S. Navy PBY-4 Airplane.*
37. Warfield, recording sent to his father, January 1942.
38. Grayson, Ralston, and Warfield interviews.
39. "*Maréchal Joffre*, War History." The remainder of the account describing the ship's passage to Surabaja is based on the "War History"; Warfield, *Maréchal Joffre* Report; and the Grayson, Ralston and Warfield interviews.
40. Chay Diary.
41. "Ops. PW-10."
42. McCabe interview.
43. Eisenbach interview.
44. Barrett Diary.

## Chapter 4

1. Pollock Narrative.
2. Ibid.
3. Pollock, letter to the author.
4. Pollock interview.
5. Pollock, letter to the author.
6. Edmonds, *They Fought with What They Had*, p. 63.
7. Pollock interview.
8. Edmonds, op.cit., p. 63.
9. Reid, "Advance Party" unpublished account, 8 May 1980.
10. Kelly interview.
11. Reid, letter to the author.
12. Reid interview. Unless otherwise noted, the following conversation is from that source.
13. Palm interview. Unless otherwise noted, the following conversation is from that source.
14. Ibid.
15. Ibid.
16. Kelly interview.
17. Swenson interview.
18. Ibid.
19. Pollock interview; and Pollock letter to the author.
20. Roberts interview.
21. Ibid.
22. Antonides and Roberts interviews. The account that follows is taken from those sources.

23. Swenson interview; and Official Navy Press Release, "PatWing-10—Story of a Gallant Squadron and its Exploits from Philippines to Australia," 24 May 1942. (Hereafter cited as Navy Press Release). The account that follows is based on those sources.

24. Hart Narrative.

25. Bowers, "Personal Narrative of Philippine Campaign." (Hereafter cited as Bowers Narrative).

26. Ibid.

27. Pollock, letter to the author.

28. "Status of Certain Personnel (Patrol Wing Ten)"; and "Status of Aircraft," 14 February 1942.

29. Hart Narrative.

*Chapter 5*

1. "PatWing-10 War Diary"; and Wagner Narrative.

2. Ibid.

3. Hyland interview.

4. McCabe interview.

5. Dawley, "Bombing Attack at Jolo, 27 December 1941, and Subsequent Incidents; Report of." 29 January 1942. (Hereafter cited as the Dawley Jolo Report).

6. Hyland and McCabe interviews.

7. Christman. "Dawn Bombing Attack of Jolo, Sulu 27 December 1941—Report of," (Hereafter cited as Christman Jolo Report).

8. Hyland, "Report of Bombing Raid on Island of Jolo," 3 January 1942; and McCabe, "Report of Bombing Raid on Island of Jolo," 3 January 1942. (Hereafter cited as Hyland Jolo Report and McCabe Jolo Report).

9. Jacobson interview; and McCabe Jolo Report.

10. McCabe Jolo Report.

11. Ebbe interview; and Deede, "Report of Bombing Raid on the Island of Jolo," 5 January 1942. (Hereafter cited as Deede Jolo Report).

12. Hyland Jolo Report.

13. Navy Press Release; and Deede Jolo Report.

14. Hyland interview.

15. Navy Press Release.

16. "Ops. PW-10"; and "PatWing-10 War Diary."

17. Deede Jolo Report.

18. McCabe interview; and McCabe Jolo Report.

19. Hyland interview; and Hyland Jolo Report.

20. Dawley Jolo Report.

21. Ibid.
22. McLawhorn interview.
23. Brown interview.
24. Dawley Jolo Report.
25. Ibid.
26. McLawhorn interview.
27. Dawley Jolo Report.
28. Christman Jolo Report.
29. Navy Press Release.
30. Christman Jolo Report.
31. Ibid.; and Brown, *Suez to Singapore*, pp. 475–76. The rest of P-9's account is taken from those two sources.
32. Goldsmith, "Trip to Jolo, Sulu Province for the Purpose of Investigating Stories Surrounding the Navy Catalina Flyers Missing After Raid on Japanese Shipping at Jolo on 27 December 1941—Report on," 18 May 1945; and Shepler, "Evaluation Results PBY Strike, Jolo, 27 December 1941," 27 April 1945.
33. Dawley Jolo Report. The following account is taken from that source.
34. Christman Jolo Report. The following account is taken from that source.
35. Deede Jolo Report.
36. Campbell interview.
37. Ibid. The following account is taken from that source and Campbell, "Report of Rescue of Ens. L. C. Deede, and Crew," 5 January 1942.
38. Campbell interview.
39. Operations Record Nr. 2, G. R. Squadron, 3 December 1941–16 February 1942; and Wagner Narrative.
40. Operations Record Nr. 2.
41. "PatWing-10 War Diary"; Wagner Narrative; and Winslow, *The Fleet the Gods Forgot*, pp. 91–92.
42. Campbell interview; Operations Record Nr. 2; and Wagner Narrative.
43. Operations Record Nr. 2.
44. Wagner Narrative.
45. Ibid.
46. "PatWing-10 War Diary"; and Peterson Narrative.
47. Ebbe and McCabe interviews.
48. McCabe interview.
49. USS *Heron*, Log.

50. Wagner Narrative.

51. USS *Heron*, Log.

52. Kabler, "Battle; Report of," 1 January 1942. (Hereafter cited as the Heron Report). Unless otherwise noted the following account is taken from that source.

53. USS *Heron*, Log.

54. Ibid.

55. Wachter interview.

56. USS *Heron*, Log.

57. Dawley Jolo Report.

58. Ibid.

*Chapter 6*

1. Wagner Narrative.

2. Johnson interview.

3. Chay Diary.

4. Barrett Diary.

5. Keller Narrative.

6. "PatWing-10 War Diary"; and "Status of Aircraft."

7. "PatWing-10 War Diary."

8. "Ops. PW-10"; and Peterson Narrative.

9. Ebbe interview.

10. Barrett Diary.

11. Wagner Narrative.

12. Armbruster and Ebbe interviews.

13. Chay Diary.

14. Campbell interview.

15. Barrett Diary.

16. Armbruster interview.

17. Hyland interview.

18. Ibid.

19. Pratt, "Episodes at Ambon," undated. The following account of the USS *Peary's* arrival in Ambon is taken from that source.

20. Campbell and Hyland interviews.

21. Hyland interview; and Hyland, "Report of Rescue of Australian Man at Sea on 1 January 1942," 3 January 1942.

22. Hyland interview. The following conversation is from that source.

23. Dawley Jolo Report. The following account is taken from that report.

24. Armbruster, Barrett, and Ebbe interviews.

25. Armbruster interview.

26. Ibid.

27. Ebbe interview.

28. Armbruster, Barrett, Ebbe, and Hyland interviews.

29. Pratt, "Episodes at Ambon."

30. Reid, letter to the author. The following account is taken from that source.

31. "PatWing-10 War Diary"; and Pratt, letter to the author.

32. "PatWing-10 War Diary."

33. Barrett, Hyland, McCabe, and Williamson interviews.

34. Hyland interview.

35. Hart Narrative.

36. Barrett Diary.

37. Ibid.

38. Ibid.

39. Barrett Diary; Hyland interview; and Webber Flight Log.

40. Barrett Diary.

41. Hyland interview.

42. "Ops. PW-10."

43. Hyland interview.

44. Ralston, "Official Log of Catalina Plane Nr. 28"; and Ralston and Grayson interviews. The following account is taken from those sources.

45. Barrett Diary; "PatWing-10 War Diary"; and Peterson and Wagner Narratives.

## Chapter 7

1. Donaho interview; and Operations Order 1S-42; "VP-22 January to April 1942," undated; "VP-22 Operations," undated.

2. Donaho interview; and F. O'Beirne, letter to the author.

3. Aeschliman, F. O'Beirne, and Thomas interviews.

4. F. O'Beirne, letter to the author.

5. Ibid.

6. Hop, letter to the author.

7. Armbruster, Barrett, Ebbe, and Hyland interviews.

8. Barrett Diary.

9. Reid, letter to the author.

10. Barrett Diary; and Hyland interview.

11. F. O'Beirne, letter to the author.

12. Aeschliman, Casey, and Donaho interviews.

13. Donaho interview.

14. Aeschliman interview.

15. Casey interview.

16. Aeschliman interview; and Hop, letter to the author.

17. Donaho interview.
18. Aeschliman interview.
19. Aeschliman and Casey interviews.
20. Fraser interview; and Hop, letter to the author.
21. Hop, letter to the author.
22. Ibid.; and "PatWing-10 War Diary."
23. Casey interview.
24. Aeschliman and Casey interviews.
25. Ibid.
26. Chay Diary.
27. "PatWing-10 War Diary."
28. Aeschliman, Casey, Donaho, and Fraser interviews; Chay Diary; and Hop, letter to the author.
29. Hop, letter to the author.
30. Chay Diary.
31. Van Oosten, *The Battle of the Java Sea*, p. 13.
32. Bannowsky interview.
33. Ibid.
34. Benefiel interview.
35. Bannowsky interview; and Holt, "Engagement With Enemy Aircraft," 16 January 1942.
36. Holt, "Engagement With Enemy Aircraft."
37. Bannowsky interview.
38. Benefiel interview.
39. Navy Press Release.
40. Bannowsky interview.
41. Navy Press Release.
42. Bannowsky interview.
43. Bannowsky and Benefiel interviews; and Navy Press Release.
44. Benefiel interview.
45. Bannowsky interview.
46. Ibid.
47. Holt, "Engagement With Enemy Aircraft."
48. Ralston, "Official Log of Catalina Plane Nr. 28."
49. Grayson interview.
50. Ralston, "Official Log of Catalina Plane Nr. 28."

*Chapter 8*

1. Pollock, "A Brief History of the Ground Forces of PatrolWing-10, and the Naval Defense Battalion, Mariveles, Bataan, P.I." undated. (Hereafter cited as Pollock, "A Brief History").

2. Ibid.; and Gaboury interview.

3. Pollock, "A Brief History."

4. Pollock, letter to the author.

5. Pollock, "A Brief History"; and Pollock interview. Unless otherwise noted, the account of the trips to Manila and Sangley Point are taken from those sources.

6. S1c John J. Webber escaped and returned to the American lines in Mid-February.

7. Burkholder interview.

8. Bowers Narrative; Pollock, "A Brief History"; and Utter, "History of PatWing-Ten Detachment Manila Area, 24 December 1941–29 January 1942."

9. Gaboury and Pollock interviews.

10. Gaboury interview.

11. Swenson interview.

12. Pollock, letter to the author.

13. Bowers Narrative.

14. Sackett, "The *Canopus*." 29 November 1943.

15. Pollock, "A Brief History."

16. Ibid.

17. Williamson interview.

18. Pollock, "A Brief History."

19. Gaboury interview.

20. Swenson interview.

21. Navy Press Release.

22. Pollock, "A Brief History."

23. Ibid.

24. Bowers Narrative.

25. Hogaboom, "Action Report: Bataan," *Marine Corps Gazette*, p. 26; and Prichett, "The Naval Battalion on Bataan," *Proceedings*, p. 74.

26. Sackett, "The *Canopus*."

27. Burkholder interview.

28. Swenson interview. The account that follows is taken from that source.

29. Esposito, *The West Point Atlas of American Wars*, vol. II, Map 124.

30. Hogaboom, "Action Report," p. 27; and Prichett, "Naval Battalion on Bataan," p. 74.

31. Hogaboom, "Action Report," p. 28.

32. Ibid., p. 29.

33. Gaboury interview.

34. Hogaboom, "Action Report," p. 29.

35. Williamson interview.

36. Ibid.

37. Williamson interview; and Commandant, Sixteenth Naval District to the commanding officer, USS *Seawolf*, 28 January 1942.

*Chapter 9*

1. "Status of Aircraft."

2. Barrett and Chay Diaries.

3. Reid, letter to the author.

4. Bray, letter to the author.

5. Barrett, Ebbe, Hyland, and McCabe interviews.

6. Wagner Narrative.

7. Hyland interview.

8. Barrett Diary; F. O'Beirne interview; and Pratt, letter to the author.

9. Davis interview.

10. Davis, "Encounter Between PBY-5 and Jap Fighter," 7 January 1942; Navy Press Release; and Pollock, letter to the author. The account that follows is taken from those sources.

11. Aeschliman, Casey, Donaho, and Hyland interviews; and Barrett Diary. The account that follows is taken from those sources.

12. Barrett Diary.

13. Chay Diary.

14. Reid, letter to the author.

15. Hyland interview.

16. Barrett Diary.

17. Hyland and McCabe interviews.

18. Pratt, letter to the author.

19. Pratt, "Appointment in Kendari," *Shipmate*, p. 15.

20. Ibid., p. 15.

21. Nordfelt interview; and Pratt, "Report of Contact With Enemy Task Force and Attack by Aircraft on 24 January 1942," 6 January 1942.

22. Kuhn and Nordfelt interviews.

23. Pratt, letter to the author.

24. Roberts, "Scouting Flight; Report of," 26 January 1942; and Roberts interview.

25. Roberts interview.

26. Ibid.

27. Roscoe, *United States Destroyer Operations in World War II*, p. 89.

28. Roberts interview.

29. Brown and Campbell interviews.

30. Brown interview.

31. Ibid.

32. "Ops. PW-10."

33. Martin interview.

34. Edmonds, *They Fought with What They Had*, pp. 306–7.

35. Campbell interview; and Campbell, "Rescue of Army Flight Crew," undated. The following account is taken from those sources.

36. Based on conversations with the men stationed in Ambon, and a study of radio reports shown in the "PatWing-10 War Diary."

37. Willmott, *Empires in the Balance*, p. 292.

38. Moorer interview.

39. Hyland interview.

40. Hop interview; and Hop, letter to the author. The following account is based on those sources.

41. Barrett Diary; Jacobson interview; and Jacobson, "Air Patrol Conducted 30–31 January 1942 in PBY #42, Report of," 31 January 1942.

42. Jacobson interview.

43. Based on a comparison of the comments made during all the interviews.

44. Armbruster, Brown, and Burgess interviews; and Barrett and Nolan Diaries.

*Chapter 10*

1. Edmonds, *They Fought with What They Had*, pp. 312–15; and "PatWing-10 War Diary."

2. Gough, "Air Raid Morokrembangan, N.E.I." 3 February 1942.

3. "PatWing-10 War Diary."

4. Messimer, *Pawns of War*, p. 18.

5. Deede, "Special Flight, 3 February 1942; Report of." 3 February 1942.

6. Ibid.

7. Nolan Diary.

8. Chay Diary.

9. "Ops. PW-10."

10. Hyland interview; and Nolan Diary.

11. Willmott, *Empires in the Balance*, p. 295.

12. "PatWing-10 War Diary."

13. Campbell interview.

14. Edmonds, *They Fought with What They Had*, p. 313.

15. Campbell interview. The account that follows is taken from that source.

16. Barrett Diary; and Jacobson interview.

17. Barrett Diary.

18. "PatWing-10 War Diary"; and "Status of Aircraft."

19. "Ops. PW-10"; "PatWing-10 War Diary"; and "Status of Aircraft."

20. Hargrave, "Report of Aerial Combat and Resultant Experiences," 30 May 1942. The account that follows is taken from that report. (Hereafter cited as Hargrave Report).

21. "Ops. PW-10"; and "PatWing-10 War Diary."

22. "PatWing-10 War Diary."

23. Ibid.

24. Hargrave Report.

25. Aeschliman interview.

26. Martin interview.

27. "PatWing-10 War Diary"; and "Status of Aircraft."

28. Wagner Narrative.

29. A destroyer was sunk when it struck a reef. Van Oosten, *The Battle of the Java Sea*, p. 28.

30. "PatWing-10 War Diary."

31. Barrett Diary; and Roberts interview.

32. Frank O'Beirne letter to Emmet O'Beirne.

33. "Status of Aircraft."

34. Glassford Narrative.

35. Pollock interview.

36. Moorer, "Account of Action Engaged by the Crew of PBY-5 Number 18 During Period 19–23 February," 23 February 1942. (Hereafter cited as Moorer Report); and *Oakland Tribune*.

37. Moorer Report.

38. Aeschliman, Anderson, and Casey interviews. The account that follows is taken from those sources.

39. Wood, "Narrative of Events During Attack on Port Darwin, Australia, 19 February 1942, and Subsequent Events there to," 21 February 1942; and F. O'Beirne, "Supplementary Report on Details Concerning Japanese Air Attack on Darwin on 19 February 1942," 21 February 1942. Unless otherwise stated the following account is from those sources. (Hereafter cited as Wood Report and O'Beirne Supplement).

40. Ebbe interview.

41. Burham interview.

42. Martin interview.

43. Wood Report.

44. Grant, "Saga of the USS *Preston*," undated.

45. Wood Report.

46. Ibid.; and "PatWing-10 War Diary."

47. Wood Report.
48. Aeschliman and Anderson interviews.

*Chapter 11*

1. "PatWing-10 War Diary."
2. Antonides interview.
3. Brown interview.
4. Glassford Narrative.
5. Ibid.
6. Campbell interview; "PatWing-10 War Diary"; and *The Western Mail*, Perth, Australia, 23 September 1943.
7. "PatWing-10 War Diary"; and *The Western Mail*.
8. "PatWing-10 War Diary."
9. Moorer Report. The following account is taken from that source and the Thomas interview.
10. "PatWing-10 War Diary."
11. Ibid.; and "Ops. PW-10."
12. Glassford Narrative; and Hyland interview.
13. "PatWing-10 War Diary."
14. Nolan Diary.
15. Burgess and Ebbe interviews; and Pratt, letter to the author.
16. Gillison, *Australia in the War of 1939–45*, p. 464.
17. Pratt, letter to the author. The preceding account is taken from that source.
18. Messimer, *Pawns of War*, p. 51.
19. Kuhn and Nordfelt interviews; Nolan Diary; and Pratt, letter to the author.
20. Messimer, *Pawns of War*, pp. 119–28; and "PatWing-10 War Diary."
21. Costello, *The Pacific War*, p. 221; and Edmonds, *They Fought with What They Had*, p. 423.
22. Roscoe, *Destroyer Operations*, p. 105; and Van Oosten, *Battle of Java Sea*, p. 52–53.
23. Van Oosten, *Battle of Java Sea*, p. 53.
24. Campbell interview; "PatWing-10 War Diary"; and Peterson Narrative.
25. Wagner Narrative.
26. Ibid.
27. Van Oosten, *Battle of Java Sea*, p. 54.
28. *The Western Mail*.
29. Van Oosten, *Battle of Java Sea*, p. 55.
30. Campbell interview.

31. "Ops. PW-10" and "Status of Aircraft."

32. Van Oosten, *Battle of Java Sea*, p. 69.

33. "PatWing-10 War Diary."

34. McCabe interview.

35. Campbell interview.

36. Eisenbach interview; and "PatWing-10 War Diary."

37. Ibid.; and Campbell and Hyland interviews.

38. Eisenbach interview.

39. "PatWing-10 War Diary."

40. Hyland interview.

41. Campbell interview.

42. Hyland interview. A few days later, P-3 was started without a problem by two Dutch pilots who flew it to Perth.

43. Wagner Narrative.

44. Hyland interview.

45. Campbell interview.

46. "PatWing-10 War Diary."

47. Gillison, *Australia in the War*, p. 465.

48. Armbruster interview.

49. *Daily Mirror*, Sydney, Australia.

50. Ibid.

51. Armbruster interview.

52. Bray Narrative.

53. Messimer, *Pawns of War*, p. 201. After the *Langley* went down, the survivors were put aboard the USS *Pecos* (AO-6), which was also sunk on 1 March. The loss of life was enormous.

54. Eisenbach and Hyland interviews.

55. "Status of Aircraft." There was a fourth plane, P-3. But after it arrived in Perth it was retained by the Dutch.

*Chapter 12*

1. Barrett Diary.

2. Hyland interview.

3. Barrett Diary.

4. E. O'Beirne interview.

5. "PatWing-10 War Diary."

6. Hyland interview.

7. Antonides interview.

8. Ibid.

9. E. O'Beirne interview.

*Chapter 13*

1. The Americans also controlled the smaller islands between those two places, but the forces there were too small and too scattered to effectively resist the Japanese. Esposito, Map 126.
2. "PatWing-10 War Diary."
3. Pollock, letter to the author; and Wainwright, *General Wainwright's Story*, pp. 96–99.
4. Blaine, Gardnier, and Whitlow interviews; Pollock, "Operations Flight Gridiron," undated; and Wainwright, op. cit., pp. 96–99.
5. "PatWing-10 War Diary."
6. Underbrink, *Destination Corregidor*, p. 192.
7. Pollock, "Operation Flight Gridiron." Unless otherwise noted the following account was taken from that source.
8. Whitlow interview.
9. Blaine interview.
10. Gardnier interview.
11. Pollock, "Operation Flight Gridiron."
12. Pollock interview; Pollock, letter to the author; and Underbrink, *Destination Corregidor*, p. 200.
13. Underbrink, *Destination Corregidor*, p. 200.
14. Pollock, letter to the author.
15. Blaine interview. There were also two sisters, Geneva and Ressa Jenkens, aboard the two planes. Geneva was captured on Mindanao, Ressa made it to Australia aboard Deede's plane. Pollock, "Operation Flight Gridiron"; and Whitlow interview.
16. Pollock, "Operation Flight Gridiron."
17. Pollock, "Trouble Report of PBY 101-P-1," 1 August 1942.
18. Blaine interview.
19. *San Francisco Chronicle.*
20. McGuigan, letter to Pollock, 10 August 1943.
21. Blaine interview.
22. Ibid.
23. Pollock, letter to the author.
24. Pollock, "Trouble Report of PBY 101-P-1."
25. Pollock interview.
26. Ibid.; and McGuigan, letter to Pollock.
27. Pollock, "Trouble Report of PBY 101-P-1."
28. Pollock, letter to the author.
29. Ibid.
30. Pollock interview.

31. Ibid.
32. Pollock, letter to the author.
33. Ibid.

## Chapter 14

1. Burkholder interview. The account that follows, describing events on Corregidor, is taken from that source.

2. Belote, *Corregidor: The Saga of a Fortress*, pp. 9–12; Gaboury interview. The account that follows, describing events at Fort Hughes, is taken from those sources.

3. Blaine, Gardnier, and Whitlow interviews. Unless otherwise noted, the account that follows is taken from those sources.

4. Pollock, letter to the author; and Underbrink, p. 206.

5. The surrender conversation was related to the author by Sally Blaine.

# Bibliography

*Correspondence and Interviews*

Aeschliman, Edwin F. VP-22.
Anderson, Martin L. VP-22.
Antonides, Joseph. PW-10 Staff.
Armbruster, Albert A. VP-101.
Bannowsky, Clarence J. VP-22.
Barrett, Robert R. VP-102.
Benefiel, Murl. VP-22.
Blaine, Sally. Army Nurse.
Brant, Joe E. VP-22.
Brown, Ira W. VP-101.
Burgess, Andrew L. VP-101.
Burham, Donald E. VP-22.
Burkholder, Arthur, Jr. PW-10 HQ.
Campbell, Duncan. VP-101.
Casey, Herbert L. VP-22.
Chay, Donald. Utility Squadron.
Davis, Douglas C. VP-22.
Donaho, D. G. VP-22.
Ebbe, Gordon K. VP-101.

Eisenbach, Charles. VP-101.
Fraser, Charles W. VP-22.
Gaboury, George. VP-102.
Gardnier, Helen. Army Nurse.
Grayson, Jack L. VP-101.
Hop, Harvey. VP-22.
Hyland, John J. VP-102.
Jacobson, Arthur. VP-101.
Johnson, Dale R. VP-101.
Kelly, Donald. VP-102.
Kuhn, Elmer. USS *Childs*.
LeBaron, Allan G.
Martin, Jack D. VP-22.
McCabe, Thomas E. L. VP-102.
McLawhorn, Everen C. VP-101.
Moorer, Thomas H. VP-22.
Nolan, James. VP-102.
Nordfelt, Rodney. USS *Childs*.
O'Beirne, Emmet. VP-21.
O'Beirne, Frank. VP-22.
Palm, Edgar. VP-101.
Pollock, Thomas F. VP-102.
Pratt, J. L. USS *Childs*.
Roberts, Richard S. VP-101.
Ralston, Frank. VP-102.
Reid, Andrew. VP-102.
Ruzak, Joseph J. VP-22.
Swenson, H. R. VP-102.
Thomas, Ralph. VP-22.
Van Bibber, Charles E. VP-22.
Wachter, T. P. USS *Heron*.
Warfield, Thomas G. MS *Maréchal Joffre*-USS *Rochambeau*
Webber, George W. VP-101.
Whitlow, Evelyn. Army Nurse.
Williamson, Lowell H. VP-102.
Ziegler, M. D. VP-101.

*Diaries, Flight Logs, and Letters to Family*

Barrett, Robert R. Diary and letters to his family.
Brant, Joe E. Flight log.
Chay, Donald. Diary.

Ebbe, Gordon K. Diary, and letters to his family.
Martin, Jack D. Flight log.
Nolan, James. Diary.
O'Beirne, Frank. Letter to his brother.
Pollock, Thomas F. Flight log and letters to his family.
Ruzak, Joseph J. Flight log.
Thomas, Ralph. Flight log.
Warfield, Thomas G. Diary.
Webber, George W. Flight log.

*Documents*

The following documents were gathered from several sources. Those followed by a microfilm number came from the Naval Historical Center, Washington Navy Yard, Washington, D.C. 20374. Those followed by NHC came from the same source but are printed copies. Documents from other sources are noted with the entry. All are in the author's possession.

Barthes, A. "Scouting Flight; Report of," 23 January 1942. AR-129-81.
Barthes, A. "Scouting Flight; Report of." 26 January 1942. AR-129-81.
Bellinger, P. N. L. "Operation Orders 1S-42." 2 January 1942. F. O'Beirne Papers.
Bellinger, P. N. L. "Operations in Far East." 14 March 1942. NHC.
Bellinger, P. N. L. "Operations on 7 December 1941." 20 December 1941. R. Thomas Papers.
Bergstrom, E. W. "Report of Patrol Flight on 28 and 29 January 1942." 30 January 1942. AR-129-81.
Bowers, Thomas K. "Personal Narrative of Philippine Campaign from 8 December 1941 to 29 April 1942." Undated. NRS-159.
Bull, Richard. "Contact with Jap Transports; 23 January 1942." 25 January 1942. AR-129-81.
Campbell, D. A. "Report of Rescue of Ensign L. C. Deede." 5 January 1942. T. E. L. McCabe Papers.
Campbell, D. A. "Rescue of Army Flight Crew." Undated. AR-129-81.
Champlin, Malcolm M. "Narrative by." 5 September 1944. AR-129-81.
Christman, E. L. "Dawn Bombing Attack of Jolo, Sulu, P.I., 27 December 1941; Report of." Undated. AR-129-81 and NRS-159.
Dawley, Jack B. "Bombing Attack at Jolo, Sulu, 27 December 1941, and Subsequent Incidents; Report of." 4 February 1942. AR-129-81.
Davis, J. F. "Encounter between PBY-5 and Jap Fighter." 27 January 1942. AR-129-81.
Deede, L. C. "Report of Bombing Raid on the Island of Jolo." 5 January 1942. T. E. L. McCabe Papers.

Deede, L. C. "Scouting Flight; Report of Number 27." 25 January 1942. AR-129-81.

Deede, L. C. "Special Flight, 3 February 1942; Report of." 3 February 1942. AR-129-81.

Donaho, D. G. "Awards, Recommendations for." 9 October 1942. AR-129-81.

Forrestal, James. "Presidential Unit Citation to Patrol Squadron One Hundred One." Undated. D. G. Donaho Papers.

Forrestal, James. "Presidential Unit Citation to Patrol Squadron One Hundred Two." Undated. D. G. Donaho Papers.

Geer, L. E. "Scouting Flight; Report of Patrol Number 8." 29 January 1941. AR-129-81.

General Dynamics (Consolidated Aircraft Corporation). *Pilots' Handbook, U.S. Navy PBY-3 Airplane.* Undated. Convair Division, San Diego, California, 92138.

General Headquarters, General Staff Allied Translator and Interpreter Section. "An Account of the Imperial Navy's Activities in the Philippines at the Beginning of the War." 15 May 1946. NRS-1974-25.

Glassford, William. "Confidential War Diary of, 29 November 1941 to 15 March 1942." Includes special message and personal memos. NRS-1970-7.

Glassford, William. "Narrative of Events in the South-West Pacific from 14 February to 5 April 1942." 16 May 1942. NRS-1970-7.

Glassford, William. "Navy Cross; Award of." Undated. NRS-1970-7.

Goldsmith, John M. "Trip to Jolo, Sulu Province, P.I., for the Purpose of Investigating Stories Surrounding the Navy Catalina Fliers missing after Raid on Japanese Shipping at Jolo on 27 December 1941; Report on." 18 May 1945. T. Pollock Papers.

Gough, W. V. "Scouting Flight; Report of." Undated. AR-129-81.

Grant, E. "Action Report, Malalag Bay, Mindanao, P.I." 8 December 1941. NHC.

Grayson, J. L. "Bombing Mission; Report of." 8 February 1942. AR-129-81.

Grayson, J. L. "Scouting Flight; Report of." 25 January 1942. AR-129-81.

Hargrave, W. W. "Report of Aerial Combat and Resultant Experiences." 30 May 1942. AR-129-81.

Hart, Thomas C. "Commendation for Ensign D. A. Campbell." 22 January 1942. AR-129-81.

Hart, Thomas C. "Narrative of Events, Asiatic Fleet, Leading up to War and from 8 December 1941 to 15 February 1942." 11 June 1942. NHC.

Holt, C. H. "Engagement with Enemy Aircraft 16 January 1942." Undated. D. G. Donaho Papers.

Hyland, J. J. "Flight to Evacuate Dutch Personnel from Ambon; Report of." 29 January 1942. AR-129-81.

Hyland, J. J. "Report of Bombing Raid on Island of Jolo." 3 January 1942. AR-129-81.

Hyland, J. J. "Report of Rescue Australian Man at Sea on 1 January 1942." 3 January 1942. AR-129-81.

Jacobson, A. L. "Air Patrol conducted 30-31 January 1942 in PBY #42; Report of." 31 January 1942. AR-129-81.

Jacobson, A. L. "Report on Air Patrol Conducted on 26 and 27 January 1942." Undated. AR-129-81.

Kabler, W. L. "Battle; Report of." 1 January 1942. AR-129-81.

Keller, C. A. "Contact with Enemy Forces on 10 December 1941; Report of." T. Pollock Papers and AR-129-81.

Keller, C. A. "Philippine and South Pacific Activities of Patrol Wing 10." 8 March 1943. AR-129-81.

McCabe, T. E. L. "Bombing Raid on Island of Jolo; Report of." 3 January 1942. T. E. L. McCabe Papers.

McCabe, T. E. L. "Report of Bombing Raid of Island of Jolo." 3 January 1942. AR-129-81.

McGuigan, S. L. "Narrative." Undated. T. Pollock Papers.

Moorer, Thomas E. "Account of Action Engaged in by Crew of PBY-5 Number 18 during Period 19-23 February." 23 February 1942. NRS-159 and AR-129-81.

"Navy Rewards PatWing 10 Heroes." Official Navy Press Release, 28 June 1942. J. L. Pratt Papers.

"PatWing 10: Story of a Gallant Squadron and its Exploits from Philippines to Australia." Official Navy Press Release, 24 May 1942. J. L. Pratt Papers.

Neale, E. T. "Orders to Lieutenant (j.g.) T. F. Pollock, USN." 17 February 1942. AR-129-81.

Neale, E. T. "Plane 101-P-45 Missing; Report of." 8 February 1942. AR-129-81.

O'Beirne, Frank. "Flight to Australia and Adjacent Islands; Report of." 9 September 1941. F. O'Beirne Papers.

O'Beirne, Frank. "Instructions for BAOE BAOE Patrol." 22 January 1942. F. O'Beirne Papers.

O'Beirne, Frank. "Kalabahi Patrol." Undated. F. O'Beirne Papers.

O'Beirne, Frank. "Report of Japanese Air Attack on Darwin on 19 February 1942 as Witnessed from USS *William B. Preston.*" 21 February 1942. F. O'Beirne Papers.

O'Beirne, Frank. "Squadron Administrative Organization." 11 February 1942. F. O'Beirne Papers.

O'Beirne, Frank. "Squadron's Personnel in *William B. Preston.*" 7 February 1942. F. O'Beirne Papers.

O'Beirne, Frank. "Supplementary Report on Details Concerning Japanese Air Attack on Darwin on 19 February 1942." 21 February 1942. F. O'Beirne Papers.

"Operations of Patrol Wing Ten from 7 December 1941 to 5 March 1942." Undated. T. E. L. McCabe Papers.

"Partial Officer Personnel Listing, December 1941–February 1942." Undated. T. Pollock Papers and AR-129-81.

Peterson, J. V. "Bombing Attack on Japanese Battleship on 10 December 1941; Report on." 31 December 1941. NHC.

Peterson, J. V. "Dawn Bombing Attack on Jolo, Sulu, P.I., 27 December 1941; Report of." 12 February 1942. NHC.

Peterson, J. V. "Enemy Aircraft Destroyed by Aircraft and Aircraft Tenders, Period 7 December 1941 to 1 March 1942, and Operational Losses During that Period." 11 January 1944. NRS-1974-25.

Peterson, J. V. "Narrative." 1 May 1943. NRS-194.

Peterson, J. V. "Report on Rescue of Ensign L. C. Deede and Crew." 7 January 1942. NHC.

Peterson, J. V. "Status of Aircraft." 2 February 1942. AR-129-81.

Pollock, Thomas F. "A Brief History of the Ground Forces of PatrolWing 10 and the Naval Defense Battalion, Mariveles, Bataan, P.I." Undated. T. Pollock Papers.

Pollock, Thomas F. "Decorations, Recommendation for." Undated. T. Pollock Papers.

Pollock, Thomas F. "Operation Flight Gridiron, 27 April–3 May 1942." Undated. T. Pollock Papers.

Pollock, Thomas F. "Trouble Report of PBY 101-P-1." 1 August 1942. T. Pollock Papers.

Pratt, John L. "A Running Account of the Cruise of the *Childs.*" 3 March 1945. J. Pratt Papers.

Pratt, John L. "Episodes at Ambon." Undated. Unpublished Account. J. Pratt Papers.

Pratt, John L. "Report of Contact with Enemy Task Force, and Attack by Aircraft, on 24 January 1942." 26 January 1942. NRS-159.

Pratt, John L. "*Childs'* Operations from December 1941 through February

1942; Manila Bay to Exmouth Gulf." Undated. This is a chart showing the *Childs*'s movements and special events. J. Pratt Papers.

Purnell, W. R. "Temporary Additional Duty; Travel Orders to Lieutenant (j.g.) Thomas F. Pollock, USN." 26 April 1942. T. Pollock Papers.

Ralston, Frank. "Official Log of Catalina Plane Nr. 28." Undated. F. Ralston papers.

"Record of Planes of VP-101." Undated. T. Pollock Papers.

Reid, Andrew H. "Advance Party." 8 May 1980. Unpublished Account. A. Reid Papers.

Renard, J. C. "War Activities, Utility Squadron, Asiatic Fleet." Undated. NRS-1974-25.

Roberts, R. S. "Scouting Flight; Report of." 26 January 1942. AR-129-81.

Robinson, W. S. "Report of Patrol, 27 January 1942." Undated. AR-129-81.

Robinson, W. S. "Scouting Flight; Report of." 23 January 1942. AR-129-81.

Rockwell, F. W. "Passengers aboard USS *Seawolf*, Authorization for." 28 January 1942. T. Pollock Papers.

"Roster, USS *Houston*, (Flagship), United States Asiatic Fleet and Station, October–November–December 1941." J. Pratt Papers.

Sackett, E. L. "The *Canopus*." Undated. T. Pollock Papers.

Shepler, Dwight C. "Evaluation Results PBY Strike, Jolo, 27 December 1941." 27 April 1945. T. Pollock Papers.

"Status of Aircraft." Undated. AR-129-81.

"Status of Certain Personnel (Patrol Wing Ten)." 21 September 1942. T. Pollock Papers.

Utter, H. T. "History of Pat Wing Ten Detachment Manila Area, 24 December 1941–29 January 1942." Undated. NRS-159.

"VP-22, January–April 1942." Undated. D. G. Donaho Papers.

"VP-22 Operations." Undated. R. Thomas Papers.

Wagner, F. D. "Bombing Attack at Jolo, Sulu, 27 December 1941, and Subsequent Incidents; Report of." 10 February 1942. T. Pollock Papers.

Wagner, F. D. "Miscellaneous Instructions." 12 January 1942. F. O'Beirne Papers.

Wood, L. O. "Narrative of Events During Attack on Port Darwin, Australia, 19 February 1942, and subsequent Events thereto." 21 February 1942. AR-129-81.

*Muster Rolls and Ships' Logs*

The following documents were obtained from the National Archives, Navy and Old Army Branch, Military Archives Division, Washington, D.C. 20408.

VP-22. 30 September 1941 to 18 April 1942.
VP-101. 31 January 1939 to 30 September 1942.
VP-102. 31 January 1939 to 18 April 1942.
USS *Childs*, Deck Log.
USS *Heron*, Deck Log.
USS *Maréchal Joffre*, Deck Log. (renamed USS *Rochambeau*).
USS *William B. Preston*, Deck Log.

*Foreign Documents and Newspapers*

"Operations Record, No. 2, G. R. Squadron, 3 December 1941 – 16 February 1942." Australian War Memorial, Canberra.
*Daily Mirror.* Sydney, Australia. 1943.
*The Western Mail.* Perth, Australia. 1943.

USS *Maréchal Joffre* Documents

These documents were all obtained from Thomas G. Warfield, captain of the *Maréchal Joffre* after she was seized, and during her escape to Australia.

CINCAF to MS *Maréchal Joffre*, Sailing Orders, 18 December 1941.
Crew List, MS *Maréchal Joffre*, 18 December 1941 – 1 June 1942. Undated.
*Maréchal Joffre:* Report and Recommendations. 26 March 1942.
MS *Maréchal Joffre:* War History, December 1941 – March 1945. Sailing Directions through Corregidor Minefields for Vessels Leaving Manila, 24 November 1941.

*Books*

Belote, James H. and William M. *Corregidor: The Saga of a Fortress.* New York and London: Harper and Row, 1967.
Brereton, Lewis H. *The Brereton Diaries: 3 October 1941 – 8 May 1945.* New York: William Morrow & Co., 1946.
Brown, Cecil. *Suez to Singapore.* New York: Random House, 1942.
Costello, John. *The Pacific War.* New York: Rawson, Wade Publishers, 1981.
Edmonds, Walter D. *They Fought With What They Had.* Boston: Little, Brown & Co., 1951.
Esposito, Vincent J., ed. *The West Point Atlas of American Wars*, vol. II, 1900 – 1953. New York, Washington, and London: Praeger, 1964.
Gillison, Douglas. *Australia in the War of 1939 – 45*, vol. I. Canberra: Australian War Memorial, 1962.
Knott, Richard. *Black Cat Raiders of WW II.* Annapolis: Nautical and Aviation Publishing Company of America, 1981.
Messimer, Dwight R. *Pawns of War: The Loss of the USS Langley and USS Pecos.* Annapolis: Naval Institute Press, 1983.

Okumiya, Masatake, Jiro Horikoshi, and Martin Cadin. *Zero*. New York: Ballantine, 1956.

Roscoe, Theodore. *Destroyer Operations in WW II*. Annapolis: U.S. Naval Institute, 1953.

Underbrink, Robert L. *Destination Corregidor*. Annapolis: Naval Institute Press, 1971.

Van Oosten, F. C. *The Battle of the Java Sea*. Annapolis: Naval Institute Press, 1976.

Wainwright, Jonathan M., and Robert Considine, ed. *General Wainwright's Story*. New York: Doubleday and Company, 1948.

Willmott, H. P. *Empires in the Balance: Japanese and Allied Pacific Strategies to April 1942*. Annapolis: Naval Institute Press, 1982.

Winslow, W. G. *The Fleet the Gods Forgot*. Annapolis: Naval Institute Press, 1982.

*Magazines and Periodicals.*

Davison, T. W. "Notes on Japanese Preparations for the Philippines Invasion." *Proceedings*, September 1955.

Hogaboom, William F. "Action Report: Bataan." *Marine Corps Gazette*, April 1946.

Parker, T. C. "The Epic of Corregidor-Bataan, December 24, 1941–May 4, 1942." *Proceedings*, January 1943.

Pratt, John L. "Appointment in Kendari." *Shipmate*, January–February 1975.

Prichett, William F. "The Naval Battalion on Bataan." *Proceedings*, November 1960.

Shimada, Koichi. "Japanese Naval Air Operations in the Philippines Invasion." *Proceedings*, January 1955.

Van Vleet, Clarke. "South Pacific Saga: The Story of Patrol Wing Ten." *Naval Aviation News*, February 1977.

*Newspapers*

*Chicago Daily News*, 1942.
*Oakland Tribune*, 1942.
*San Francisco Chronicle*, 1942.

# Index